INFORMATION SYSTEMS MANAGEMENT
Handbook

JAE SHIM, ANIQUE QURESHI, JOEL SIEGEL

2002 SUPPLEMENT

PRENTICE HALL

This publication is designed to provide accurate and authoritative information in regard to the subject matter covered. It is sold with the understanding that the publisher is not engaged in rendering legal, accounting, or other professional service. If legal advice or other expert assistance is required, the services of a competent professional person should be sought.

—From a Declaration of Principles jointly adopted by a Committee of the American Bar Association and a Committee of Publishers and Associations.

Printed in the United States of America

10 9 8 7 6 5 4 3 2 1

ISBN 0-13-092640-X

ATTENTION: CORPORATIONS AND SCHOOLS

Prentice Hall books are available at quantity discounts with bulk purchase for educational, business, or sales promotional use. For information, please write to: Prentice Hall Special Sales, 240 Frisch Court, Paramus, New Jersey 07652. Please supply: title of book, ISBN, quantity, how the book will be used, date needed.

PRENTICE HALL
Paramus, NJ 07652

On the World Wide Web at http://www.phdirect.com

ACKNOWLEDGMENTS

We are very appreciative to John Hiatt for her outstanding editorial work and input to this Supplement. Thanks also go to Roberta M. Siegel for her expertise in information systems management.

CONTENTS

Chapter 13D   Electronic Banking and Payments 217

Chapter 13E   Intranets and Extranets 229

Appendix A

General-Security-Issues Worksheet 345

Appendix B

Access-Security Worksheet 347

Appendix C

Security-Controls Worksheet 349

Appendix D

Firewall-Personnel-Security Worksheet 353

Appendix E

Computer-Facilities-Protection Worksheet 357

Appendix F

Common Services, Features, and Definitions Related
to the Internet Service-Provider Market 359

ABOUT THE AUTHORS

Jae K. Shim, Ph.D., is a Professor of Business Administration and Computer Science at California State University, Long Beach. Dr. Shim received his Ph.D. degree from the University of California at Berkeley. He is the President of the National Business Review Foundation, a management and computer consulting firm. Dr. Shim has published about 50 articles in professional journals, including *Journal of Systems Management, Financial Management, Journal of Operational Research, Omega, Data Management, Management Accounting, Simulation and Games, Long Range Planning, Journal of Business Forecasting, Decision Sciences, Management Science,* and *Econometrica.* Dr. Shim has more than 45 books to his credit and is a recipient of the Credit Research Foundation Outstanding Paper Award for his article on financial modeling. He is also a recipient of a Ford Foundation Award, Mellon Research Fellowship, and Arthur Andersen Research Grant. For over twenty years Dr. Shim has been an industrial consultant in the areas of information systems development and applications, corporate planning, modeling, business forecasting, and financial modeling.

Anique Qureshi, Ph.D., CPA, CIA, is a computer consultant to companies and Associate Professor of Accounting and Information Systems at Queens College of the City University of New York. Dr. Qureshi has contributed chapters to books published by Prentice-Hall and McGraw-Hill. His articles have appeared in *Accounting Technology, The CPA Journal, National Public Accountant, Management Accountant,* and *Internal Auditing.* Dr. Qureshi is proficient in programming languages such as C/C++, Java, and Visual

Basic. Besides having expertise with many software packages, he maintains the web page for the Department of Accounting and Information Systems at Queens College.

Joel G. Siegel, Ph.D., CPA, is a computer consultant to businesses and Professor of Accounting and Information Systems at Queens College of the City University of New York. He was previously associated with Coopers and Lybrand, LLP, and Arthur Andersen, LLP. He served as a consultant to numerous organizations including Citicorp, International Telephone and Telegraph, Person-Wolinsky Associates, and the American Institute of CPAs. Dr. Siegel is the author of about 60 books. His books have been published by Prentice-Hall, Richard Irwin, McGraw-Hill, HarperCollins, John Wiley, Macmillan, Probus, International Publishing, Barron's, Glenlake, and the American Institute of CPAs. He has authored approximately 200 articles on business and computer topics. His articles have appeared in various journals including *Computers in Accounting, Decision Sciences, Financial Executive, Financial Analysts Journal, The CPA Journal, National Public Accountant,* and *Practical Accountant.* In 1972, he received the Outstanding Educator of America Award. Dr. Siegel is listed in *Who's Who Among Writers* and *Who's Who in the World.* Dr. Siegel is the former chairperson of the National Oversight Board.

WHAT THIS SUPPLEMENT WILL DO FOR YOU

This Supplement to the Information Systems Management Handbook both expands on areas covered in the main volume as well as presents relevant and timely new material. The 2002 Supplement also updates the reader on current developments and emerging trends. Keeping abreast of new areas of interest in information systems will ensure the continued success of the IS professional.

The major problem facing IS professionals today is having the appropriate computer security to safeguard the integrity and accuracy of the systems and to prevent misuse of the system. Recent developments to strengthen computer security, including firewalls, are fully explained in this Supplement.

Hiring considerations are important to ensure that the best possible staff is hired and properly trained. Outsourcing may be appropriate in certain areas or under specific circumstances. These include considerations regarding costs, risk, time, and review work. Attributes of effective outsourcing are provided here, along with what important points the IS managers should monitor.

IS managers must be familiar with capital budgeting. This is the process of making long-term planning decisions for alternative investment opportunities related to computer systems and hardware. Is a particular proposed acquisition economically feasible? What alternatives are available?

Peer-to-peer networks and server-based networks are discussed in this book, including application considerations, network security, and speed. A guide to client/server computing is presented to help IS managers maximize the use of their computer resources. The server process receives requests from client processes, executes database retrieval and updates, manages data integrity, and dispatches responses to client requests.

Recent developments related to Intranets and Extranets are provided to make better use of them in business operations. Efficient use of Intranets and Extranets will improve revenue generation, enhance productivity, lower costs, and reduce labor hours. We enumerate many applications of Intranets within the entity and Extranets with outsiders such as customers and suppliers.

Internet marketing can assist a business in maximizing both sales and increasing market share. Online marketing strategies and advertising guidelines are detailed here. Information service providers are examined in terms of benefits and drawbacks. Setting up an effective web page to attract new business is also explored.

Electronic banking and payments are an important aspect of electronic commerce. Coverage includes business-to-business and individual-to-business transactions. Online payments for merchandise and services, electronic bill payments, and banking are discussed.

A contingency plan should be in place to guard against the adverse effects of a disruption of a computer system. A contingency plan instructs IS professionals on what to do before, during, and after a disruption to minimize financial losses, data losses, and lost time. By following the contingency-planning tips recommended here, companies can resume their day-to-day activities in both a timely and efficient manner.

A NOTE REGARDING ORGANIZATION

The main volume of the *Information Systems Management Handbook* is arranged in chapters numbered one through sixteen. There are also six appendices included at the end of the book, which represent additional sources of relevant material.

There are many new chapters included within this supplement that relate to a chapter in the main volume, but which are significantly unique to warrant a separate heading. These new chapters have the same number as the related chapter in the main volume, but are also given an alphabetical designation. For instance, in this Supplement, you'll find Chapter 7A, Database Design, Chapter 10A Building Client Server Systems, and so on. These chapters are entirely new, yet intricately related to the main chapter.

Like the main volume, this Supplement also contains many informative and helpful appendices. These appendices take the form of worksheets, checklists, and resource lists and are directly connected to the material presented in this volume.

FIREWALLS

Firewalls are used to control access between two networks; their purpose is to allow authorized traffic and restrict unauthorized traffic. Firewalls are not used to cut off communications at the network's parameters. Firewalls are used to selectively allow the passing of data between untrusted networks and trusted networks. Firewalls should be used whenever trusted networks are connected to untrusted networks.

Firewalls are frequently used when connecting an organization's network to the Internet. The Internet should always be assumed to be untrusted. Internet firewalls are sometimes referred to as secure Internet gateways. A gateway is simply a computer that relays communications between networks. A firewall may consist of various components, filters, or screens that are used to restrict transmission of certain types of traffic. A gateway computer provides relay services to complement the filters or screen.

Firewalls may also be used within an organization, such as between segments of WANS (Wide Area Networks). While it is possible to use application-level security to protect critical data in a networked environment, security can be greatly enhanced by using firewalls and segregating networks.

Security administrators are concerned about attackers breaking into the organization's network. Anyone with motivation to obtain access may launch an attack. A network is susceptible to direct attacks by hackers or automated attacks, such as by worms.

Firewalls may be configured to allow outgoing data to travel freely across the firewall, but restrict incoming data. Other configurations are also

1

possible, such as allowing only e-mails and no other communications to go through the firewall. Firewalls may be configured to allow internal users unrestricted access to outside services, while preventing any outside traffic from getting inside. Firewalls may be configured to prevent unauthenticated interactive logins from external networks.

Some firewalls place greater emphasis on restricting unauthorized traffic while others are more concerned with permitting traffic. Senior management should be consulted in deciding how to configure the firewall and what type of access to permit or deny.

ADVANTAGES AND LIMITATIONS

Firewalls offer some advantages over dial-in modem connections. Logging and auditing functions for security purposes are available with firewalls. Security data, such as the number of unsuccessful login attempts or password failures, is readily available.

Firewalls have their limitations. Firewalls are not meant to provide all-purpose access-control protection. They cannot, for example, prevent an authorized internal user from launching an attack from behind the firewall. An overwhelming majority of security breaches involve internal authorized users, and firewalls are ineffective against internal attacks. Caution: Internal users behind the firewall may steal proprietary data.

Firewalls are not designed to provide protection against viruses, Trojan horses, and other malicious programs. Many firewalls can be configured to provide some level of protection, but the protection is not perfect. Many viruses are spread thorough the macros of shared documents. The documents with viruses in their macros may be sent through the Internet as e-mail attachments. Users may be downloading infected programs from untrusted web sites.

A virus may infect a network from several sources. Network-to-network transfers are not the only source of viruses. Other sources, including floppy disks should be considered in setting a virus-protection policy.

The best way to reduce risks related to a malicious code is not firewalls. Rather, automatic virus-scanning software should be installed on all machines. Appropriate antivirus policies and procedures are a must. Firewalls should be one part of the organization's security plan and should not be expected to serve comprehensive security needs.

Firewalls are not suitable for protecting all types of data. It may be unwise to make top-secret proprietary information available on a network, even if it is protected using a firewall. The nature of the data to be protected should be considered by senior management in determining whether the data should even be accessible via the Internet.

The costs associated with setting up a firewall vary considerably. A firewall system may cost virtually nothing or it may cost hundreds of thousands of dollars. It is essential to consider not only the initial setup costs, but also the expenses in supporting and maintaining the firewall.

COMMERCIAL FIREWALLS

The following pages list firewall vendors, their products, and appropriate contact information:

Product Vendor*	E-mail	OS/Hardware Platforms	Contact
Actane Controller Actane	info@actane.com	SNMP PC	Le California Bat D2 2, Rue Jean Andreani 13084 Aix-En-Provence Cedex 2 France
AFS 2000 Internet Device Internet Devices	sales@internetdevices.com		(408) 541-1400 x314
AltaVista Firewall AltaVista		UNIX, WNT WS, PC	
Ascend Secure Access Firewall Ascend	info@ascend.com	PC	One Ascend Plaza 1701 Harbor Bay Parkway Alameda, CA 94502 USA (510) 769-6001

---

* The source of this listing is: www.waterw.com/~manowar/vendor.html. Please check this web site for the latest information.

aVirt Gateway aVirt Gateway Solutions	sales@aVirt.com	PC	51 West Center, Suite 604 Orem, UT 84043 USA (800)-41-AVIRT or (801) 802-7450
BIGfire Biodata and AB Systems	sales@biodata.com.sg		Burg Lichtenfels D-35104 Lichtenfels, Germany 6454-912070
BorderManager Novell Consulting	Sales	Novell	Sales
BorderWare BorderWare Technologies	info@borderware.com	POS,PC	90 Burnhamthorpe Road West, Suite 1402 Mississauga, Ontario L5B 3C3 Europe: 181 893 6066 North America: (905) 804-1855
Brimstone SOS Corporation	sales@soscorp.com	any PC	40 Broad Street, Suite 2175 New York, NY 10004 USA (800)-SOS-UNIX or (212) 809-5900
Bull S.A.:Firewall and Netwall Bull	www.bullsoft.com	UNIX/NT	.1.30.87.63.88
Centri Cisco	info@cisco.com	WNT PC	170 W. Tasman Dr. San Jose, CA 95134 USA (408) 526-4000
Cisco IOS Firewall Cisco	info@cisco.com	Router	170 W. Tasman Dr. San Jose, CA 95134 USA (408) 526-4000
Cisco PIX Cisco	info@cisco.com	POS	170 W. Tasman Dr. San Jose, CA 95134 USA (408) 526-4000

Citadel Citadel Data Security	info@cdsec.com	UNIX PC	Unit 3, 46 Orange Street Cape Town, 8001 South Africa (21) 23-6065
Conclave Internet Dynamics	sales@interdyn.com	NT PC	3717 E. Thousand Oaks Blvd. Westlake, CA 91362 USA (630) 953-7706
CONNECT:Firewall Sterling Commerce	connect@sterling.com	SUN WS	4600 Lakehurst Court Dublin, OH 43016-2000 USA 1-800-700-5579 or (33) 1 4417-6400
ConSeal PC Signal 9 Solutions	firewall@signal9.com	W95 PC	(613) 599-9010
COOL-FIRE Symbolic	mt@symbolic.it		Viale Mentana 29 I-43100 Parma, Italy 521 776180
Cowboyz Firewall cowboyz.com	mark@cowboyz.com	Many	117 SW Taylor Street Portland, OR 97204 USA (503) 241-1990

CryptoSystem
  PyroWall
  RADGUARD
	info@radguard.com		24 Raoul Wallenberg
			Street
			Tel Aviv 69719
			Israel
			972 3 645 5444

CSM Proxy Plus CSM-USA	Var_sales@csm-usa.com	Many PC WS	360 So. Ft. Lane, Suite # 1B Layton, UT 84041 USA (801) 547-0914
CyberGuard CyberGuard Corporation	info@cybg.com	UNIX WS PC	2000 W. Commercial Blvd Ft. Lauderdale, FL 33309 USA (954) 958-3900

Cybershield Data General		UNIX WS	(508) 898-5000
CyberwallPLUS Network-1	sales@network-1.com	WNT PC	1601 Trapelo Rd. Waltham, MA 02451-7305 USA (781) 522-3400
CYCON Labyrinth CYCON Technologies	labyrinth@cycon.com	UNIX PC	11240 Waples Mill Rd., Suite 403 Fairfax, VA 22030 USA (703) 383-0247
Digital Firewall Service Digital Equipment Corporation	e-mail directory	UNIX,WNT	United States Contact: Dick Calandrella at (508) 496-8626

DEC SecurityGate for
  OpenVMS[*]
  Digital Equipment Corporation
	e-mail directory	VMS	contacts or
			(508) 568-6868
			(voice)

Elron Firewall Elron Software	info@elronsoftware.com	POS NT	7 New England Executive Park Burlington, MA 01803-0977 USA (781) 993-6000

enterWorks
  NetSeer Light
  enterWorks.com
	Michael Lazar		19886 Ashburn
			Road
			Ashburn, VA
			20147 USA
			(800) 505-5144 or
			(703) 724-3800

ExFilter V1.1.2	exfilter@exnet.com or exfilter@exnet.co.uk	SUN WS	
F100 Netasq Secure	info@netasq.com	WNT PC	3, rue Archimede 59650 Villeneuve d'Ascq, France 320 619 630
FLUX EF Enhanced Firewall INS Inter Networking Systems	flux-info@ins.de	FluxOS	INS GmbH, P.O.Box 101312, D-44543 Castrop-Rauxel, Germany 2305 1010

Firewall-1
  Check Point Software
  Technologies
	sales@CheckPoint.com	UNIX,WNT
		many
			400 Seaport
			Court, Suite 105
			Redwood City,
			CA 94063 USA
			(800) 429-4391

Fort Knox Firewall Device Internet Devices	sales@internetdevices.com	PC	(408) 541-1400 x314
Freegate FreeGate Corporation	info@freegate.com		1208 E. Arques Sunnyvale, CA 94086 USA (408) 617-1000
Fuego Firewall Cendio Systems	info@cendio.se	any	Teknikringen 8 583 30 Linköping, Sweden 13 214600

Gauntlet
  Trusted Information Systems
  Network Associates
	tis@tis.com(us)
	info@eu.tis.com(non-us)
		SOL HPUX
		BSDI WNT
			Contact Info

GEMINI Trusted Security
  Firewall
  Gemini Computers
	tft@geminisecure.com		(408) 373-8500

GFX Internet Firewall System
  GNAT Box
  Global Technology Associates
	gfx-sales@gta.com
	gb-sales@gta.com
		UNIX/POS
		PC
			3504 Lake Lynda
			Drive, Suite 160
			Orlando, FL
			32817 USA
			(800) 775-4GTA
			or (407) 380-0220

GlobeServer Data Quest Information Systems	info@dqisystems.com	LINUX PC	7509 Kingston Pike, Suite 313 Knoxville, TN 37919 USA (423) 588-4757
HSC GateKeeper Herve Schauer Consultants	info@hsc.fr		142, rue de Rivoli 75039 Paris Cedex 01 France (1) 46.38.89.90

IBM Firewall for AIX IBM	peter_crotty@vnet.ibm.com	AIX WS	IBM Internet Firewall PO Box 12195, Mail Drop B44A/B501 RTP, NC 27709 USA (919) 254-5074
ICE.Block J. River, Inc.	info@jriver.com	UNIX PC	125 North First Street Minneapolis, MN 55401 USA (612) 339-2521
Instant Internet Deerfield Communications	info@deerfield.com	WNT,W95 PC	(517) 732-8856
Interceptor and InstaGate Technologic	info@tlogic.com	PC	2990 Gateway Dr., Suite 950 Norcross, GA 30071 USA (800) 615-9911
InterLock MCI Worldcom Advanced Networks	info@ans.net	SUN WS	1875 Campus Commons Dr. Reston, VA 22091 USA (800) 456-8267 or (703) 758-7700
Inter-Ceptor Network Security International			John Shepherd at (516) 674-0238
IPAD 1200 Netmatrix Internet Co.	sales@ipad-canada.com	POS	Netmatrix Corporation #36001, 6449 Crowchild Tr. SW Calgary, Alberta Canada T3E 7C6 (403) 686-1169
IRX Firewall Livingston Enterprises	info@livingston.com sales@livingston.com	Router	4464 Willow Road Pleasanton, CA 94588 USA (510) 737-2100
IWare Internetware	Paul Singh	Novell	505 W. Olive Ave., Suite 420 Sunnyvale, CA 94086 USA (408) 244-6141

iWay-One BateTech Software	www.workgroup.co.za sales@batetech.com	WNT	7550 W. Yale Ave, B130 Denver, CO 80227 USA (303) 763-8333
Juniper Obtuse Systems	info@obtuse.com		Alberta, Canada
KarlBridge/KarlBrouter KarlNet Inc	sales@KarlNet.com	Bridge/ Router	Columbus, OH, USA (614) 263-KARL
Kwall Firewall BSJ Enterprises	info@kwall.com		
LANguard GFI FAX & VOICE Ltd.	ngalea@gfifax.com	WNT PC	1-888-2GFIFAX
Lucent Managed Firewall Lucent Technologies	firewall@lucent.com	WNT UNIX POS	480 Red Hill Road Middletown, NJ 07748 USA (800) 288-9785
LuciGate LUCIDATA	admin@lucidata.com	POS	Lucidata House, Selwyn Close Great Shelford, CAMBRIDGE, CB2 5HA (0)1223 846100
MIMEsweeper Integralis	info@us.integralis.com	WNT PC	U.K. (0)1734 306060 (The zero from the UK) In the US: (206) 889-5841
M>Wall MATRAnet	info@matranet.com	UNIX WNT WS PC	18 rue Grange Dame Rose BP 262-78147 Velizy Cedex France (0)1 34 58 44 58

NetCS
  NetCS Informationstechnik
  GmbH
	Oliver Korfmacher	Router	Katharinenstrasse 18
			D-10711 Berlin,
			Germany
			Voice: 30/89660-0

NetGate(tm) SmallWorks	info@smallworks.com	SUN WS	(512) 338-0619

NetGuard Control Center
  (was Guardian)
  LanOptics
	sales@lanoptics.com	WNT,W95
		PC
			2445 Midway Rd.
			Carrollton, TX
			75006 USA
			(972) 738-6900

NetRoad/FireWARE/FireWALL Ukiah Software		WNT NWR PC	
NetSafe Siemens Nixdorf	info@swn.sni.be	UNIX WS	SNS RD21 Rue de Niverlie 11 B-5020 Namur Belgium (0)81/55.47.00
Netscreen-100 Netscreen Technologies	info@netscreen.com	POS	4699 Old Ironsides Drive, Suite 300 Santa Clara, CA 95054 USA (408) 970-8889
Net SecurityMaster SOLsoft SA	info@solsoft.com	UNIX WNT WS PC	4 bis, rue de la Gare 92300 Levallois- Perret France 147 155 500
Netra Server Sun MicroSystems		SUN WS	SunSoft, Inc. 2550 Garcia Ave. Mountain View, CA 94043 USA (800) SUN-SOFT outside US: (415) 960-3200

Network Systems ATM
  Firewall
  BorderGuard
  Network Control Facility
  The Security Router
  StorageTek Network Systems
  Group
	webmaster@network.com		(800) NET INFO

Nokia IP & VPN Series Nokia Telecommunications	info@iprg.nokia.com	Router	232 Java Drive Sunnyvale, CA 94089-1318 USA (408) 990-2000

Norman Firewall Norman Data Defense Systems	norman@norman.com	UNIX WS PS	3040 Williams Dr. 6th Floor Fairfax, VA 22031 USA (703) 573-8802
Novix FireFox		Novell	(800) 230-6090
Orion Zebu Systems	info@zebu.com		Samantha Agee (206) 781-9566
Phoenix Adaptive Firewall Progressive Systems	sales@progressive- systems.com		2000 West Henderson Rd., Suite 400 Columbus, OH 43220 USA (614) 326-4600
PORTUS & PORTUS-ES Livermore Software Labratories	portusinfo@lsli.com	ALL ALL	1830 S. Kirkwood, Suite 205 Houston, TX 77077 USA (281) 759-3274
PrivateNet NEC Technologies	info@privatenet.nec.com	BSD UNIX	(800) 668-4869, Department Code: YCB
Pyramid Firewall DataTec	antoniob@datatec.co.uk	UNIX POS	650 Wharfedale Rd. Winnersh Wokingham Berkshire RG41 5TP UK 0118 925 6213
Quiotix	jbs@Quiotix.com		
Raptor Axent Technologies	info@axent.com	UNIX,WNT WS,PC	2400 Research Blvd. Rockville, MD 20850 USA (888)44-AXENT

SecureLan SecureAccess
  SecureFrame
  Cylink
			8229 Boone Blvd.,
			Suite 650
			Vienna, VA
			22182 USA
			(800) 449-1162

SecurIT Firewall Milkyway Networks	Info@milkyway.com	UNIX WNT WS PC	150-2650 Queensview Drive Ottawa, Ontario, Canada K2B 8H6 (800) 206-0922
Sidewinder, SecureZone, and Secure Computing Firewall for NT Secure Computing	sales@securecomputing.com	PC	Contact Info Worldwide US (408) 487-1900
Site Patrol BBN Planet Corp	Gregg Lebovitz		
SonicWall SonicWALL	info@sonicwall.com	Any POS	5400 Betsy Ross Drive, Suite 206 Santa Clara, CA 95054 USA (408) 844-9900
SPF-100/SPF-200 Sun MicroSystems	sunscreen@incog.com	POS WS, PC	Mountain View, CA 94043 USA (415) 960-3200
Sygate SyberGen		W95, WNT PC	
TUNIX Firewall TUNIX Open System Consultants	sales@tunix.nl	BSDI, PC, UNIX	Toernooiveld 124 6525 EC Nijmegen, Netherlands 24.3528819
TurnStyle Firewall System (TFS) TurnStyle Internet Module (TIM) Atlantic Systems Group	US Sales and Marketing Canada	UNIX	USA: (516) 737-6435 CAN: (506) 453-3505
VCS Firewall The Knowledge Group	sales@ktgroup.co.uk	UNIX PC	Concorde Road Patchway, Bristol UK (0)117 900 7500
VPCom Ashley Laurent	Jeffrey Goodwin	UNIX NT	707 West Avenue, Suite 201 Austin, TX 78701 USA (512) 322-0676

Watchguard WatchGuard Technologies	sales@watchguard.com	All PC	Contacts (888) 682-1855 or (206) 521-8340
WebSENSE NetPartners Internet Solutions	sales@netpart.com		9210 Sky Park Court San Diego, CA 92123 USA (800) 723-1166 or (619) 505-3020
WinGate Deerfield Communications	info@deerfield.com	WNT,W95 PC	(517) 732-8856
ZapNet! IPRoute/Secure	info@iproute.com	WNT PC	Suite 400-120, 10945 State Bridge Road Alpharetta, GA 30202 USA (770) 772-4567

FIREWALL RESELLERS

The following is a list of firewall resellers, their products, and services, and appropriate contact information:

ompany	Products/Services	E-mail	Contact
Alexander Open Systems	Firewalls and Security consulting	Sales@aos5.com	10055 Lakeview Ave. Lenexa, KS 66219 USA (913) 307-2300
ANR	NetGuard Control Center and Security consulting	info@anr.co.il	20 Admonit St. Netanya 42204 Israel 972.9.885.0480
Approved Technologies	Network Security and Internet Management	sales@approvedtech.com	110 East 42nd Street, Suite 800 New York , NY 10017-5611 USA (212) 476-4761
Astra Network	Security and network consulting, Firewall installation & admin	infosec@man.net	2633 Portage Ave. Winnipeg, MB Canada R3J 0P7 (204) 987-7050

Atlantic Computing Technology	BorderWare	info@atlantic.com	84 Round Hill Road Wethersfield, CT 06109 USA (203) 257-7163
ARTICON Information Systems GmbH	BorderWare		
Bell Atlantic Network Integration	Network and firewall design.	sales.lead@bani.com	52 East Swedesford Road Frazer, PA 19355 USA (800) 742-2264
BRAK Systems	Firewall-1, WebSENSE and others	tony@brak.com	1 City Centre Drive, Suite 801 Mississauga, Ontario L6S 4T2 Canada (905) 272-3076
Breakwater Security Associates	Many firewalls and security consulting	info@breakwater.net	(206) 770-0700
Cadre Computer Resources	Firewall-1, Secured ISP, Internet development	info@ccr.com	3000 Chemed Center 255 East Fifth Street Cincinnati, OH 45202-4726 USA (513) 762–7350
C-CURE	Information Security Architects	luc.dooms@c-cure.be	K. Rogierstraat 27 B-2000 Antwerpen Belgium (0)3 216.50.50
Centaur Communication GmbH	Firewall-1, and others, Security consulting	info@centaur.de	Urbanstrasse 68 74074 Heilbronn Germany 7131 799 0
Citadel Security Management Systems	Gauntlet, many others, and Internet consulting	infocit@citadel.com.au	726 High Street Armadale VIC AU 03 9500 2990
CleverMinds	Gauntlet, others, and security consulting	Jack Boyle	Bedford, MA (USA) (781) 275-2749
Cohesive Systems	Centri Firewall Information services	info@gi.net	755 Page Mill Road, Suite A-101 Palo Alto, CA 94304 USA (800) 682-5550

Cornerstone Solutions	Firewall-1	info@cornerstones.com	1315 Directors Row, Suite 205 Fort Wayne, IN 46808 USA (219) 496-8259
Collage Communications	Many firewalls and network services	cyberguard@CollCom.COM	12 Tulip Lane Palo Alto, CA 94303 USA
Comark	Firewall-1, and others, Security consulting	webteam@comark.net	444 Scott Drive Bloomingdale, IL 60108 USA (630) 924-6700
Comcad GmbH	Firewall-1 others, and security and network services	frank.recktenwald@ comcad.de	Industriestr. 23 51399 Burscheid Germany 2174.6770
Comnet Solutions	Shareware firewall:Mediator One	firewall@comnet.com.au	ComNet Solutions Pty Ltd Unit 4/12 Old Castle Hill Road Castle Hill, NSW 2154 Australia 2.899.5700
Computer Software Manufaktur (CSM)	CSM Proxy & Proxy Plus Internet Gateway with fw features	sales@csm-usa.com	P.O. Box 1105 Layton, UT 84041 USA (801) 547-0914
Com Tech Communications	Firewall-1 and others, Online Security Services	rof@comtech.com.au	Australia 0412.163374
Conjungi	Gauntlet	simon@conjungi.com	Seattle, WA (USA)
ConnecT GmbH	NetSentry II, BorderWare, Atlas ATM, FireBox, and others	security@connect-gmbh.de	Pichlmayrstr. 11 83024 Rosenheim Germany 0049 8031 38959 0
CONTACTS ONLINE	Secure 4U	secure4u@ contactsonline.com.sg	10 Anson Road, # 05-16 International Plaza, Singapore 079903 (65) 456 6790

CREDO NET	Raptorand Security Consulting	info@credo.net	22941 Triton Way, Suite 241 Laguna Hills, CA 92654 USA (888) 88-CREDO
Crocodial Communications	Firewall-1and Security Consulting	Vertrieb@crocodial.de	Ruhrstrasse 61 D-22761 Hamburg Germany 40.8532640
CyberCorp	NetGuard Control Center	amuse@ cyberservices.com	2934 West Royal Lane, Suite 3136 Irving, TX 75063 USA (972) 738-6916
Cypress Systems	Raptor	rmck	P. O. Box 9070 McLean, VA 22102-0070 USA (703) 273-2150
Data General	Cybershield and Raptor	sense@dg.com	4400 Computer Drive Westboro, MA 01580 USA (800) 4DG-OPEN
Decision-Science Applications	BorderWareFireWall-1 Sidewinder and more	infosec@dsava.com	1110 N. Glebe Rd., Suite 400 Arlington, VA 22201 USA (703) 875-9600 or 243-2500
Deerfield Communications	WinGate Instant Internet	info@deerfield.com	(517) 732-8856
DFC International Ltd.	IBM Firewall	sales@dfc.com	52 Mowatt Court Thornhill, Ontario L3T 6V5 Canada (905) 731-6449
Digital Pathways UK	Sidewinder		
Dimension Data Security	Firewall-1and security products	mouritz@ddsecurity.co.za	158 Jan Smuts Ave. Rosebank P.O. Box 3234 Parklands 2121 South Africa (0)11-283-5116

DNS Telecom	SecureNet and SecureSite, Watchguard and others	preynes@dnstelecom.fr	Immeuble La Fayette 2 place des vosges 92051 Paris la Difense 5 France (0)1 43 34 10 17
Dynavar Networking	Ascend, Cisco PIX and many others	sales@dynavar.com	#300, 1550 - 5th Street SW Calgary, Alberta, Canada T2R 1K3 (403) 571-5000
East Coast Software	NetGuard Control Centerand Security Consulting	infotec@ eastcoastsw.com.au	PO Box 6494, St. Kilda Road Central Melbourne, Victoria 3004 AU 61-3-9821-4848
ElectricMail	Firewall-1and Internet products	info@elmail.co.uk	Merlin Place, Milton Road Cambridge, UK (0) 1223501 333
EMJ America	AFS 2000,BorderWare and others.	mrktusa@emji.net	1434 Farrington Road Apex, NC 27502 USA (800) 548-2319
Enstar Networking	Firewall-1and Security consulting	baustin@enstar.com	8304 Esters Blvd., Suite 840 Dallas, TX 75063 USA (800) 367-4254
Enterprise System Solutions	BorderWare		
FishNet Consulting Services	Firewall-1, others and Security consulting	info@kcfishnet.com	7007 College Blvd. Suite 450 Overland Park, KS 66211-2424 USA (913) 498-0711
Garrison Technologies	Security Consulting, Firewalls, audits, etc.	sales@garrison.com	100 Congress Ave., Suite 2100 Austin TX 78701 USA (512) 302-0882

GearSource	NetGuard Control Center PIX	Sales@GearSource.Com	5015 Victor Street Dallas, TX 75214 USA (214) 821-7909
Global Data Systems	Firewalls and Security	sorourke@gdsconnect.com	5 Pond Park Road, Suite 2 Hingham, MA 02043 USA (781) 740-8818
Global Technology Associates	GTA firewalls and security services	david@globaltech.co.uk	71 Portland Road, Worthing West Sussex BN11 1QG England 44 (0) 1903.20.51.51
Graphics Computer Systems	Firewall-1 and security services	sales@gcs.com.au	97 Highbury Road Burwood, Victoria, Australia 3125 61 3.9888.8522
Haystack Labs now owned by Network Associates	Stalker Intrusion detection system	info@haystack.com	10713 RR620N, Suite 521 Austin, TX 78726 USA (512) 918-3555
Herve Schauer Consultants	HSC GateKeeper	info@hsc.fr	142, rue de Rivoli 75039 Paris Cedex 01 France (1) 46.38.89.90
HomeCom Internet Security Services	Firewall and Security sales and consulting	security@homecom.com	1900 Gallows Rd. Vienna, VA 22182 USA (703) 847-1702
IConNet	Internet in a Rack (IR) Network hardware and software	info@iconnet.net	
Inflo Communications Limited	Raptor firewalls and others	sales@inflo.co.uk	Mountcharles Road Donegal Town Co. Donegal, Ireland 73 23111
Ingress Consulting Group	BorderWare and others	sales@nohackers.com	60 Guild Street Norwood, MA 02062 USA 888-INGRESS

Integralis UK Integralis USA	MIMEsweeper	msw.support @integralis.co.uk info@us.integralis.com	U.K. (0)1734 306060 (The zero from the UK) In the US: (206) 889-5841
Intercede Ltd.	MilkyWay SecureIT	sales@intercede.co.uk	1 Castle Street, Hinckley, Leicestershire LE10 1DA UK (0)1455 250 266
INTERNET GmbH	BorderWare Consulting	Ingmar Schraub	Am Burgacker 23 D-69488 Birkenau, Germany 6201-3999-59
ISP	NetGuard Control Center	info@isp.es	Panama, 22 08034-Barcelona, Spain 932041212
Jerboa	Vendor Independent Security and Firewall Consulting	info@jerboa.com	Box 382648 Cambridge, MA 02238 USA (617) 492-8084
Kerna Communications Ltd	Security consultants, firewall installation and support	sales@kerna.ie	3 Arbourfield Terrace, Dundrum, Dublin 14, Ireland 1-2964396
The Knowledge Group	VCS Firewall and Security products	sales@ktgroup.co.uk	Concorde Road Patchway, Bristol UK (0)117 900 7500
LANhouse	Ascend,Centri Firewall, Communications consulting	sales@lanhouse.com Gauntlet and Security	510 King Street East, Suite 202 Toronto, Ontario, Canada M5A 1M1 (416) 367-2300
LURHQ Corporation	Security Consulting, Firewalls, Web Server Security	info@lurhq.com	Post Office Box 2861 Conway, SC 29526 USA (843) 347-1075
M-Computers	SonicWall and other Sonic Systems products	info@m-computers.de	AlboinstraBe 36-42 12103 Berlin Germany 30-75 49 44-0

Madison Technology Group	Security/FW Design & Implementation	Steveng@microlan.com	331 Madison Ave., 6th Floor New York, NY 10017 USA (212) 883-1000
Master Software Technology	AltaVista and CS consulting	sales@masteredge.com	92 Montvale Ave. Stoneham, MA 02180 USA (617) 438-8330
media communications eur ab	Gauntlet Security consulting	sales@medcom.se	Box 1144, 111 81 Stockholm, Sweden 8 20 85 85
Mergent International	Gauntlet Security consulting	info@mergent.com	(800) 688-1199
Midwest Systems	Gauntlet Sidewinder VAR	lschwanke @midwest-sys.com	2800 Southcross Drive West, Burnsville, MN 55306 USA (612) 894-4020
MPS Ltd	M>Wall and Security consulting	johnt@mpsuk.com	The Manor Stables Great Somerford Nr Chippenham Wiltshire SN15 5EH England (0)1249 721414
NetCon Systems	Firewall-1. Firewall and network security implementation	info@netconsystems.com	300 Arboretum Place, Suite 140 Richmond, VA 23236 USA (804) 560-9638
NetGuard	NetGuard Control Center	solutions@ntguard.com	11350 Random Hill Road, Suite 750 Fairfax, VA 22030 USA (703) 359-8150
NetPartners Internet Solutions	WebSENSE, Firewall-1, Raptor, and others	sales@netpart.com	9665 Chesapeake Dr., Suite 350 San Diego, CA 92123 USA (800) 723-1166 or (619) 505-3020

Netrex	Secure Internet Solutions Firewall-1	info@netrex.com	3000 Town Center, Suite 1100 Southfield, MI 48075 USA 800.3.NETREX
Network Associates	Gauntlet, and many security products	contacts	3965 Freedom Circle Santa Clara, CA 95054 USA (408) 988-3832
Network Security	Firewall-1, NetScreen and others	info@nsec.net	369 River Road North Tonawanda, NY 14120 USA (716) 692-8183
Newlink	Firewall-1, and WatchGuard	contacts	Velizy Plus 1 rue bis petit clamart 78140 Velizy France 146-013-100
Obtuse Systems	Juniper	info@obtuse.com	Alberta, Canada
OMNILINK Internet Service Center	Gauntlet	info@omnilink.net	Hahnstrasse 70 60528 Frankfurt, Germany (69) 66 44 10
Orbis Internet	Sidewinder and Security consulting	dan@orbis.net	475 Cleveland Avenue North, Suite 222 St. Paul, MN 55104 USA (612) 603-9030
PC-Privacy	ConSeal and Security consulting	info@pc-privacy.com	4138-2 Falcon Place Waldorf, MD 20603 USA (301) 638-0341
Qualix	Firewall-1 and security products	qdirect@qualix.com	177 Bovet Road, 2nd Floor San Mateo, CA 94402 USA; Johannesburg South Africa: (650) 572-0200

Racal Airtech Ltd	Raptor Security services	Sohbat Ali	Meadow View House Long Crendon, Aylesbury Buckinghamshire, UK HP18 9EQ 01844.201800
Racal Gaurdata	Raptor Security services	Sohbat Ali	480 Spring Park Place, Suite 900 Herndon, VA 22070 USA (703) 471-0892
Reese Web	Raptor	pp001261@interramp.com	Rocky Point Harbour 3309 Diamond Knot Circle Tampa, FL 33607 USA (813) 286-7065
Sandman Security of Smoke N' Mirrors Inc.	Firewall-1 Raptor and others	Ben Taylor	1165 Herndon Pkwy, Suite 200 Herndon, VA 20170 USA (703) 318-1440
Sea Change Pacific Region	BorderWare	jalsop@seachange.com michael@seawest	5159 Beckton Road Victoria, British Columbia V8Y 2C2 Canada (604) 658-5448
Sea Change Europe Ltd	BorderWare	jalsop@seachange.com peter@sea-europe.co.uk	470 London Road Slough, Berks, SL3 8QY UK 44-1753-581800
Secure Network Systems	Many firewalls and Security and Network consulting	sales@ securenetworkgroup.com	1008 New Hampshire Lawrence, KS 66044 USA (785) 843-8855
SecureXpert Labs FSC Internet Corp	Security consulting and information FireWall1 and others	security@securexpert.com	
Serverware Group plc	iWay-One	sale@serverwr. demon.co.uk	(44)1732-464624
Sherwood Data Systems Ltd	KarlBridge/KarlBrouter	sales@gbnet.com	High Wycombe, UK (0)1494 464264

Silicon Graphics	Gauntlet and Security	Sales	39001 West 12 Mile Rd. Farmington, MI 48331-2903 USA (800) 800-7441
Siemens Nixdorf	TrustedWeb	info@trustedweb.com	Fitzwilliam Court, Leeson Close Dublin 2, Ireland
SkyNet Czech Republic	Gauntlet	Roman.Pavlik@SkyNet.CZ	Kabatnikova 5 602 00 Brno Czech Republic 5 41 24 59 79
SMC Electronic Commerce Ltd	Gauntlet, many other FWs, and Security consulting	info@smcgroup.co.za	52 Wierda Rd. West Wierda Vally, Sandton, South Africa 11 2694005
Softway Pty Ltd	Gauntlet and Security consulting	enquiries@softway.com.au	P.O. Box 305 Strawberry Hills, NSW 2012 Australia 2 9698-2322
Stallion Ltd.	Firewall-1 and Security services	stallion@stallion.ee	Mustamäe tee 55, Tallinn 10621, Estonia 6 567720
Stonesoft Corporation	Stonebeat and Firewall-1	info@stone.fi	Taivalm=E4ki 9 FIN-02200 Espoo, Finland 9 4767 11 9 4767 1282
StorageTek Network Systems Group	ATM,NCF,BorderGuard	webmaster@network.com	(800) NET INFO
Sun Tzu Security	Firewalls and Security consulting	info@suntzu.net	(414) 289-0966
Symbolic	COOL-FIRE and Security services	mt@symbolic.it	Viale Mentana 29 I-43100 Parma, Italy 521 776180
Technology Management Systems	BlackHole	tmsinc@erols.com	Vienna, VA 22181 USA (703) 768-3139

Technology Transition Services	Fort Knox Firewall and security consulting	sales@techtranserv.com	100 Blue Run Rd. Indianola, PA 15051 USA
Trident Data Systems	SunScreen Firewall-1 and Security Consulting	Anthony_Dinga (east) Bob_Hermann (west) Charlie_Johnson (midwest)	5933 W. Century Blvd., Suite 700 Los Angeles, CA 90045 USA (310) 645-6483
Tripcom Systems	Firewall-1 and Internet consulting	Adam Horwitz	Naperville, IL, USA (708) 778-9531
Trusted Information Systems	Gauntlet	tis@tis.com(us) info@eu.tis.com(non-us)	Contact Info (301) 854-6889 or (410) 442-1673
Trusted Network Solutions	Gauntlet and Security consulting		Johannesburg, South Africa
UNIXPAC AUSTRALIA	Raptor and Network consulting	info@unixpac.com.au	Cremorne, Australia (02) 9953 8366 or 1 800 022 137
UUnet	Raptor and others Security consulting	info@uu.net	UUNET Technologies, Inc. 3060 Williams Drive Fairfax, VA 22031-4648 USA (800) 488-6383 or (703) 206-5600
V-ONE	SMARTWALL and Security Consulting	sales@v-one.com	20250 Century Blvd. Germantown, MD 20874 USA (301) 515-5200
Vanstar	All major Security products and consulting	Jrecor@vanstar.com	30800 Telegraph Rd., Suite 1850 Bingham Farms, MI 48312 USA (810) 540-6493
Ward Consulting Limited	Firewall-1 and others. Security consulting	sales@ward.ie	Unit 2504, Citywest Business Campus Dublin 24, Ireland 1-6420100

We Connect People Inc.	Security, FWs, Internet Consulting, and more	sales@wcpinc.com	California, USA (408) 421-0857
WheelGroup	NetRanger/NetSonar Intrusion detection and other security products	sales@wheelgroup.com	13750 San Pedro, Suite 670 San Antonio, TX 78232 USA (210) 494-3383
X Open Systems Pty Ltd	Security, FWs, and network services	info@xplus.com.AU	P.O. Box 6456 Shoppingworld North Sydney, NSW 2059 AU 2 9957 6152
Zeuros Limited	Raptor and Network services	support@zeuros.co.uk	Tudor Barn, Frog Lane Rotherwick, Hampshire, RG27 9BE UK 44 (0) 1256 760081
ZONEOFTRUST.COM	Security Products, FWs and Services	info@zoneoftrust.com	22941 Triton Way, 2nd Floor Laguna Hills, CA 92653 USA (714) 859-0196

4
HIRING AND OUTSOURCING

WHY COMPANIES OUTSOURCE

Outsourcing is prevalent in *Information Technology (IT)*. The Outsourcing Institute's* *Annual Survey of Outsourcing End Users* reveals the following top ten reasons for why companies outsource:

- Reduce and control operating costs
- Improve company focus
- Gain access to world-class capabilities
- Free internal resources for other purposes
- Resources are not available internally
- Accelerate reengineering benefits
- Function difficult to manage/out of control
- Make capital funds available
- Share risks
- Cash infusion

Outsourcing IT lets an organization focus on its core business functions. Every organization has limited resources. By outsourcing, an organi-

---

*www.outsourcing.com

zation can shift its energies away from noncore functions and can concentrate on serving the needs of its customers. Noncore functions, such as IT, may not necessarily be operating at peak efficiency when in-house IT facilities and staff are used. Outsourcing IT gives the organization an opportunity to use a world-class IT provider and achieve benefits from reengineering.

A world-class IT provider can make extensive investments in the latest and most efficient technologies and can give its staff the best training. An IT provider's staff is exposed to problem solving for many clients. This allows the IT provider's staff to gain better experience and develop greater expertise and specialization. The ability to work in a challenging environment often gives the IT provider an edge in recruiting the best staff and talent.

An IT vendor's cost structure is likely to be lower than that of an organization that tries to perform all functions itself. Economies of scale resulting from greater specialization can reduce operating costs and give it a competitive advantage.

THE OUTSOURCING PROCESS

Outsourcing frequently involves selling/transferring facilities, hardware, software, and other assets to the IT provider. In some cases, the IT vendor hires the organization's information technology staff. The IT provider/vendor uses these assets and personnel to provide services to the organization/client.

The sale or transfer of assets (usually at book value) may be a significant source of cash to the client organization. The book value of the assets is equal to their historical cost (original purchase price) less accumulated depreciation. The market value of the assets is often less than their book value. If the sale takes place at book value, then the difference between the book value and market value is treated as a loan from the IT vendor to the client organization; the loan is repaid as the client pays IT fees over the term of the service contract.

Outsourcing reduces the need to invest in noncore activities. With limited resources, it often makes business sense to invest in an organization's core functions. Outsourcing eliminates the need for capital expenditures in IT; instead the fees for IT are treated as operating expenses. Sometimes, outsourcing can improve certain financial ratios of an organization by eliminating IT assets as well as liabilities.

UNDERSTANDING THE RISKS OF OUTSOURCING

The risks of outsourcing include

- loss of control over the function or process,
- loss of flexibility and the inability to meet changes in the marketplace,
- failure to improve performance or achieve projected financial benefits.

However, eliminating the in-house IT function reduces certain risks. Technologies can change rapidly. Keeping up with the state of the art in IT technology may not be possible for an in-house IT department. IT resources, such as access to highly specialized personnel, may not be available internally, and outsourcing may be an organization's only option.

It is a mistake to outsource the IT function if the organization's primary reason is to outsource a poorly managed, costly, or misunderstood function. Outsourcing is not the solution to a problem that the organization itself doesn't understand. If the organization is unable to communicate its needs to the IT provider, it will not benefit from outsourcing the IT function.

REEVALUATING THE NEED TO OUTSOURCE

The organization should reevaluate the merits of outsourcing at regular intervals (e.g., three to five years). Changes in technology, internal dynamics, market conditions, or industry can affect the outsourcing decision.

SELECTING AN OUTSOURCING VENDOR

The Outsourcing Institute's *Annual Survey of Outsourcing End Users* reveals the following top factors in selecting outsource vendors:

- Commitment to quality
- Price

- References/reputation
- Flexible contract terms
- Scope of resources
- Additional value-added capability
- Cultural match
- Existing relationship
- Location

USING EXTERNAL CONSULTANTS

An outside consultant can be useful in making the outsourcing decision, especially when outsourcing threatens to disrupt the organizational status quo. Outside consultants can also help management during the evaluation and negotiation process. Outsourcing vendors typically have greater experience in negotiating outsourcing contracts. Also, obtaining unbiased help from outside consultants can help level the playing field.

SELECTING THE OUTSOURCING TEAM

Once the decision to outsource has been made, a management team should be selected. The team should consist of personnel from various departments, including

- Legal
- Finance
- Human resources
- Information technology

The team should be responsible for oversight and management of the outsourcing agreement. The team should play an integral role in drafting and negotiating the outsourcing contract.

The legal staff should be involved in all phases of negotiating the outsourcing contract. There should be a clear understanding of the relationship and the expectations between the organization and the vendor.

SUCCESSFUL OUTSOURCING

The Outsourcing Institute's *Annual Survey of Outsourcing End Users* gives the following top factors for successful outsourcing:

- Understanding company goals and objectives
- A strategic vision and plan
- Selecting the right vendor
- Ongoing management of the relationships
- A properly structured contract
- Open communication with affected individual/groups
- Senior-executive support and involvement
- Careful attention to personnel issues
- Near-term financial justification
- Use of outside expertise

CONTRACTING CONSIDERATIONS

Some of the important considerations in an outsourcing contract are:

- Time period
- Renewal option
- Levels of service
- Ownership and confidentiality of data
- Performance measurement
- Performance incentives and penalties
- Financial stability of the IT vendor
- Circumstances for modifying agreement

The contract should be sufficiently detailed to avoid misunderstandings. However, when contractual requirements are too detailed, problems may arise. They may leave little room for innovation. The organization and the IT vendor may be unable to take advantage of new opportunities or changes in environment. Some flexibility in the outsourcing agreement can benefit outsourcing partners.

Despite best intentions, the parties may be unable to work with each other. The outsourcing contract should clearly define conditions that will terminate the relationship with the IT vendor.

OUTSOURCING WEB HOSTING

Even if other IT functions are performed in-house, many organizations are outsourcing their web-hosting function. Outsourcing web-hosting is popular for several reasons:

- Web-based systems are complex; most organizations lack the expertise.
- Many organizations are unable to recruit top quality IT professionals.
- Most organizations lack the time and manpower to support web operations twenty-four hours a day.
- Web-hosting organizations can often provide the services at a significantly lower cost.

Factors to consider in selecting a web-hosting company include

- High-speed, network backbone
- Highly reliable network
- Expertise in managing Internet systems
- Ability to monitor and manage customers' web operations twenty-four hours a day
- Sufficient bandwidth to meet increased user demand
- Security to protect against unauthorized access

DEVELOPING A STRATEGIC OUTSOURCING RELATIONSHIP

This section discusses *Strategic Sourcing Architecture* developed by the Warren Company.* Developing a strategic outsourcing relationship benefits both the organization and its outsourcing provider. Senior management should

---

*Blumberg, Les, *How to Engage in a Strategic Sourcing Relationship,* www.outsourcing.com (The Warren Company, One Richmond Square, Providence, RI)

approve and authorize an evaluation of strategic outsourcing opportunities for the IT function. Senior-management support for nontraditional outsourcing is crucial. They must set the outsourcing strategy and objectives and provide an atmosphere that encourages innovation.

The outsourcing strategy should be:

- A part of the organization's overall strategic plan, and
- In line with the organization's goals

Individuals responsible for implementing the outsourcing plan should understand the organization's goals and objectives and how outsourcing fits into the organization's overall strategy. The following steps are identified by Blumberg:

- Identify the process(es) to be considered for outsourcing.
- Tentatively determine which type of sourcing relationship is appropriate.
- Assess organizational readiness.
- Develop and document a preliminary Outsourcing Mission, Strategy, and Goals (OMSAG) statement.

The first step in determining an outsourcing strategy is to identify functions or processes that may be outsourced. Common areas for outsourcing include

- Client/server systems
- Data centers
- Desktop systems
- End-user support services
- Internet services
- Network management
- Personnel training
- Reengineering and quality management
- Repair and maintenance

- Software development
- Web hosting

Next, a determination must be made about which type of outsourcing relationship is appropriate. In other words, one must determine how to integrate operations with the outsourcing vendor and which objectives are important. For instance, if cost reduction and low price are the primary objectives, a traditional IT outsourcing relationship with the vendor is likely to be most appropriate.

For certain low-value-added processes, the costs of analytical effort and relationship building may not justify anything but traditional IT-vendor outsourcing. Blumberg explains how outsourcing relationships can vary based on an organization's objectives (see Fig. 4–1).

Some organizations use two or more vendors to create a competitive environment. Each vendor is given a specific portion of the work, with the remainder available for either vendor. For instance, two vendors might each be given 35% of the work. The remaining 30% will be given annually to the vendor with the greatest cost reductions or productivity improvements. The competition approach encourages the vendors to perform their best and not to take the client organization for granted.

The competitive approach has its limitations. The IT vendors' focus becomes that of winning instead of really working with each other to do what is in the best interest of the client organization. In other words, this kind of competitive arrangement discourages the competing vendors from sharing their best practices.

Another approach is to use two or more vendors and give each vendor functions where the vendor has greatest expertise. For instance, one IT vendor may be assigned the function of application development, whereas another IT vendor may be responsible for ongoing maintenance, service, and support. This type of relationship emphasizes the need for a tight complementary alliance. The two vendors are expected to cooperate; yet at the same time, one vendor serves as a check on the other.

These kinds of strategic arrangements typically require significant effort to ensure that the alliance is well managed.

*Figure 4–1
Major Stage Differentiators

	Transaction-Based		Relationship-Based		
	Stage 1:	**Stage 2:**	**Stage 3:**	**Stage 4:**	**Stage 5:**
	Transaction Oriented Outsourcing	*Cosourcing Partner Relationships*	*Strategic Sourcing Strategic Relationships*	*Value-Chain Networking Shared Asset Relationships*	*Entrepreneurial Venturing/ Hybrid Spin-off Relationships*
Motive for Outsourcing	Fix immediate problem	Leverage resources, technology	Positioning vehicle for the future	Cocreating future value, focus on asset influence/ pooling	Capture of specific breakthrough bypass business opportunity
Provider Selection	Vendor-procurement based	Negotiated partner selection	Strategic-alliance architecture based	Strategic-alliance architecture based	Strategic-alliance architecture based
Measures	Better, cheaper, faster	Productivity, Leverage, Best-in-class, Value-added projects	System-integration trust measures	System-integration trust measures	System-integration trust measures
Strategic Orientation	Short-term	Medium- to long-term	Long-term	Long-term, open-ended	Long-term, open-ended
Structure	Transactional	Hybrid of transactional/ relational	Relational	Completely relationship based	Primarily relational leading to stand-alone entity
Pricing Framework	Low-bidder	Cost-cognizant but not dominant Sometimes shared risk/reward	Win-win, shared risk/reward	Win-win, shared risk/reward	Win-win, shared risk/reward

*Source: Blumberg, Les, *How to Engage in a Strategic Sourcing Relationship*, www.outsourcing.com

FIGURE 4–1
MAJOR STAGE DIFFERENTIATORS (*continued*)

	Transaction-Based		Relationship-Based		
	Stage 1:	**Stage 2:**	**Stage 3:**	**Stage 4:**	**Stage 5:**
	Transaction Oriented Outsourcing	*Cosourcing Partner Relationships*	*Strategic Sourcing Strategic Relationships*	*Value-Chain Networking Shared Asset Relationships*	*Entrepreneurial Venturing/ Hybrid Spin-off Relationships*
Strategic Planning	Little or none	Significant resources for decision	Extensive planning and due diligence	Intimately linked to corporate vision	Driven from distinct new venture plan
Formal Control	High	Low-level collaborative mechanisms	Based on shared outcomes/ objectives	Control exercised through collaboration	Medium to low
Integration Level	Very little or none	Loose integration	Very substantial	Very high	Very high
Trust	Low	Based on partnering	High levels of mutual trust	Highest degree of mutual trust based on performance	Highest degree of mutual trust based on performance, Joint expansion of opportunity

Characteristics of a Well-Structured Alliance

Blumberg gives the following as characteristics of a well-structured out-sourcing alliance:

- *Strategic synergy:* Can the two (or more) organizations together achieve a high level of benefits?

- *Growth opportunity:* Can the relationship—and its benefits—be expanded?

- *Less risk:* Does the relationship reduce the level of risk for your organization?

- *Excellent chemistry:* Is there a good "fit" between your organization and the provider(s)' organization?
- *Clarity of purpose:* Are the goals and benefits explicit and clear?
- *Win-win:* Does each party benefit fairly from the relationship?

Outsourcing Mission, Strategy, and Goals Statement

The organization's outsourcing objectives and strategic rationale are summarized in the Outsourcing Mission, Strategy, and Goals (OMSAG) statement. The OMSAG statement should describe:

- Objectives and benefits of outsourcing
- Processes or functions to be outsourced
- How outsourcing is a part of the organization's overall strategy
- How outsourcing affects your organization's core and expanded core activities
- Risks
- Expected duration of the outsourcing relationship
- Number of outsourcing partners
- Nature of outsourcing: competitive versus cooperative

Senior management must understand why it wishes to outsource certain functions. Blumberg has proposed the following:

- Consider how specific target customers (internal or external) are affected—how the relationship's product or service makes the customer more
  - Successful
  - Profitable
  - Competitive
  - Efficient
  - Effective
  - Productive
  - Satisfied
- Seek validation from target customers.
- Describe explicit, quantified benefits.

- Fix the date when measurable success is expected.
- Assess the feasibility of reaching goals.
- Consider the advantage of an alliance versus other approaches.

SOLE OUTSOURCING

Sole outsourcing occurs when an organization selects a single vendor to perform a function without obtaining competitive bids. The primary advantage of sole outsourcing is that it frees the organization's time and resources by shortening the procurement cycle. However, sometimes the only way to get the best price and service is through open competition, rather than through sole sourcing.

Selecting an IT outsourcing vendor through a formal Request for Proposal (RFP) may take several months or even a year or two. For certain critical functions, the organization may not be able to afford such a delay.

Many vendors are unwilling to absorb the costs associated with an RFP. A formal RFP can be expensive, time consuming, and complex. If the competing outsourcing vendors are to submit an accurate bid, the vendors must have a detailed understanding of the job specification.

Industry benchmarking can help overcome some of the problems associated with sole outsourcing. An organization considering sole outsourcing can use industry benchmarking to ensure that the terms, conditions, and service levels in the agreement are consistent with those of the industry.

Caution must be exercised when engaging in sole outsourcing to avoid the appearance of impropriety. It should not appear that one vendor received preferential treatment over another in the selection process. Due diligence must be exercised, and there must be no suggestion of a lack of fiduciary responsibility.

5A

CAPITAL BUDGETING AND ECONOMIC FEASIBILITY STUDY

Capital budgeting is the process of making long-term planning decisions for alternative investment opportunities. There are many investment decisions that the company may have to make in order to grow. Examples of capital budgeting applications are installation of a new information system (IS), lease or purchase, new-product development, product-line selection, keep or sell a business segment, and which asset to invest in. A careful cost-benefit analysis must be performed to determine a project's economic feasibility of a capital expenditure project.

This chapter covers

- Types and special features of capital budgeting decisions
- Concept of time value of the money
- Several popular capital-budgeting techniques
- Effect of Modified Accelerated Cost Recovery System (MACRS) on capital budgeting decisions
- How to determine the cost of capital
- How to make lease-purchase decisions
- Economic feasibility study for a new information system

---

*www.outsourcing.com

39

TYPES OF INVESTMENT PROJECTS

There are typically two types of long-term capital expenditure decisions.

1. *Selection decisions* in terms of obtaining new facilities or expanding existing ones: Examples include

   - Investments in property, plant, and equipment as well as other types of assets
   - Resource commitments in the form of new-product development, market research, introduction of an IS system, refunding of long-term debt, and so on
   - Mergers and acquisitions in the form of buying another company to add a new product line

2. *Replacement decisions* in terms of replacing existing facilities with new ones. Examples include replacing an old machine with a high-tech machine.

FEATURES OF INVESTMENT PROJECTS

Long-term investments have three important features.

1. They typically involve a large amount of initial cash outlays, which tend to have a long-term impact on the firm's future profitability. Therefore, this initial cash outlay needs to be justified on a cost-benefit basis.

2. There are expected recurring cash inflows (for example, increased revenues, savings in cash operating expenses, etc.) over the life of the investment project. This frequently requires considering the *time value of money*.

3. Income taxes could make a difference in the accept-or-reject decision. Therefore, income tax factors must be taken into account in every capital-budgeting decision.

UNDERSTANDING THE CONCEPT OF TIME VALUE OF MONEY

A dollar now is worth more than a dollar to be received later. This statement sums up an important principle: money has a time value. The truth of this principle is not that inflation might make the dollar received at a later time worth less in buying power. The reason is that you could invest the dollar now and have more than a dollar at the specified later date.

Time value of money is a critical consideration in financial and investment decisions. For example, compound-interest calculations are needed to determine future sums of money resulting from an investment. Discounting, or the calculation of present value, inversely related to compounding, is used to evaluate the future cash flow associated with capital-budgeting projects. There are plenty of applications of time value of money in accounting and finance.

Calculating Future Values—How Money Grows

A dollar in hand today is worth more than a dollar to be received tomorrow because of the interest it could earn from putting it in a savings account or placing it in an investment account. Compounding interest means that interest earns interest. For the discussion of the concepts of compounding and time value, let us define

F_n = future value: the amount of money at the end of year n
P = principal
i = annual interest rate
n = number of years

Then,

F_1 = the amount of money at the end of year 1
  = principal and interest = $P + iP = P(1 + i)$
F_2 = the amount of money at the end of year 2
  = $F_1(1 + i) = P(1 + i)(1 + i) = P(1 + i)^2$

The future value of an investment compounded annually at rate i for n years is

$$F_n = P(1 + i)^n = P \cdot T1(i,n)$$

where T1 (i,n) is the compound amount of $1 and can be found in Table 5A-1.

Example 1 You place $1,000 in a savings account earning 8% interest compounded annually. How much money will you have in the account at the end of four years?

$$F_n = P(1 + i)^n$$
$$F_4 = \$1,000 \ (1 + 0.08)^4 = \$1,000 \ T1(8\%, 4 \ years)$$

From Table 5A-1, the T1 for 4 years at 8% is 1.361.

Therefore, $F_4 = \$1,000 \ (1.361) = \$1,361.$

Example 2 You invested a large sum of money in the stock of Delta Corporation. The company paid a $3 dividend per share. The dividend is expected to increase by 20% per year for the next three years. You wish to project the dividends for years one through three.

$$F_n = P(1+i)^n$$
$$F_1 = \$3(1 + 0.2)^1 = \$3 \ T1(20\%, 1) = \$3 \ (1.200) = \$3.60$$
$$F_2 = \$3(1 + 0.2)^2 = \$3 \ T1(20\%, 2) = \$3 \ (1.440) = \$4.32$$
$$F_3 = \$3(1 + 0.2)^3 = \$3 \ T1(20\%, 3) = \$3 \ (1.728) = \$5.18$$

Future Value of an Annuity

An annuity is defined as a series of payments (or receipts) of a fixed amount for a specified number of periods. Each payment is assumed to occur at the end of the period. The future value of an annuity is a compound annuity, which involves depositing or investing an equal sum of money at the end of each year for a certain number of years and allowing it to grow.

TABLE 5A–1 FUTURE VALUE OF $1 = T1 (I, N)

Periods	4%	6%	8%	10%	12%	14%	20%
1	1.040	1.060	1.080	1.100	1.120	1.140	1.200
2	1.082	1.124	1.166	1.210	1.254	1.300	1.440
3	1.125	1.191	1.260	1.331	1.405	1.482	1.728
4	1.170	1.263	1.361	1.464	1.574	1.689	2.074
5	1.217	1.338	1.469	1.611	1.762	1.925	2.488
6	1.265	1.419	1.587	1.772	1.974	2.195	2.986
7	1.316	1.504	1.714	1.949	2.211	2.502	3.583
8	1.369	1.594	1.851	2.144	2.476	2.853	4.300
9	1.423	1.690	1.999	2.359	2.773	3.252	5.160
10	1.480	1.791	2.159	2.594	3.106	3.707	6.192
11	1.540	1.898	2.332	2.853	3.479	4.226	7.430
12	1.601	2.012	2.518	3.139	3.896	4.818	8.916
13	1.665	2.133	2.720	3.452	4.364	5.492	10.699
14	1.732	2.261	2.937	3.798	4.887	6.261	12.839
15	1.801	2.397	3.172	4.177	5.474	7.138	15.407
20	2.191	3.207	4.661	6.728	9.646	13.743	38.338
30	3.243	5.744	10.063	17.450	29.960	50.950	237.380
40	4.801	10.286	21.725	45.260	93.051	188.880	1469.800

Let S_n = the future value on an n-year annuity
A = the amount of an annuity

Then we can write

$$S_n = A(1 + i)^{n-1} + A(1 + i)^{n-2} + \ldots + A(1 + i)^0$$

$$= A[(1 + i)^{n-1} + (1 + i)^{n-2} + \ldots + (1 + i)^0]$$

$$= A \cdot \sum_{t=0}^{n-1} (1 + i)^t = A \bullet \left[\frac{(1 + i)^n - 1}{i} \right] = A \cdot T2(i,n)$$

where T2(i,n) represents the future value of an annuity of $1 for n years compounded at i percent and can be found in Table 5A-2.

TABLE 5A–2 FUTURE VALUE OF $1 = T2 (I, N)

Periods	4%	6%	8%	10%	12%	14%	20%
1	1.000	1.000	1.000	1.000	1.000	1.000	1.000
2	2.040	2.060	2.080	2.100	2.120	2.140	2.220
3	3.122	3.184	3.246	3.310	3.374	3.440	3.640
4	4.247	4.375	4.506	4.641	4.779	4.921	5.368
5	5.416	5.637	5.867	6.105	6.353	6.610	7.442
6	6.633	6.975	7.336	7.716	8.115	8.536	9.930
7	7.898	8.394	8.923	9.487	10.089	10.730	12.916
8	9.214	9.898	10.637	11.436	12.300	13.233	16.499
9	10.583	11.491	12.488	13.580	14.776	16.085	20.799
10	12.006	13.181	14.487	15.938	17.549	19.337	25.959
11	13.486	14.972	16.646	18.531	20.655	23.045	32.150
12	15.026	16.870	18.977	21.395	24.133	27.271	39.580
13	16.627	18.882	21.495	24.523	28.029	32.089	48.497
14	18.292	21.015	24.215	27.976	32.393	37.581	59.196
15	20.024	23.276	27.152	31.773	37.280	43.842	72.035
20	29.778	36.778	45.762	57.276	75.052	91.025	186.690
30	56.085	79.058	113.283	164.496	241.330	356.790	1181.900
40	95.026	154.762	259.057	442.597	767.090	1342.000	7343.900

Example 3 You wish to determine the sum of money you will have in a savings account at the end of six years by depositing $1,000 at the end of each year for the next six years. The annual interest rate is 8%. The T2(8%,6 years) is given in Table 5A-2 as 7.336. Therefore,

$$S_6 = \$1,000 \; T2(8\%,6) = \$1,000 \; (7.336) = \$7,336$$

Example 4 You deposit $30,000 semiannually into a fund for ten years. The annual interest rate is 8%. The amount accumulated at the end of the tenth year is calculated as follows:

$$S_n = A. \; T2(i, n)$$

where $A = \$30,000$

$i = 8\%/2 = 4\%$

$n = 10 \times 2 = 20$

Therefore,

$S_n = \$30,000\ T2(4\%, 20)$
$= \$30,000\ (29.778) = \$893,340$

Calculating Present Value—How Much Money Is Worth Now

Present value is the present worth of future sums of money. The process of calculating present values, or discounting, is actually the opposite of finding the compounded future value. In connection with present-value calculations, the interest rate i is called the *discount rate*. The discount rate we use is more commonly called the *cost of capital*, which is the minimum rate of return required by the investor.

Recall that $F_n = P(1 + i)^n$

Therefore,

$$P = \frac{F_n}{(1 + i)^n} = F_n \left[\frac{1}{(1 + i)^n} \right] = F_n \cdot T3(i,n)$$

where T3(i,n) represents the present value of $1 and is given in Table 5A-3.

Example 5 You have been given an opportunity to receive $20,000 six years from now. If you can earn 10% on your investments, what is the most you should pay for this opportunity? To answer this question, you must compute the present value of $20,000 to be received six years from now at a 10% rate of discount. F_6 is $20,000, i is 10%, and *n* is six years. T3(10%,6) from Table 5A-3 is 0.565.

$$P = \$20,000 \left[\frac{1}{(1 + 0.1)^6} \right] = \$20,000\ T3(10\%,6) = \$20,000(0.564) = \$11,280$$

TABLE 5A–3 FUTURE VALUE OF $1 = T_3 (I, N)

Periods	4%	5%	6%	8%	10%	12%	14%	16%	18%	20%	22%	24%	26%	28%	30%	40%
1	0.962	0.952	0.943	0.926	0.909	0.893	0.877	0.862	0.847	0.833	0.820	0.806	0.794	0.781	0.769	0.714
2	0.925	0.907	0.890	0.857	0.826	0.797	0.769	0.743	0.718	0.694	0.672	0.650	0.630	0.610	0.592	0.510
3	0.889	0.864	0.840	0.794	0.751	0.712	0.675	0.641	0.609	0.579	0.551	0.524	0.500	0.477	0.455	0.364
4	0.855	0.823	0.792	0.735	0.683	0.636	0.592	0.552	0.516	0.482	0.451	0.423	0.397	0.373	0.350	0.260
5	0.822	0.784	0.747	0.681	0.621	0.567	0.519	0.476	0.437	0.402	0.370	0.341	0.315	0.291	0.269	0.186
6	0.790	0.746	0.705	0.630	0.564	0.507	0.456	0.410	0.370	0.335	0.303	0.275	0.250	0.227	0.207	0.133
7	0.760	0.711	0.665	0.583	0.513	0.452	0.400	0.354	0.314	0.279	0.249	0.222	0.198	0.178	0.159	0.095
8	0.731	0.677	0.627	0.540	0.467	0.404	0.351	0.305	0.266	0.233	0.204	0.179	0.157	0.139	0.123	0.068
9	0.703	0.645	0.592	0.500	0.424	0.361	0.308	0.263	0.225	0.194	0.167	0.144	0.125	0.108	0.094	0.048
10	0.676	0.614	0.558	0.463	0.386	0.322	0.270	0.227	0.191	0.162	0.137	0.116	0.099	0.085	0.073	0.035
11	0.650	0.585	0.527	0.429	0.350	0.287	0.237	0.195	0.162	0.135	0.112	0.094	0.079	0.066	0.056	0.025
12	0.625	0.557	0.497	0.397	0.319	0.257	0.208	0.168	0.137	0.112	0.092	0.076	0.062	0.052	0.043	0.018
13	0.601	0.530	0.469	0.368	0.290	0.229	0.182	0.145	0.116	0.093	0.075	0.061	0.050	0.040	0.033	0.013
14	0.577	0.505	0.442	0.340	0.263	0.205	0.160	0.125	0.099	0.078	0.062	0.049	0.039	0.032	0.025	0.009
15	0.555	0.481	0.417	0.315	0.239	0.183	0.140	0.108	0.084	0.065	0.051	0.040	0.031	0.025	0.020	0.006
16	0.534	0.458	0.394	0.292	0.218	0.163	0.123	0.093	0.071	0.054	0.042	0.032	0.025	0.019	0.015	0.005
17	0.513	0.436	0.371	0.270	0.198	0.146	0.108	0.080	0.060	0.045	0.034	0.026	0.020	0.015	0.012	0.003
18	0.494	0.416	0.350	0.250	0.180	0.130	0.095	0.069	0.051	0.038	0.028	0.021	0.016	0.012	0.009	0.002
19	0.475	0.396	0.331	0.232	0.164	0.116	0.083	0.060	0.043	0.031	0.023	0.017	0.012	0.009	0.007	0.002
20	0.456	0.377	0.312	0.215	0.149	0.104	0.073	0.051	0.037	0.026	0.019	0.014	0.010	0.007	0.005	0.001
21	0.439	0.359	0.294	0.199	0.135	0.093	0.064	0.044	0.031	0.022	0.015	0.011	0.008	0.006	0.004	0.001
22	0.422	0.342	0.278	0.184	0.123	0.083	0.056	0.038	0.026	0.018	0.013	0.009	0.006	0.004	0.003	0.001
23	0.406	0.326	0.262	0.170	0.112	0.074	0.049	0.033	0.022	0.015	0.010	0.007	0.005	0.003	0.002	
24	0.390	0.310	0.247	0.158	0.102	0.066	0.043	0.028	0.019	0.013	0.008	0.006	0.004	0.003	0.002	
25	0.375	0.295	0.233	0.146	0.092	0.059	0.038	0.024	0.016	0.010	0.007	0.005	0.003	0.002	0.001	
26	0.361	0.281	0.220	0.135	0.084	0.053	0.033	0.021	0.014	0.009	0.006	0.004	0.002	0.002	0.001	
27	0.347	0.268	0.207	0.125	0.076	0.047	0.029	0.018	0.011	0.007	0.005	0.003	0.002	0.001	0.001	
28	0.333	0.255	0.196	0.116	0.069	0.042	0.026	0.016	0.010	0.006	0.004	0.002	0.002	0.001	0.001	
29	0.321	0.243	0.185	0.107	0.063	0.037	0.022	0.014	0.008	0.005	0.003	0.002	0.001	0.001	0.001	
30	0.308	0.231	0.174	0.099	0.057	0.033	0.020	0.012	0.007	0.004	0.003	0.002	0.001	0.001		
40	0.208	0.142	0.097	0.046	0.022	0.011	0.005	0.003	0.001	0.001						

This means that you can earn 10% on your investment, and you would be indifferent to receiving $11,280 now or $20,000 six years from today since the amounts are time equivalent. In other words, you could invest $11,300 today at 10% and have $20,000 in six years.

Present Value of Mixed Streams of Cash Flows

The present value of a series of mixed payments (or receipts) is the sum of the present value of each individual payment. We know that the present value of each individual payment is the payment times the appropriate T3 value.

Example 6 You are thinking of starting a new product line that initially costs $32,000. Your annual projected cash inflows are

1 $10,000

2 $20,000

3 $5,000

If you must earn a minimum of 10% on your investment, should you undertake this new product line?

The present value of this series of mixed streams of cash inflows is calculated as follows:

Year	Cash inflows	x T3(10%, n)	Present Value
1	$10,000	0.909	$ 9,090
2	$20,000	0.826	$16,520
3	$ 5,000	0.751	$ 3,755
			$29,365

Since the present value of your projected cash inflows is less than the initial investment, you should not undertake this project.

Present Value of an Annuity

Interest received from bonds, pension funds, and insurance obligations involve annuities. To compare these financial instruments, we need to know the present value of each.

The present value of an annuity (P_n) can be found by using the following equation:

$$P_n = A. \frac{1}{(1+i)^1} + \frac{1}{(1+i)^2} \cdots + A. \frac{1}{(1+i)^n}$$

$$= A. \left[\frac{1}{(1+i)^1} + \frac{1}{(1+i)^2} + \cdots + \frac{1}{(1+i)^n} \right]$$

$$= A. \sum_{t=1}^{n} \frac{1}{(1+i)^t} = A. \frac{1}{i} \left[1 - \frac{1}{(1+i)} \right] = A. T4(i,n)$$

where T4(i,n) represents the present value of an annuity of $1 discounted at i percent for n years and is found in Table 5A-4.

Example 7 Assume that the cash inflows in Example 6 form an annuity of $10,000 for three years. Then the present value is

$$P_n = A \cdot T4(i,n)$$
$$P_3 = \$10,000 \, T4(10\%, 3 \, years) = \$10,000 \, (2.487) = \$24,870$$

Use of Financial Calculators and Spreadsheet Programs

There are many financial calculators that contain preprogrammed formulas to perform many present-value and future applications. They include *Hewlett-Packard 10B, Sharpe EL733,* and *Texas Instrument BA35*. Furthermore, spreadsheet software such as *Excel* has built-in financial functions to perform many such applications.

MEASURING INVESTMENT WORTH

Several methods of evaluating investment projects are as follows:

1. Payback period
2. Net present value (NPV)
3. Internal rate of return (IRR)

TABLE 5A–4 PRESENT VALUE OF AN ANNUITY OF $1 = T_4 (I, N)

Periods	4%	5%	6%	8%	10%	12%	14%	16%	18%	20%	22%	24%	26%	28%	30%	40%
1	0.962	0.952	0.943	0.926	0.909	0.893	0.877	0.862	0.847	0.833	0.820	0.806	0.794	0.781	0.769	0.714
2	1.886	1.859	1.833	1.783	1.736	1.690	1.647	1.605	1.566	1.528	1.492	1.457	1.424	1.392	1.361	1.224
3	2.775	2.723	2.673	2.577	2.487	2.402	2.322	2.246	2.174	2.106	2.042	1.981	1.868	1.816	1.816	1.589
4	3.630	3.546	3.465	3.312	3.170	3.037	2.914	2.798	2.690	2.589	2.494	2.404	2.320	2.241	2.166	1.879
5	4.452	4.330	4.212	3.993	3.791	3.605	3.433	3.274	3.127	2.991	2.864	2.745	2.635	2.532	2.436	2.035
6	5.242	5.076	4.917	4.623	4.355	4.111	3.889	3.685	3.498	3.326	3.167	3.020	2.885	2.759	2.643	2.168
7	6.002	5.786	5.582	5.206	4.868	4.564	4.288	4.039	3.812	3.605	3.416	3.242	3.083	2.937	2.802	2.263
8	6.733	6.463	6.210	5.747	5.335	4.968	4.639	4.344	4.078	3.837	3.619	3.421	3.241	3.076	2.925	2.331
9	7.435	7.108	6.802	6.247	5.759	5.328	4.946	4.607	4.303	4.031	3.786	3.566	3.366	3.184	3.019	2.379
10	8.111	7.722	7.360	6.710	6.145	5.650	5.216	4.833	4.494	4.192	3.923	3.682	3.465	3.269	3.092	2.414
11	8.760	8.306	7.887	7.139	6.495	5.988	5.453	5.029	4.656	4.327	4.035	3.776	3.544	3.335	3.147	2.438
12	9.385	8.863	8.384	7.536	6.814	6.194	5.660	5.197	4.793	4.439	4.127	3.851	3.606	3.387	3.190	2.456
13	9.986	9.394	8.853	7.904	7.103	6.424	5.842	5.342	4.910	4.533	4.203	3.912	3.656	3.427	3.223	2.468
14	10.563	9.899	9.295	8.244	7.367	6.628	6.002	5.468	5.008	4.611	4.265	3.962	3.695	3.459	3.249	2.477
15	11.118	10.380	9.712	8.559	7.606	6.811	6.142	5.575	5.092	4.675	4.315	4.001	3.726	3.483	3.268	2.484
16	11.652	10.838	10.106	8.851	7.824	6.974	6.265	5.669	5.162	4.730	4.357	4.033	3.751	3.503	3.283	2.489
17	12.166	11.274	10.477	9.122	8.022	7.120	6.373	5.749	5.222	4.775	4.391	4.059	3.771	3.518	3.295	2.492
18	12.659	11.690	10.828	9.372	8.201	7.250	6.467	5.818	5.273	4.812	4.419	4.080	3.786	3.529	3.304	2.494
19	13.134	12.085	11.158	9.604	8.365	7.366	6.550	5.877	5.316	4.844	4.442	4.097	3.799	3.539	3.311	2.496
20	13.590	12.462	11.470	9.818	8.514	7.469	6.623	5.929	5.353	4.870	4.460	4.110	3.808	3.546	3.316	2.497
21	14.029	12.821	11.764	10.017	8.649	7.562	6.687	5.973	5.384	4.891	4.476	4.121	3.816	3.551	3.320	2.498
22	14.451	13.163	12.042	10.201	8.772	7.645	6.743	6.011	5.410	4.909	4.488	4.130	3.822	3.556	3.323	2.498
23	14.857	13.489	12.303	10.371	8.883	7.718	6.792	6.044	5.432	4.925	4.499	4.137	3.827	3.559	3.325	2.499
24	15.247	13.799	12.550	10.529	8.985	7.784	6.835	6.073	5.451	4.937	4.507	4.143	3.831	3.562	3.327	2.499
25	15.622	14.094	12.783	10.675	9.077	7.843	6.873	6.097	5.467	4.948	4.514	4.147	3.834	3.564	3.329	2.499
26	15.983	14.375	13.003	10.810	9.161	7.896	6.906	6.118	5.480	4.956	4.520	4.151	3.837	3.566	3.330	2.500
27	16.330	14.643	13.211	10.935	9.237	7.943	6.935	6.136	5.492	4.964	4.525	4.154	3.839	3.567	3.331	2.500
28	16.663	14.898	13.406	11.051	9.307	7.984	6.961	6.152	5.502	4.970	4.528	4.157	3.840	3.568	3.331	2.500
29	16.984	15.141	13.591	11.158	9.370	8.022	6.983	6.166	5.510	4.975	4.531	4.159	3.841	3.569	3.332	2.500
30	17.292	15.373	13.765	11.258	9.427	8.055	7.003	6.177	5.517	4.979	4.534	4.160	3.842	3.569	3.332	2.500
40	19.793	17.159	15.046	11.925	9.779	8.244	7.105	6.234	5.548	4.997	4.544	4.166	3.846	3.571	3.333	2.500

The NPV method and the IRR method are called *discounted cash flow (DCF) methods.* Each of these methods is discussed hereafter.

Payback Period The payback period measures the length of time required to recover the amount of initial investment. It is computed by dividing the initial investment by the cash inflows through increased revenues or cost savings.

Example 8 Assume:

Cost of investment	$18,000
Annual after-tax cash savings	$3,000

Then, the payback period is

$$Payback\ period = \frac{Initial\ investment}{Cost\ savings} = \frac{\$18,000}{\$3,000} = 6\ years$$

Decision rule: Choose the project with the shorter payback period. The rationale behind this choice is: The shorter the payback period, the less risky the project, and the greater the liquidity.

Example 9 Consider the two projects whose after-tax cash inflows are not even. Assume each project costs $1,000.

	Cash Inflow	
Year	*A($)*	*B($)*
1	*100*	*500*
2	*200*	*400*
3	*300*	*300*
4	*400*	*100*
5	*500*	
6	*600*	

When cash inflows are not even, the payback period has to be found by trial and error. The payback period of project A is ($1,000 = $100 + $200 + $300 + $400) four years. The payback period of project B is $1,000 = $500 + $400 + $100).

$$2 \text{ years} + \frac{\$100}{\$300} = 2 \text{ } 1/3 \text{ years}$$

Project B is the project of choice in this case, since it has the shorter payback period.

The advantages of using the payback-period method of evaluating an investment project are that (1) it is simple to compute and easy to understand, and (2) it handles investment risk effectively.

The shortcomings of this method are that (1) it does not recognize the time value of money, and (2) it ignores the impact of cash inflows received after the payback period; essentially, cash flows after the payback period determine profitability of an investment.

Net Present Value Net present value (NPV) is the excess of the present value (PV) of cash inflows generated by the project over the amount of the initial investment (I):

$$NPV = PV - I$$

The present value of future cash flows is computed using the so-called cost of capital (or minimum required rate of return) as the discount rate. When cash inflows are uniform, the present value would be

$$PV = A \cdot T4 \text{ } (i, n)$$

where A is the amount of the annuity. The value of T4 is found in Table 5A–4.

Decision rule: If NPV is positive, accept the project. Otherwise, reject it.

Example 10 Consider the following investment:

Initial investment	$12,950
Estimated life	10 years
Annual cash inflows	$3,000
Cost of capital (minimum required rate of return)	12%

Present value of the cash inflows is

PV = A.T4(i,n)

    = $3,000. T4(12%,10 years)

= $3,000 (5.650)		$16,950
Initial investment (I)		12,950
Net present value (NPV = PV − I)		$ 4,000

Since the NPV of the investment is positive, the investment should be accepted.

The advantages of the NPV method are that it obviously recognizes the time value of money and it is easy to compute whether the cash flows form an annuity or vary from period to period.

Internal Rate of Return Internal rate of return (IRR), also called *time adjusted rate of return*, is defined as the rate of interest that equates I with the PV of future cash inflows.

In other words,

at IRR I = PV or NPV = 0

Decision rule: Accept the project if the IRR exceeds the cost of capital. Otherwise, reject it.

Example 11 Assume the same data given in Example 10, and set the following equality (I = PV):

$12,950 = $3,000 . T4(i,10 years)

$$T4(i,10 \text{ years}) = \frac{\$12,950}{\$3,000} = 4.317$$

which stands somewhere between 18% and 20% in the 10-year line of Table 5A–4. The interpolation follows:

PV of an Annuity of $1 Factor
T4(i,10 years)

18%	4.494	4.494
IRR	4.317	
20%	———	4.192
Difference	0.177	0.302

Therefore,

$$IRR = 18\% + \frac{0.177}{0.302} \ (20\% - 18\%)$$

$$= 18\% + 0.586(2\%) = 18\% + 1.17\% = 19.17\%$$

Since the IRR of the investment is greater than the cost of capital (12%), accept the project.

The advantage of using the IRR method is that it does consider the time value of money and, therefore, is more exact and realistic than the ARR method.

The shortcomings of this method are that (1) it is time-consuming to compute, especially when the cash inflows are not even, although most financial calculators and PCs have a key to calculate IRR, and (2) it fails to recognize the varying sizes of investment in competing projects.

Can a Computer Help?

Note: Spreadsheet programs can be used in making IRR calculations. For example, Lotus 1-2-3 has a function @IRR(*guess, range*). 1-2-3 considers negative numbers as cash outflows such as the initial investment and positive numbers as cash inflows. Many financial calculators have similar features. As in Example 13, suppose you want to calculate the IRR of a $12,950 investment (the value −12950 entered in cell A3 that is followed by ten monthly cash inflows of $3,000 in cells B3...K3. Using a guess of 12% (the value of .12, which is in effect the cost of capital), your formula would be @IRR(.12,A3...K3) and 1-2-3 would return 19.14%, as shown here.

	A	*B*	*C*	*D*	*E*	*F*	*G*	*H*	*I*	*J*	*K*
1	0	1	2	3	4	5	6	7	8	9	10
2	-------	-------	-------	-------	-------	-------	-------	-------	-------	-------	-------
3	−12950	3000	3000	3000	3000	3000	3000	3000	3000	3000	3000
4	=======	=======	=======	=======	=======	=======	=======	=======	=======	=======	=======
5											

HOW DO INCOME TAXES AFFECT INVESTMENT DECISIONS?

Income taxes make a difference in many capital budgeting decisions. The project that is attractive on a before-tax basis may have to be rejected on an after-tax basis and vice versa. Income taxes typically affect both the amount and the timing of cash flows. Since net income, not cash inflows, is subject to tax, after-tax cash inflows are not usually the same as after-tax net income.

Calculating After-Tax Cash Flows

Let us define:

S = Sales

E = Cash operating expenses

d = Depreciation

t = Tax rate

Then, before-tax cash inflows (or cash savings) = S – E and net income = S – E – d.

By definition,

After-tax cash inflows = Before-tax cash inflows – Taxes
        = (S – E) – (S – E – d) (t)

Rearranging gives the short-cut formula:

After-tax cash inflows = (S – E) (1 – t) + (d)(t) or
        = (S – E – d) (1 – t) + d

The deductibility of depreciation from sales in arriving at taxable net income reduces income tax payments and thus serves as a *tax shield.*

Tax shield = Tax savings on depreciation = (d) (t)

Example 12 Assume:

S = $12,000
E = $10,000
d = $500 per year using the straight-line method
t = 30%

Then,

$$\text{After-tax cash inflow} = (\$12{,}000 - \$10{,}000)\,(1 - .3) + (\$500)(.3)$$
$$= (\$2{,}000)(.7) + (\$500)(.3)$$
$$= \$1{,}400 + \$150 = \$1{,}550$$

Note that a tax shield = tax savings on depreciation = (d)(t)
$$= (\$500)(.3) = \$150$$

Since the tax shield is dt, the higher the depreciation deduction, the higher the tax savings on depreciation. Therefore, an accelerated depreciation method (such as double-declining balance) produces higher tax savings than the straight-line method. Accelerated methods produce higher present values for the tax savings, which may make a given investment more attractive.

Example 13 The Navistar Company estimates that it can save $2,500 a year in cash operating costs for the next ten years if it buys a special-purpose machine at a cost of $10,000. No residual value is expected. Depreciation is by straight-line. Assume that the income-tax rate is 30%, and the after-tax cost of capital (minimum required rate of return) is 10%. After-tax cash savings can be calculated as follows:

Depreciation by straight-line is $10,000/10 = $1,000 per year. Thus,

$$\text{After-tax cash savings} = (S - E)\,(1 - t) + (d)(t)$$
$$= \$2{,}500(1 - .3) + \$1{,}000(.3)$$
$$= \$1{,}750 + \$300 = \$2{,}050$$

To see if this machine should be purchased, the net present value can be calculated.

$$PV = \$2{,}050\ T4(10\%,\ 10\ \text{years}) = \$2{,}050\ (6.145) = \$12{,}597.25$$

$$\text{Thus, } NPV = PV - I = \$12{,}597.25 - \$10{,}000 = \$2{,}597.25$$

Since NPV is positive, the machine should be bought.

Example 14 Shalimar Corporation has provided its revenues and cash operating costs (excluding depreciation) for the old and the new machine, as follows:

	Revenue	*Annual Cash Operating Costs*	*Net Profit before Depreciation and Taxes*
Old machine	$150,000	$70,000	$80,000
New machine	$180,000	$60,000	$120,000

Assume that the annual depreciation of the old machine and the new machine will be $30,000 and $50,000, respectively. Assume further that the tax rate is 46%.

To arrive at net profit after taxes, we first have to deduct depreciation expense from the net profit before depreciation and taxes, as follows:

	Net Profits after Taxes	*Add Depreciation*	*After-Tax Cash Inflows*
Old machine	($80,000 − $30,000)(1 − 0.46) = $27,000	$30,000	$57,000
New machine	($120,000 − $50,000)(1 − 0.46) = $37,800	$50,000	$87,800

Subtracting the after-tax cash inflows of the old machine from the cash inflows of the new machine results in the relevant, or incremental, cash inflows for each year.

Therefore, in this example, the relevant or incremental cash inflows for each year are $87,800 − $57,000 = $30,800.

Alternatively, the incremental cash inflows after taxes can be computed, using the following simple formula:

After-tax incremental cash inflows = (increase in revenues)(1 − tax rate)
− (increase in cash charges)(1 − tax rate)
+ (increase in depreciation expenses)(tax rate)

Example 15 Using the data in Example 14, after-tax incremental cash inflows for each year are:

Increase in revenue × (1 − tax rate):
   ($180,000 − $150,000) (1 − 0.46) $16,200
− Increase in cash charges × (1-tax rate):
   ($60,000 − $70,000) (1 − 0.46)   −(−5,400)
+ Increase in depreciation expense ×
   tax rate: ($50,000 − $30,000) (0.46)   9,200
                                        $30,800

HOW DOES MACRS AFFECT INVESTMENT DECISIONS?

Although the traditional depreciation methods can be used for computing depreciation for book purposes, 1981 saw a new way of computing depreciation deductions for tax purposes. The current rule is called the *Modified Accelerated Cost Recovery System* (MACRS) rule, as enacted by Congress in 1981 and then modified somewhat in 1986 under the Tax Reform Act of 1986. This rule is characterized as follows:

1. It abandons the concept of useful life and accelerates depreciation deductions by placing all depreciable assets into one of eight age-property classes. It calculates deductions, based on an allowable percentage of the asset's original cost (see Tables 5A–5 and 5A–6).

With a shorter asset tax life than useful life, the company would be able to deduct depreciation more quickly and save more in income taxes in the earlier years, thereby making an investment more attractive. The rationale behind the system is that this way the government encourages the company to invest in facilities and increase its productive capacity and efficiency. (Remember that the higher the d, the larger the tax shield (d)(t)).

2. Since the allowable percentages in Table 5A–5 add up to 100%, there is no need to consider the salvage value of an asset in computing depreciation.

3. The company may elect the straight-line method. The straight-line convention must follow what is called the *half-year convention*. This means that the company can deduct only half of the regular straight-line depreciation amount in the first year.

The reason for electing to use the MACRS optional straight-line method is that some firms may prefer to stretch out depreciation deductions using the straight-line method rather than to accelerate them. Those firms are the ones that just start out or have little or no income and wish to show more income on their income statements.

Table 5A–5
Modified Accelerated Cost Recovery System
Classification of Assets

Year	3-year	5-year	Property class 7-year	10-year	15-year	20-year
1	33.3%	20.0%	14.3%	10.0%	5.0%	3.8%
2	44.5	32.0	24.5	18.0	9.5	7.2
3	14.8a	19.2	17.5	14.4	8.6	6.7
4	7.4	11.5a	12.5	11.5	7.7	6.2
5		11.5	8.9a	9.2	6.9	5.7
6		5.8	8.9	7.4	6.2	5.3
7			8.9	6.6a	5.9a	4.9
8			4.5	6.6	5.9	4.5a
9				6.5	5.9	4.5
10				6.5	5.9	4.5
11				3.3	5.9	4.5
12					5.9	4.5
13					5.9	4.5
14					5.9	4.5
15					5.9	4.5
16					3.0	4.4
17						4.4
18						4.4
19						4.4
20						4.4
21	___	___	___	___	___	2.2
Total	100%	100%	100%	100%	100%	100%

a. Denotes the year of changeover to straight-line depreciation.

Example 16 Assume that a machine falls under a three-year property class and costs $3,000 initially. The straight-line option under MACRS differs from the traditional straight-line method in that under this method the company would deduct only $500 depreciation in the first year and the fourth year ($3,000/3 years = $1,000; $1,000/2 = $500). The table on page 60 compares the straight-line with half-year convention with the MACRS.

TABLE 5A–6
MACRS TABLES BY PROPERTY CLASS

MACRS Property Class & Depreciation Method	Useful Life (ADR Midpoint Life) "a"	Examples of Assets
3-year property 200% declining balance	4 years or less	Most small tools are included; the law specifically excludes autos and light trucks from this property class.
5-year property 200% declining balance	More than 4 years to less than 10 years	Autos and light trucks, computers, typewriters, copiers, duplicating equipment, heavy general-purpose trucks, and research and experimentation equipment are included.
7-year property 200% declining balance	10 years or more to less than 16 years	Office furniture and fixtures and most items of machinery and equipment used in production are included.
10-year property 200% declining balance	16 years or more to less than 20 years	Various machinery and equipment, such as that used in petroleum distilling and refining and in the milling of grain, are included.
15-year property 150% declining balance	20 years or more to less than 25 years	Sewage treatment plants, telephone and electrical distribution facilities, and land improvements are included.
20-year property 150% declining balance	25 years or more	Service stations and other real property with an ADR midpoint life of less than 27.5 years are included.
27.5-year property Straight-line	Not applicable	All residential rental property is included.
31.5-year property Straight-line	Not applicable	All nonresidential real property is included.

"a" The term ADR midpoint life means the "useful life" of an asset in a business sense; the appropriate ADR midpoint lives for assets are designated in the Tax Regulations.

Year	Straight-line (half-year) Depreciation	Cost		MACRS %	MACRS Deduction
1	$500	$3,000	X	33.3%	$999
2	1,000	3,000	X	44.5	1,335
3	1,000	3,000	X	14.8	444
4	<u>500</u>	3,000	X	7.4	<u>222</u>
	<u>$3,000</u>				<u>$3,000</u>

Example 17 A machine costs $10,000. Annual cash inflows are expected to be $5,000. The machine will be depreciated using the MACRS rule and will fall under the three-year property class. The cost of capital after taxes is 10%. The estimated life of the machine is four years. The salvage value of the machine at the end of the fourth year is expected to be $1,200. The tax rate is 30%.

The formula for computation of after-tax cash inflows $(S - E)(1 - t)+ (d)(t)$ needs to be computed separately. The NPV analysis can be performed as follows:

					Present value factor @ 10%	Present value
Initial investment: $10,000					1.000	$(10,000.00)
$(S - E)(1 - t)$:						
$5,000 (1 − .3) = $3,500 for 4 years					3.170(a)	$11,095.00
$(d)(t)$:						
Year	Cost	MACRS %	d	(d)(t)		
1	$10,000 X	33.3%	$3,330	$999	.909(b)	908.09
2	$10,000 X	44.5	4,450	1,335	.826(b)	1,102.71
3	$10,000 X	14.8	1,480	444	.751(b)	333.44
4	$10,000 X	7.4	740	222	.683(b)	151.63

Salvage value:

$1,200 in year 4: $1,200 (1 − .3) = $840(c)	.683(b)	<u>573.72</u>
Net present value (NPV)		<u>$4,164.59</u>

(a) T4(10%, 4 years) = 3.170 (from Table 5A-4).
(b) T3 values obtained from Table 5A-3.
(c) Any salvage value received under the MACRS rules is a *taxable gain* (the excess of the selling price over book value, $1,200 in this example), since the book value will be zero at the end of the life of the machine.

Since NPV = PV − I = \$4,164.59 is positive, the machine should be bought.

UNDERSTANDING THE COST OF CAPITAL

The cost of capital is defined as the rate of return that is necessary to maintain the market value of the firm (or price of the firm's stock). Project managers must know that the cost of capital, often called the *minimum required rate of return*, was used either as a discount rate under the NPV method or as a hurdle rate under the IRR method. The cost of capital is computed as a weighted average of the various capital components, which are items on the righthand side of the balance sheet such as debt, preferred stock, common stock, and retained earnings.

Cost of Debt

The cost of debt is stated on an after-tax basis, since the interest on the debt is tax deductible. However, the cost of preferred stock is the stated annual dividend rate. This rate is not adjusted for income taxes because the preferred dividend, unlike debt interest, is not a deductible expense in computing corporate income taxes.

Example 18 Assume that the Hume Company issues a \$1,000, 8%, 20-year bond whose net proceeds are \$940. The tax rate is 40%. Then, the after-tax cost of debt is:

$$8.00\% \ (1 - 0.4) = 4.8\%$$

Example 18A Suppose that the Hume company has preferred stock that pays a \$12 dividend per share and sells for \$100 per share in the market. Then the cost of preferred stock is:

$$\frac{Dividend\ per\ share}{Price\ per\ share} = \frac{\$12}{\$100} = 12\%$$

Cost of Common Stock

The cost of common stock is generally viewed as the rate of return investors require on a firm's common stock. One way to measure the cost of common stock is to use the *Gordon's growth model.* The model is

$$P_o = \frac{D_1}{r - g}$$

where P_o = value (or market price) of common stock
D_1 = dividend to be received in 1 year
r = investor's required rate of return
g = rate of growth (assumed to be constant over time)

Solving the model for r results in the formula for the cost of common stock:

$$r = \frac{D_1}{P_o} + g$$

Example 19 Assume that the market price of the Hume Company's stock is $40. The dividend to be paid at the end of the coming year is $4 per share and is expected to grow at a constant annual rate of 6%. Then the cost of this common stock is:

$$\frac{D_1}{P_o} + g = \frac{\$4}{\$40} + 6\% = 16\%$$

Cost of Retained Earnings

The cost of retained earnings is closely related to the cost of existing common stock, since the cost of equity obtained by retained earnings is the same as the rate of return investors require on the firm's common stock.

Measuring the Overall Cost of Capital

The firm's overall cost of capital is the weighted average of the individual capital costs, with the weights being the proportions of each type of capital used.

Σ (percentage of the total capital structure supplied by each source of capital x cost of capital for each source)

The computation of overall cost of capital is illustrated in the following example.

Example 20 Assume that the capital structure at the latest statement date is indicative of the proportions of financing that the company intends to use over time:

		Cost
Mortgage bonds ($1,000 par)	$20,000,000	4.80% (from Example 17)
Preferred stock ($100 par)	5,000,000	12.00 (from Example 18)
Common stock ($40 par)	20,000,000	16.00 (from Example 19)
Retained earnings	5,000,000	16.00
Total	$50,000,000	

These proportions would be applied to the following assumed individual explicit after-tax costs:

Source	*Weights*	*Cost*	*Weighted Cost*
Debt	40%(a)	4.80%	1.92%(b)
Preferred stock	10	12.00%	1.20
Common stock	40	16.00%	6.40
Retained earnings	10	16.00%	1.60
	100%		11.12%

(a) $20,000,000/$50,000,000 = .40 = 40%
(b) 4.80% x 40% = 1.92%

Overall cost of capital is 11.12%.

By computing a company's cost of capital, we can determine its minimum rate of return, which is used as the discount rate in present-value calculations. A company's cost of capital is also an indicator of risk. For example, if your company's cost of financing increases, it is being viewed as more risky by investors and creditors, who are demanding higher return on their investments in the form of higher dividend and interest rates.

MAKING LEASE-VERSUS-BUY DECISIONS

The lease-purchase decision is one commonly confronting firms considering the acquisition of new assets. It is a hybrid capital budgeting decision that forces a company to compare the leasing and financing (purchasing) alternatives.

There are tax benefits of leasing equipment rather than financing it with a term loan. Depending upon your needs and the nature of your business, the entire lease payment may be fully deductible as a business expense, thereby reducing your taxable income. With a loan, only the interest and depreciation can be used for deductions. Another benefit a lease offers is 100% financing plus an additional 10% of the equipment's costs to cover "soft costs," such as taxes, shipping, and installation. Some term loans offer 100% financing but, typically, they cover the cost of equipment only.

A lease can help you manage your cash flow. The payments are usually lower than for a term loan. Since a lease payment requires no down payment or deposit, you can get the equipment you need without depleting your reserve capital. The types of businesses that most often lease equipment to generate revenue are manufacturing, transportation, printing, and professional corporations, such as medical, law, or accounting firms. Leasing works well for such companies since they can keep their equipment current without having to dip into capital to do it. Since the businesses' capital is not being used for equipment, they can use it for business development and expansion.

A loan is your best choice, however, if you wish to keep the equipment and build equity quickly. Loans can be structured so you can own the equipment outright at the end of the term. *Note:* If you are sure you want to retain your equipment beyond the lease term and prefer to know the full cost of the financing up front, you may choose a Lease Purchase option. As its name implies, this option requires no additional payment to own the equipment at the end of the lease.

To make an intelligent financial decision on a lease-purchase, an after-tax, cash outflow, *present-value* comparison is needed. There are special steps to take when making this comparison. When considering a lease, take the following steps:

1. Find the annual lease payment. Since the annual lease payment is typically made in advance, the formula used is

$$\text{Amount of lease} = A + A.T4(i, n - 1) \text{ or } A = \frac{\text{Amount of lease}}{1 + T4\ (i, n - 1)}$$

Notice we use n – 1 rather than n.

2. Find the after-tax cash outflows.

3. Find the present value of the after-tax cash outflows.

When considering a purchase, take the following steps:

1. Find the annual loan amortization by using

$$A = \frac{\text{Amount of loan for the purchase}}{T4\ (i, n - 1)}$$

The step may not be necessary since this amount is usually available.

2. Calculate the interest. The interest is segregated from the principal in each of the annual loan payments because only the interest is tax-deductible.

3. Find the cash outflows by adding interest and depreciation (plus any maintenance costs), and then compute the after-tax outflows.

4. Find the present value of the after-tax cash outflows, using Table 5A–3.

Example 21 A firm has decided to acquire a computer system costing $100,000 that has an expected life of five years, after which the system is not expected to have any residual value. The system can be purchased by borrowing or it can be leased. If leasing is used, the lessor requires a 12% return. As is customary, lease payments are made in advance, that is, at the end of the year prior to each of the ten years. The tax rate is 50% and the firm's cost of capital, or after-tax cost of borrowing, is 8%.

First compute the present value of the after-tax cash outflows associated with the leasing alternative.

1. Find the annual lease payment:

$$A = \frac{\text{Amount of lease}}{1 + T4\ (i, n - 1)}$$

$$= \frac{\$100,000}{1 + T4\ (12\%, 4\ years)} = \frac{\$100,000}{1 + 3.3073} = \frac{\$100,000}{4.3073} = \$23,216\ (rounded)$$

Steps 2 and 3 can be done in the same schedule, as follows:

Year	(1) Lease Payment($)	(2) Tax Savings($)	(3)=(1)–(2) After-Tax Cash Outflow($)	(4) PV at 8%	(5)=(3) x (4) PV of Cash Out-flow($,Rounded)
0	23,216		23,216	1.000	23,216
1–4	23,216	11,608[a]	11,608	3.3121[b]	38,447
5		11,608	(11,608)	0.6806[a]	(7,900)
					53,763

a $23,216 X 50%
b From Table 5A.4
c From Table 5A.3

If the asset is purchased, the firm is assumed to finance it entirely with a 10% unsecured term loan. Straight-line depreciation is used with no salvage value. Therefore, the annual depreciation is $20,000 ($100,000/5 years). In this alternative, first find the annual loan payment by using:

$$A = \frac{Amount\ of\ loan}{T4\ (i,n)}$$

$$A = \frac{\$100,000}{T4(10\%, 5\ years)} = \frac{\$100,000}{3.7906} = \$26,381\ (rounded)$$

2. Calculate the interest by setting up a loan amortization schedule.

Yr	(1) Loan Payment($)	(2) Beginning-of-Yr Principal($)	(3)=(2)(10%) Interest($)	(4)=(1)–(3) Principal($)	(5)=(2)–(4) End-of-Yr Principal
1	26,381	100,000	10,000	16,381	83,619
2	26,381	83,619	8,362	18,019	65,600
3	26,381	65,600	6,560	19,821	45,779
4	26,381	45,779	4,578	21,803	23,976
5	26,381	23,976[a]	2,398	23,983[a]	

a Because of rounding errors, there is a slight difference between (2) and (4)

Steps 3 (cash outflows) and 4 (present values of those outflows) can be done as shown in Table 5A–7.

The sum of the present values of the cash outflows for leasing and purchasing by borrowing shows that purchasing is preferable because the PV of borrowing is less than the PV of leasing ($52,008 versus $53,763). The incremental savings is $1,675.

ECONOMIC FEASIBILITY STUDY FOR A NEW INFORMATION SYSTEM

Determining economic feasibility requires a careful investigation of the costs and benefits of a proposed information system. The basic framework for feasibility analysis is the *capital budgeting* model in which cost savings and other benefits, as well as initial outlay costs, operating costs, and other cash outflows, are translated into dollar estimates.

The estimated benefits are compared with the costs to determine whether the system is cost beneficial. Where possible, benefits and costs that are not easily quantifiable should be estimated and included in the feasibility analysis. If they cannot be accurately estimated, they should be listed and the likelihood of their occurring and the expected impact on the organization evaluated. Some of thc tangible and intangible benefits a company might obtain from a new system are cost savings; improved customer service, productivity, decision making, and data processing; better management control; and increased job satisfaction and employee morale.

Equipment costs are an initial outlay cost if the system is purchased and an operating cost if rented or leased. Equipment costs vary from a few thousand for microcomputer systems to millions of dollars for enormous mainframes. Equipment costs are usually less than the cost of acquiring software and maintaining, supporting, and operating the system. Software acquisition costs include the purchase price of software as well as the time and effort required to design, program, test, and document software. The personnel costs associated with hiring, training, and relocating staff can be substantial. Site-preparation costs may be incurred for large computer systems. There are costs involved in installing the new system and converting files to the appropriate format and storage media.

The primary operating cost is maintaining the system. There may be significant annual cash outflows for equipment replacement and expansion and software updates. Human-resource costs include the salaries of systems analysts, programmers, operators, data-entry operators, and management.

TABLE 5A–7
LEASE VERSUS PURCHASE EVALUATION REPORT

	Leasing		Purchase/Borrow				Present Value Factor	Discounted Cash Flow	
Year	Lease Payments	Net After-Tax Cash Flow	Loan Payments	Interest Expense	Depreciation Expense	Net After-Tax Cash Flow		Leasing	Purchase
0	$23,216	$23,216					1	$23,216	
1	23,216	11,608	$26,381	$10,000	$20,000	$11,381	0.9259	10,748	10,538
2	23,216	11,608	26,381	8,362	20,000	12,200	0.8573	9,952	10,459
3	23,216	11,608	26,381	6,560	20,000	13,101	0.7938	9,214	10,400
4	23,216	11,608	26,381	4,578	20,000	14,092	0.735	8,532	10,358
5		(11,608)	26,381	2,398	20,000	15,182	0.6806	(7,900)	10,333
	$92,864	$58,040	$131,905	$31,898	$100,000	$65,956		$53,761	$52,087

	Lease Proposal	Purchase Proposal
Cost of machine	$100,000	$100,000
Terms of payment	5 years	5 years
Interest rate	12%	10%
Downpayment		
Monthly lease payment at the end of the year	$23,216	
Monthly loan payment		$26,381
Depreciation		Straight line
Residual purchase price	0%	0
Corporate tax bracket	50%	50%
After-tax cost of capital	8%	8%

Costs are also incurred for supplies, overhead, and other operating costs. Initial cash outlay and operating costs are summarized in Table 5A–8.

During systems design, several alternative approaches to meeting system requirements are developed. Various feasibility measures such as technical, operational, legal, and scheduling feasibility are then used to narrow the list of alternatives. Economic feasibility and capital-budgeting techniques, which were discussed earlier, are used to evaluate the benefit-cost aspects of the alternatives.

Example 22 Sophie, an information systems (IS) project manager for the MYK chain of discount stores, is contemplating installation of a new IS system that is flexible, efficient, timely, and responsive to user and customer needs. The new system aims at improving the company's business processes. After the analysis Sophie's IS project team decided they wanted the corporate office to gather daily sales data from each store. Analyzing the prior day's sales will help the company adapt quickly to customer needs. Providing sales data to suppliers will help avoid stockouts and overstocking.

Coordinating buying at the corporate office will help MYK to minimize inventory levels and negotiate lower wholesale prices. Stores will send orders electronically the day they are prepared. Based on store orders, the previous day's sales figures, and warehouse inventory, MYK will send purchase orders to suppliers. Suppliers will process orders and ship goods to regional warehouses or directly to the stores the day orders are received. Each store will have the flexibility to respond to local sales trends and conditions by placing local orders. Accounts payable will be centralized so the firm can make payments electronically.

Sophie's team conducted an economic feasibility study and determined that the project makes excellent use of funds. As shown in Table 5A–9, they estimated that initial outlay costs for the system are $4.32 million (initial systems design and new hardware $1.8 million each, software $375,000, and training, site preparation, and conversion $250,000 each).

The team estimated what it would cost to operate the system for its estimated six-year life, as well as what the system would save the company. The following recurring costs were identified: hardware expansion, additional software and software updates, systems maintenance, added personnel to operate the system, communication charges, and overhead. The system will also save the company money by eliminating clerical jobs, generating working capital savings, increasing sales and profits, and decreasing warehouse costs. The costs and savings for years one through six, which are expected to rise from year to year, are shown in Table 5A–9.

Hardware
  Central processing unit
  Peripherals
  Special input/output devices
  Communications hardware
  Upgrade and expansion costs

Software
  Application, system, general-purpose, utility, and communications software
  Updated versions of software
  Application software design, programming, modification, and testing

Installation
  Freight and delivery charges
  Setup and connection fees

Conversion
  Systems testing
  File and data conversions
  Parallel operations

Documentation
  Systems documentation
  Training-program documentation
  Operating standards and procedures

Site preparation
  Air-conditioning, humidity, and dust controls
  Physical security (access)
  Fire and water protection
  Cabling, wiring, and outlets
  Furnishing and fixtures

Staff
  Supervisors
  Analysts and programmers
  Computer operators
  Input (data conversion) personnel
  Recruitment and staff training

Maintenance/backup
  Hardware/software maintenance
  Backup and recovery operations
  Power supply protection

Supplies and overhead
  Preprinted forms
  Data storage devices
  Supplies (paper, ribbons, toner)
  Utilities and power

Others
  Legal and consulting fees
  Insurance

Economic Feasibility Study for a New Information System

	Initial Outlay		Years				
	0	1	2	3	4	5	6
Initial outlay costs (I)							
Initial system design	$ 1,800,000						
Hardware	1,800,000						
Software	375,000						
Training	185,000						
Site preparation	250,000						
Conversion	250,000						
Total	$ 4,660,000						
Recurring costs							
Hardware expansion			$ 250,000	$ 290,000	$ 330,000	$ 370,000	$ 390,000
Software			160,000	210,000	230,000	245,000	260,000
Systems maintenance		$ 70,000	120,000	130,000	140,000	150,000	160,000
Personnel costs		485,000	800,000	900,000	1,000,000	1,100,000	1,300,000
Communication charges		99,000	160,000	180,000	200,000	220,000	250,000
Overhead		310,000	420,000	490,000	560,000	600,000	640,000
Total		$ 964,000	$ 1,910,000	$ 2,200,000	$ 2,460,000	$ 2,685,000	$ 3,000,000
Cash savings							
Clerical cost savings		$ 500,000	$ 1,110,000	$ 1,350,000	$ 1,500,000	1,700,000	1,950,000
Working capital savings		1,000,000	1,200,000	1,500,000	1,500,000	1,500,000	1,500,000
Increased sales and profits			500,000	900,000	1,200,000	1,500,000	1,800,000
Reduced warehouse costs			400,000	800,000	1,200,000	1,600,000	2,000,000
Total		$ 1,500,000	$ 3,210,000	$ 4,550,000	$ 5,400,000	$ 6,300,000	$ 7,250,000
Cash savings minus recurring costs		536,000	1,300,000	2,350,000	2,940,000	3,615,000	4,250,000
Less income taxes (34%)	34%	(182,240)	(442,000)	(799,000)	(999,600)	(1,229,100)	(1,445,000)
Cash savings (net of tax)		$ 353,760	$ 858,000	$ 1,551,000	$ 1,940,400	$ 2,385,900	$ 2,805,000
Tax shield from depreciation		316,880	507,008	304,205	182,206	182,206	91,895
Net cash inflow (net savings)							
after taxes	$ (4,660,000)	$ 670,640	$ 1,365,008	$ 1,855,205	$ 2,122,606	$ 2,568,106	$ 2,896,895

Tax savings from depreciation deduction

Year	MACRS	Depreciation	Tax savings
1	20.00%	$ 932,000	$ 316,880
2	32.00%	1,491,200	507,008
3	19.20%	894,720	304,205
4	11.50%	535,900	182,206
5	11.50%	535,900	182,206
6	5.80%	270,280	91,895

Net present value calculations @ a cost of capital of 10%

Year	Net savings	PV factor	PV
0	$ (4,660,000)	1.0000	$ (4,660,000)
1	670,640	0.9091	609,679
2	1,365,008	0.8265	1,128,179
3	1,855,205	0.7513	1,393,815
4	2,122,606	0.6830	1,449,740
5	2,568,106	0.6209	1,594,537
6	2,896,895	0.5645	1,635,297
		NPV	$ 3,151,248
		IRR	26.26%

Sophie calculated the annual savings minus the recurring additional costs and then calculated the annual after-tax cash savings under the MACRS tax rule. The $4.66-million system can be depreciated over the six-year period. For example, the depreciation in year one of $932,000 reduces net income by that amount. Since the company does not have to pay taxes on the $1 million, at their tax rate of 34% they end up saving an additional $316,880 in year one. Finally, Sophie calculated the net savings for each year.

Sophie used MYK's cost of capital of 10% to calculate the net present value (NPV) of the investment, which is over $3 million. The internal rate of return (IRR) is a respectable 26%. Sophie realized how advantageous it would be for the company to borrow the money (at 10% interest rates) in order to produce a 26% return on that borrowed money. In addition, pay-back (the point at which the initial cost is recovered) occurs in the fourth year. NPV and IRR are calculated as shown in Table 5A–9.

Sophie presented the system and its cost-benefit calculations to top management. Challenges to her estimates (various "what-if" scenarios) were plugged into the Excel model so that management could see the effect of the changed assumptions. This spreadsheet analysis was intended to ensure a positive return of the new system under future uncertainty.

CONCLUSION

We have examined the process of evaluating capital expenditure projects. We have also discussed several commonly used criteria for evaluating capital budgeting projects, including the NPV and IRR methods. Since income taxes could make a difference in the accept-or-reject decision, tax factors must be taken into account in every decision. Although the traditional depreciation methods still can be used for computing depreciation for book purposes, 1981 saw a new way of computing depreciation deductions for tax purposes. The rule is called the modified accelerated cost recovery system (MACRS). It was enacted by Congress in 1981 and then modified somewhat in 1986 under the Tax Reform Act of 1986. Lease-purchase decisions were also treated on an after-tax basis. Also presented is an example of economic feasibility study for a new information system.

7A

DATABASE DESIGN

This chapter discusses all the essential aspects to database design, including design objectives, processes, relationships, keys, integrity rules, entity-relationship model, normalization, and object-oriented database model.

DESIGN OBJECTIVES

A database is a collection of inter-related information concerning a certain topic and business applications. It helps companies, from start-up to huge, organize related information in a logical fashion for easy access, storage, and retrieval.

The first step in designing a database is much like designing a building or a house. We first outline the layout on a paper or blueprint and then physically build it based on the information gathered. In a database world, we first create a conceptual data model. This model describes the structure of the data to be stored in the database regardless of how and where it will be stored physically. Once the conceptual design stage has been rigorously analyzed and tested, we move on to the physical design stage where methods for physically implementing the structures outlined in the conceptual design are examined, selected, and implemented.

CONCEPTUAL AND PHYSICAL DESIGN

Data models are our mechanism for representing data structures. A number of data models are available to support the conceptual and physical design processes. The process of designing a database focuses on how data will be represented and how units and blocks of data will be organized and interconnected rather than on specifying the values of specific data items. The design process builds a structure that can be used to store and process data and is analogous to designing and building a factory to produce physical products. Just as the factory must be designed and built before the products can be produced, the database structure must be designed and implemented before actual data items can be stored and processed.

In designing a database, we first create a *conceptual data model* that describes the structure of the data to be stored in the database without specifying how and where it will be physically stored or the physical methods used to retrieve it. Once a conceptual design has been developed and analyzed, we move on to the *physical* design stage. Here, alternative methods of physically implementing the structures specified in the conceptual design are examined and an appropriate method is selected and implemented. This produces a database that supports the structures for storage and retrieval developed in the conceptual design phase. These steps are roughly equivalent to first designing a factory layout on paper, and then physically building the structure and installing the equipment.

The data model most commonly used to support the conceptual design stage is the entity-relationship (E-R) model (to be discussed later).

DESIGN PROCESS

A well-designed database is one that allows broader sharing of organizational data while reducing data duplication and improving data consistency at the same time. With this said, a design process is a task that should be taken seriously to achieve a well-structured database.

There are a couple of steps in the design process that need to be met before a database is ready to be implemented for production use. These steps are outlined below:

- Eliminate repeating groups.
- Eliminate partial dependencies.
- Eliminate transitive dependencies.

These three steps are also known as *normalization*, which will be described later.

RELATIONAL DATABASES EXPLAINED

Explaining a relational database is best done by example:

> Assume you are running a mail-order service and you want to keep track of sales to customers. Essentially you want to store the following information:

- *Customer information*—Name, address, phone number.
- *Orders*—The product, quantity, price, customer.
- *Product information*—The product, description, price, supplier.
- *Suppliers*—Name, address, phone number, products supplied.

In a flat file database you would need to have a number of tables (two to be exact), each of which holds one set of information. One table would hold information about customers and their orders while the second would hold information about suppliers and their products. This is viable if each customer only orders one item and each supplier only makes one product—a very unlikely scenario!

In reality each table would store a large amount of duplicate information, and each order would entail the re-entry of all of the customer's details. At some point a typing error is likely to occur; for example, a customer's name may be incorrectly typed. Now, if you try to look at all the products ordered by a customer you would miss some because of the typing error. In addition, if a customer moves, then you will have to face a lot of typing to update all of the records. Finally, the huge amount of duplicate information takes up disk space and computer memory and will slow down the system.

Now consider the situation where you have a table containing each customer's details and only one record for each customer. You also have a table containing each order made. Assume that you give each customer a reference number (customers could share the same surname) and against each order you enter that reference number. You can now relate a customer to an order and if a customer's details change, then you only have to change one record in the customers' table. Much neater and space efficient!

A relational database will provide a link between these two tables so that you can create a query that will show you the products ordered by each customer. The same principle can be applied to suppliers and products. Finally, a link can be made between the orders and the products (via a product reference number) so that a change in the details of a product will be picked up in the orders. Therefore, a relational database saves typing, reduces the potential for errors, reduces the size of a database, and makes for much more flexible data management.

An example of a popular relational database system for personal computers is described below.

Example (Microsoft Access)

Of the many popular database management systems software packages available for personal computers, Microsoft's Access is a typical example of the growing sophistication of database software for microcomputer users.

Access is a relational database system that operates under the Microsoft Windows environment (see Figures 7A-1 and 7A-2). It is graphically oriented. Users can select and execute commands using a pointing device like a mouse; users are presented with graphical portrayals of related tables; multiple tables can be displayed at the same time by either overlapping them or displaying them in separate portions of the display area; and most functions can be selected by "clicking" a pointing device on top of graphical icons or buttons. Moreover, all the graphical services generally available to Windows applications are available to Access users (such as being able to copy and "paste" graphical images to and from Access).

Access allows users to query databases by using the simple query-by-example format—this gives them powerful functions for ordering, rearranging, filtering, and adding calculated fields. Query results (in table format) can be used subsequently as the basis for further queries or reports. Queries can also be made using the popular structured query language (SQL) for querying Access or external databases.

Reports can be easily designed graphically in a what-you-see-is-what-you-get (WYSIWYG) environment, with extensive control over fonts, font sizes, arrangement of data, shading, and highlighting. Reports can include images such as identification photos of individuals in a personnel database and graphics such as bar graphs and scatter plots of financial or production data.

Sophisticated tasks can be automated either by writing statements in a programming language (a version of BASIC) or by simply having Access "record" a user's manual steps for later "playback."

Finally, the range of help features for a confused user rivals the complexity of the database management functions available. Help programs built into the system include extensive "how-to" guides and function reference material that is indexed and searchable by key words. A feature called Cue Cards is available at all times; cue cards provide step-by-step instructions with graphical examples, guidance, and transfers to additional reference material.

FIGURE 7A-2
CATEGORIES: TABLE

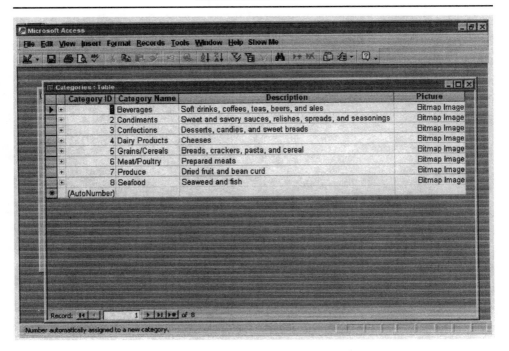

For a few hundred dollars (or less in many cases), businesses can provide a sophisticated database management system right on an employee's desktop or even in a notebook computer while he or she is away from the office.

KEYS

Keys or primary keys are used to uniquely identify a row or record in a table. Think of it as house numbers in a street identifying each house. Without the house numbers, visitors would not know where to go. Without a primary key, a database engine cannot identify individual rows.

A primary key can consist of one or more columns or fields. All columns (or combination of columns) that contain unique values are called candidate keys and the primary key can be chosen from any of these. All other remaining candidate keys are called alternate keys. A primary key consisting of one column is called a simple key, while a primary key made up of a number of columns is called a composite key.

There are no hard and fast rules about which candidate key should become the primary key but it is usual to pick one that will make a simple key and one that will not change frequently. It is quite usual for a table's primary key to be some sort of ID, such as a customer ID. The ID itself is normally a number and in Access (and many other systems) this number can automatically be assigned by the system. The benefits of using an automatically created number are that the user does not even have to consider it, it takes up very little storage space, and it is faster to add new data with one field than with a text field (tables are primarily sorted by the primary key so adding a lot of data, by importing for example, means that the data is added to the end of the table rather than the system having to slot it into the middle of the table). On the downside, auto-assigned numbers should not be used if the records will need to be renumbered or if the values must increment with no gaps (deleting a record will remove the number which will not be re-assigned).

In the example of the mail-order service, the customers would be assigned an ID number and this would be used as the primary key. In the orders table, the customer making the order is identified by his or her ID and the field containing this information is called the foreign key. The tables are joined via a relationship.

RELATIONSHIPS

Relationships "connect" tables. In other words, they link the data in one table to the data in another. Data can be linked via three types of relationship: one-to-one, one-to-many, and many-to-many.

In a one-to-one relationship, each record in one table has at most one related record in another table. This type of relationship is rare and usually only occurs because of limitations caused by the database software itself. For example, in Access a table can only consist of 255 fields and any more than this will necessitate a second table linked by a one-to-one relationship. In addition, security or performance concerns may necessitate this type of relationship.

A one-to-many relationship is by far the most common. Here one record in one table can be related to many records in another table. In the mail-order example, each customer may place many orders. Of course there can be only one order and sometimes none at all. The one-to-many relationship is also called a parent-child or master-detail relationship.

A many-to-many relationship means that for each record in one table, there can be many records in another table, and for each record in the second table, there can be many in the first. Many-to-many relationships cannot be directly represented in relational database programs and have to be built by using two or more one-to-many relationships. In the mail-order example, each customer may buy from several manufacturers and each manufacturer may supply products to many customers. In reality it is unlikely that this relationship would have to be used.

To ensure that data remains related, we can use integrity rules.

INTEGRITY RULES

There are two sets of integrity rules: general and database specific.

There are two general integrity rules and these apply to all databases. The entity integrity rule says that primary keys cannot contain null (empty) values. With a composite key, none of the individual columns can be null.

The referential integrity rule says that the database must not contain any unmatched foreign key values. What this is saying is that a record cannot be added to a table with a foreign key unless the referenced value exists in the primary table and that (to enforce this) if a record in a primary table is deleted, then the records in the child table must not be orphaned. To resolve this, three options exist—disallow the deletion, cascade the deletion to delete the records in the child table, or nullify which sets the child table values to null. (Access does not support this third option.) In addition, the child records could be re-assigned to a new parent. Access also allows you to cascade updates to a change to the primary key in the parent table. This will change the foreign key in the child table. Database specific integrity rules are specific to each database and are defined by that database.

CONCEPTUAL DESIGN—ENTITY RELATIONSHIP (E-R) MODEL

To touch a little bit on the history side, the E-R model was developed in 1976 by Peter Chen. Since then, it has undergone substantial modification. No uniformly accepted set of notation exists for the elements of the E-R model. Nevertheless, the entity-relationship model was among one of the first methodologies developed for database conceptual design.

The Entity Relationship model is the most commonly used data model to support the conceptual design stage for database development in visual form. Theoretically, a model for conceptual design of a database must consist of a mechanism for representing the metadata structures that data can take on. Entities, Attributes, and Relationships should be well represented on the conceptual model.

Let's take a closer look at how the E-R model is commonly used.

- Entities are represented in rectangles shape.

- Attributes are represented in elliptical shape with lines connecting them to the entity to which they belong.

- Relationships are represented as diamond shape with lines connecting them to the related entities.

In practice, the name of each element is written inside the shape accordingly and the primary key of an entity is always underlined. Figure 7A-3 shows a common E-R diagram.

FIGURE 7A-3
ENTITY RELATIONSHIP (E-R) DIAGRAM

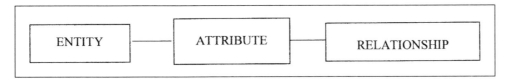

An E-R diagram of a Customer Entity is pictured in Figure 7A-4.

FIGURE 7A-4

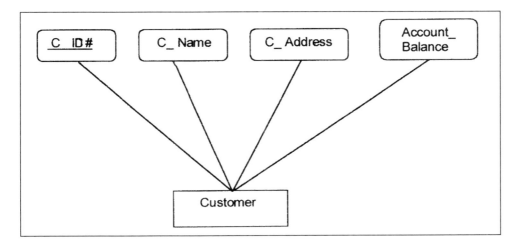

An E-R Diagram of a One-to-Many Relationship is pictured in Figure 7A-5.

If you notice in Figure 7A-5, one-to-many relationships are represented with a branched line, also widely known as a crow's foot. This crow's foot indicates that each customer may place many orders; however, each order belongs to only one customer. Additionally, the circle on the line between the Customer-Order relationship and the Order entity indicates that the relationship is optional and it is always possible that no orders exist for a given customer.

DETAILS OF E-R MODELING

To physically implement a conceptual database design, we must have physical structures that allow us to store and retrieve logically related units of data both within entities and across related entity classes. In other words, we must be able to create physically implementable structures that correspond to all the logical structures represented in our conceptual designs.

The attribute, entity occurrence, and entity class structures within entity classes correspond to the field, record, and file structures of file-oriented processing. In relational databases, the terms *column, row,* and *table* are commonly used to describe these units. A field or column name identifies a specific attribute of interest, and the value of the primary key attribute identifies a specific occurrence—the row of the table identified by the primary key value. The entire set of data for an entity class is stored in a table.

FIGURE 7A-5

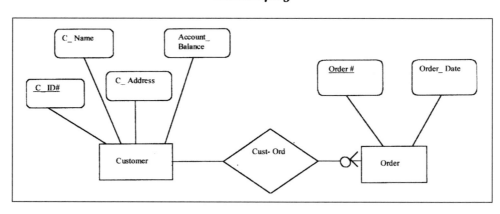

The relational model requires that all tables be flat files with records of a fixed size.

A data structure diagram can be used to describe the structure of each table. For instance, the data structure diagram for the customer table might look like this: Customer(C_ID#, C_Name, C_Account, Acct_Bal). Customer identifies the name of the table, while the items in parentheses are a list of the attributes or columns of the table. C ID# is underlined to indicate that it is the primary key of this table.

Relationships among entity types are represented in the relational model by repeating identifying data to link related tables. The relational model requires that all data structures be represented by sets of tables (entities) that can have only one-to-one or one-to-many relationships with each other. In addition, each table must have a primary key. All other attributes of a table must be functionally determined by the primary key. A process called *normalization* is used to ensure that these conditions are met. We will discuss normalization later in this chapter.

DATA INTEGRITY

Data integrity is a very important subject in a database and probably is one of the reasons that databases exist in the first place.

A Customer table in Figure 7A-6 is an example of a table that is not fully normalized.

FIGURE 7A-6
A TABLE WITH ANOMALIES

Customer Number	Customer Name	Credit Limit	Salesperson Number	Salesperson Name	Commission Rate
13728	A. Andrews	$2500	1425	Barnes	1.8%
71687	L. Morris	$1000	1872	Jones	2.0%
32763	G. Gates	$1500	1425	Barnes	1.8%
61395	V. Bass	$1000	1763	Hansen	2.2%
20698	H. Fain	$2000	1425	Barnes	1.8%
49217	R. Pate	$1500	1425	Barnes	1.8%
50387	L. Knowles	$1250	1763	Hansen	2.2%
36103	P. Dalh	$2000	1138	Roberts	2.2%
23076	H. Bain	$1750	1425	Barnes	1.8%

Normalization seeks to identify and correct data structures that are subject to anomalies when new data are added or existing data are modified or deleted. An insertion anomaly occurs if there are data items that are available and whose values should be recorded in a database, but that cannot be added to the database until the values of some other data element or elements are known. If a new salesperson named Adams is to be assigned the Salesperson number 2300 and given an initial commission rate of 1.5 percent, we cannot enter this data until at least one customer has been assigned to this salesperson. A modification anomaly occurs if a change to the value of a data item must be recorded in more than one location in a database. For example, if the commission rate for Salesperson number 1425 changes to 2.3 percent, this value must be corrected in five records of the table. A deletion anomaly occurs if the deletion of a data item in a database causes other, still valid data to be deleted as well. If the only customer assigned to the salesperson Jones is deleted, we lose the fact that salesperson Jones is assigned the salesperson number 1872 and is paid commission at the rate of 2.0 percent of sales.

The fundamental problem with Figure 7A-6 is that it contains data about two different things, two different entities. Salesperson Number, Salesperson Name, and Commission Rate are all characteristics of salespersons, while Customer Number, Customer Name, and Credit Limit are characteristics of customers. With this being said, data integrity in this table is at risk and should be normalized where each table describes only one thing, one entity.

TABLE RELATIONSHIPS AND NORMALIZATION

Normalization is most closely associated with the relational data model. However, normalization rules are used to evaluate and improve conceptual designs regardless of the data model to be used for implementation. Normalization is a process designed to achieve three goals: (1) eliminate redundant information, (2) increase data integrity, and (3) make systems more efficient.

There are four basic rules of normalization:

1. Each table must have a unique key. In a mail-order example, each customer, order, and product must be individually identifiable. This helps ensure that the system does not hold duplicate data.

2. Eliminate repeating groups. Split your data where you have repeating groups. For the mail-order system, we essentially split the data into tables of unique customers and unique products.

3. Examine multi-field key relationships. Essentially this simply says where you have a multi-field key, you may be able to split that table. A multi-field key is where your primary key is based on two or more fields.

4. Examine any remaining groups of information. If descriptive information does not directly relate to the key in that table, then move the descriptive data to a new table. In the mail-order example, the manufacturer information is split from the products table on the basis that one manufacturer could make more than one product.

If these rules are followed, then your database will have a robust structure that is also efficient.

When applying normalization rules, we think of the entities of our design in relational terms, as two-dimensional tables, or relations. Normalization assists in the process of finding the most appropriate structure for data. Database systems can operate using data that has not been fully normalized.

However, normalized data structures possess some powerful advantages over un-normalized data such as:

• To ensure that data are stored in structures that do not cause unnecessary redundancy.

• To ensure that units of data can be represented in the database as soon as their values are known.

• To ensure that the value of a unit of data in a database can be accurately and efficiently modified, and that meaningful data will not be accidentally deleted from a database.

Due to these advantages, database designers attempt to ensure that the data structures they use are normalized unless there are compelling reasons for accepting an un-normalized structure.

A relation is a two-dimensional array—a table—that meets the following restrictions: each cell of the array must contain a single-valued entry, no duplicate rows may exist, and each column must have the same meaning across all rows. Recall that each column in a relational table represents an attribute and each row represents an occurrence of an entity. Thus, we would expect that the meaning of each column would be identical across all rows of a relational table. The restriction that there be no duplicate rows means that there cannot be two completely identical entity occurrences in our table. Finally, the requirement that all cells be single-valued means that for any given entity occurrence (row), there can be only one value for each attribute (column). A table meeting these conditions can be described as a relation, and all tables used in a relational data model must be relations.

Different degrees or levels of normalization exist. We can speak of a table being un-normalized, being in first normal form, being in second normal form, and so on. Higher orders of normalization require that a table meet an ever more restrictive set of rules. Figure 7A-7 illustrates this point. We begin with a set of possible tables. At the bottom of the figure, no degree of normalization has been achieved. The first normal form (1NF) imposes the restriction that tables must contain no repeating groups of fields. For a table to be in second normal form (2NF), it must be in first normal form, and it must also meet the additional restriction of having no partial dependencies. For a table to be in third normal form (3NF), it must be in second normal form and meet the additional restriction of having no transitive dependencies. More restrictive conditions are imposed as we move to higher level normal forms until, theoretically, we arrive at conditions that assure a fully normalized relation—a table—with no anomalies. First, second, and third normal forms were first defined by E. F. Codd (1970). Since that time, additional higher levels have been discovered.

The ideal of fully normalized relations that eliminate all anomalies may be unachievable and is probably impractical. Database theorists periodically discover new sources of anomalies and develop higher degree normal forms to eliminate them. However, these very high order normal forms tend to involve rather obscure anomalies that are unlikely to occur in practice and that would be difficult to detect and correct. In the remainder of this section, we will describe normalization down to the fourth normal form. In practice, database designers are usually satisfied if their data structures achieve third normal form.

BUSINESS RULES AND LIMITATIONS OF NORMALIZATION

There are some disadvantages and limitations of normalization. Anomalies in data structures make the maintenance of a database more cumbersome

FIGURE 7A-7
LEVELS OF NORMALIZATION

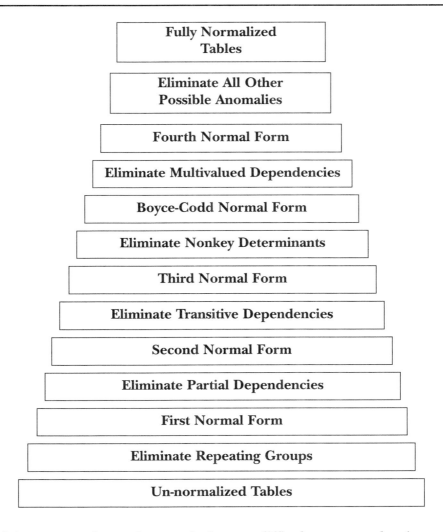

and time consuming and can make it more difficult to ensure data integrity. As we have seen, normalization is a powerful tool that can help us identify and eliminate serious anomalies in databases. Thus, there is a very strong presumption that the structure of a database should be fully normalized. Unfortunately, there are situations where judgment is required to determine whether an apparent violation of normalization should be corrected and situations exist in which business reasons compel us to deliberately maintain a table in less than fully normalized form. In addition, databases are sometimes intentionally de-normalized due to business requirements in order to improve processing efficiency. However, when a de-normalized structure is used, anomalies can result and special measures must be taken to maintain data integrity of such structures.

THE OBJECT-ORIENTED DATABASE MODEL

The most recent development in databases is the *object-oriented model*. Although no common definition for this model has yet emerged, there is agreement as to some of its features. Terminology in the object-oriented model, similar to object-oriented programming languages, consists of objects, attributes, classes, methods, and messages.

An *object* is similar to an entity in that it is the embodiment of a person, place, or thing. Similarly, *attributes* are characteristics that describe the *state* of that object—the attribute values for an object at a given period in time (e.g., the age of an employee). A *method* is an operation, action, or a behavior the object may undergo (e.g., a product may be sold). *Messages* from other objects activate operations contained within the object. Once an operation is activated, it will often send another message to a third object, which, in turn, may activate methods within that object and so on. Significantly, all the data that an object needs in order to perform an operation are logically contained *within* the object. *Encapsulation* is the term used to describe the fact that an object contains all the data and operations necessary to carry out some action.

Every object is an instance of some class. An object's class defines all the messages to which the object will respond, as well as the way in which objects of this class are implemented. Classes are typically arranged in a tree-like structure, connecting superclasses to their subclasses. The links or relationships between a superclass and a subclass is often called an *IS-A* link. The IS-A chain shows that all subclasses inherit all behaviors and attributes defined by its superclass as well as any additional behaviors and attributes of its own. For example, an object of trucks is a subclass of an object of motor vehicles; a truck "IS-A" motor vehicle.

Object-oriented databases can be particularly helpful in heterogeneous (multimedia) environments such as in many manufacturing sites. Data from design blueprints, photographic images of parts, operational acoustic signatures, test or quality control data, and geographical sales data can all be combined into one object, itself consisting of structures and operations. For companies with widely distributed offices, an object-oriented database can provide users with a transparent view of data throughout the overall system.

Object-oriented databases can be particularly useful in supporting temporal and spatial dimensions. All things change; sometimes keeping track of temporal and spatial changes—rather than just the latest version—is important. Related but slightly different versions of an object can easily be maintained in an object-oriented database.

Object-oriented databases allow firms to structure their data and use it in ways that would be impossible, or at least very difficult, with other database models. One example of a business using an object-oriented database is presented below.

Example (Object-Oriented Database at Daimler-Benz)

Daimler-Benz, the German automobile and aerospace multinational corporation known for its Mercedes cars, is a pioneer in the use of object-oriented databases for business applications. The company uses this emerging technology to integrate data stored worldwide throughout the enterprise and to expedite decision making. Cooperating with a small software vendor, Daimler-Benz integrated object databases with its existing or "legacy" information systems for distributed network applications. The new technology enables Daimler-Benz to tie its diverse database systems together and link to customers and suppliers in a network-based, distributed on-line information system.

Object-oriented databases have been around since the mid-1980s, but they were used primarily for computer-aided design and graphical information systems. Since the early 1990s, object-oriented databases have become popular for many other business applications, due to their integration with existing relational and hierarchical databases, and with networks.

This is why Daimler-Benz pioneered the large-scale use of the technology. The distributed network-based environment gives a global view of all Daimler-Benz data available worldwide. The company maintains an object database of product-model data, based on an automotive industry standard. The databases are used in design, manufacturing, and sales of both automobile and aerospace products. One reason why Daimler-Benz was willing to invest heavily in the emerging technology was that it could meet its business goals of high productivity and quality and at the same time leverage the high investment it had in existing legacy information systems.

SOURCE: Adapted from *Information Week,* November 7, 1994.

SUMMARY

Database design is the process by which the requirements of a database are modeled prior to implementation. The conceptual model of a database is a logical data model independent of any particular form of implementation. Metadata is data about the structure of data. Fundamental metadata units are: entities (persons, places, things, or events) and attributes (characteristics of entities).

If there is a one association from unit X to unit Y, we can infer that knowing the value of X allows us to uniquely identify the value of Y. This type of inferencing is used to establish data structures both within an entity class and between entity classes. An attribute, or a combination of attributes, can serve as a primary key to any entity class if, and only if, knowledge of the value of the primary key allows you to uniquely identify the values of all other attributes of that entity class. Entity classes can be related to one another in one of three ways: a one-to-one relationship, a one-to-many relationship, or a many-to-many relationship. A one association on either side of the relationship allows data from the two entity classes to be linked. If a many-to-many relationship exists between entity classes, an intersection entity must be created before the relationship can be implemented in a database.

The E-R model is the data model most commonly used in the conceptual design process. It provides mechanisms for depicting the key metadata structures of a set of data during the conceptual design process. Normalization seeks to produce data structures that facilitate efficient and error-free storage and processing. A series of normal forms have been discovered that assure certain types of anomalies are not present in tables. A table that has no repeating groups of fields is said to be in first normal form. A table that is in first normal form and has no partial dependencies is said to be in second normal form. A table that is in second normal form and has no transitive dependencies is said to be in third normal form. Although other, more restrictive, normal forms have been discovered, most database designers are satisfied with achieving third normal form.

The most recent development in databases is the *object-oriented model.* Object-oriented databases allow firms to structure their data and use it in ways that would be impossible, or at least very difficult, with other database models. Daimler-Benz is one example of a business using an object-oriented database. Also presented was popular PC database software, Microsoft Access.

8A PEER-TO-PEER AND SERVER-BASED NETWORKS

PEER-TO-PEER NETWORKS

Computer networks arose out of the need to share data and capabilities between computers. To fill this need, two basic types of networks have evolved. The first network type, known as a peer-to-peer network, is a simple, cost-effective way to share resources. Peer-to-peer networks consist of workstations connected through a network cable. This simple network design does not utilize a dedicated network server found in the server-based networks. Instead, in a peer-to-peer network all of the computers have equal functionality and act as both the client and the server. Each machine dedicates some data that will be shared to other machines on the network.

Peer-to-peer networks are best used in an environment with fewer than ten workstations, where the sharing of data and resources is not common. Centralized control on these networks is not an option because of the lack of a server. This means that network security is extremely limited. The operating systems used in peer-to-peer networks allow very basic security levels. Security consists mainly of a password. That is usually all that is required to access data that have been dedicated to be shared across the network. Microsoft Windows for Workgroups, Microsoft Windows 95/98, and Microsoft Windows NT are the most commonly used Operating Systems (OS) in this simple network design. Only a network interface card (NIC) and cabling are required to turn your stand-alone computers into a peer-to-peer network.

SERVER-BASED NETWORKS

Today's offices require a more powerful, more secure solution to their network-computing needs. These offices utilize large databases of information that simply cannot be stored and accessed on a simple workstation. The solution is the server-based network, which will be discussed in great detail. These networks offer greater opportunity for growth via resource sharing and solve many of the security issues companies need to address. By centrally administering and controlling resources, server-based networks can be much more efficient.

At the heart of these networks is the server. The server is a machine dedicated to manage the flow of data across the network. This computer can be in charge of several tasks including file-and-printer sharing, application sharing, and communication sharing. File-and-printer-sharing servers manage user access to data stored across the network. Client machines can access files located on the server for manipulation or printing by downloading the data from the server and storing the file on the client's local hard drive. Application servers allow client machines the same abilities as a file-and-print server except the files are never downloaded from the server. Instead, client machines have the ability to access and manipulate files stored only on the server. This is effective for networks with large databases of information that need to be shared among many client machines. Communication servers allow routing of e-mail messages and access to the Internet. This functionality is extremely important in today's wired world. The communication server establishes a simple gateway for all incoming and outgoing data.

PRELIMINARY CONFIGURATION CONSIDERATIONS

Before you go out and purchase the most expensive, most powerful hardware available, it is essential to examine what you are trying to accomplish. Asking yourself several simple questions will save you thousands of dollars and will greatly increase network performance. Listed here are several preliminary questions that need to be addressed.

1. What types of applications over the network are there?
2. Who will need access to the network data?

3. How large are the files being accessed?

4. How often will users access the data and will they need to manipulate them in any manner?

5. How often is it necessary to back up the data?

Application Servers

The first question gives you an insight as to the software your LAN requires. The sharing of applications is the entire purpose of a LAN. The problem is that most managers do not understand software well enough to decide which application is necessary to get the job done. LANs could require the sharing of a large database of information. In this instance you need to consider using database servers such as Microsoft Exchange Server. Other LANs are established to share information regarding project-management functions. Still other LANs require only sharing of files and the printers. No additional software would be required for this LAN other than the server software. The key is to take a look at what other people are using to run similar applications. You can then use their experiences to help you decide what combination of software and hardware is necessary.

Network Security

Question two needs to be addressed as soon as possible. By determining who can have access to what information, you will be able to protect your network from security breaches. Most networks will allow local users access to information on the server and other client workstations. However, there are security issues that must be considered among client machines in your LAN. Windows NT 4.0 Server is a popular back-end server for small office LANs. The NT 4.0 Server comes equipped with security passwords and permissions to prevent local users from gaining access to specific files and network settings. When installing Windows NT 4.0 Server onto a computer, there exists a wide variety of security options. The most basic security level is the login name and password prompt that appears every time the machine is turned on. Without this information an unauthorized user will not be able to enter the operating system. NT Server allows much higher levels of security once you enter the OS.

Firewalls

Remote clients must be considered when setting up your LAN. The majority of LANs will allow some access to outside users. It is essential to limit the access only to those individuals you specify. Also, you need to make clear to your network administrator the files and applications available to those remote users. The best tool to prevent an illegal network break-in is a "firewall." A firewall is a mechanism that acts as the traffic cop between your network and the outside world. Firewalls accomplish two main functions: permitting access to your LAN and preventing access to your LAN. The moment you connect your network to the outside world you are opening it up to viruses, hackers, and unauthorized entries. A firewall may not be able to prevent all break-ins but it does give you the ability to control what information is available to the outside world. Many corporations use a firewall system as a place to store public information about products, services, and files available for download. In this fashion, the firewall is acting as a proxy server for your network by allowing outsiders access to only specified information. Firewalls can be established to permit only e-mail messages entry into the LAN. Less stringent firewalls can be set up to allow local users to communicate freely with the outside world while at the same time preventing anyone from the outside world entering into the LAN. This may limit the functionality of your network. Therefore, you can use your firewall to block entry by certain users that are known to cause problems. For instance, if there is an outside user that is consistently breaking into your network, the firewall will be set up to block that specific user's Internet Protocol (IP) address from entering into your network.

Firewalls will not completely solve network security issues. Firewalls cannot protect against security breaches that do not go through the firewall. A firewall is only a small portion of a corporation's total security system. Network security breaches can easily occur over the telephone and fax machine. Individuals inside your network may be the cause of your security breaches. They can easily circumvent the firewall by storing important information on a floppy disk, zip disk, or compact disk. Once the information is recorded onto one of these types of media, it can easily be transported out of the building through a coat pocket or briefcase. A firewall must be part of the organizational security design. Organizations that spend thousands of dollars on firewalls but allow people to enter and leave the office with unchecked pieces of media have wasted precious resources.

Can a firewall prevent data-destroying viruses? Unfortunately there is some confusion as to the ability of a firewall to prevent against viruses. Most viruses today are spread via e-mail. These e-mail messages contain an attachment that possesses the virus. When the user opens the attachment, the virus is free to run its destructive course. According to Matt Curtin and Marcus Ranum, authors of *Firewalls FAQ,* "Firewalls can't protect very well against things like viruses. There are too many ways of encoding binary files for transfer over networks, and too many different architectures and viruses to try to search for them all." (http://www.cis.ohiostate.edu/hypertext/faq/usenet/firewalls-faq/faq.htm)

Even so, there are several companies that advertise firewall products that can scan for and detect viruses entering the network through e-mail attachments. DataTel Communications Technologies advertises its Interscan product line as being able to stop the spread of viruses into the network. Interscan performs the following function:

1. Internet e-mail is routed through the network to the antivirus gateway, where e-mail attachments are detached and scanned for viruses.

2. If an infected attachment is detected, the antivirus firewall routes the infected attachment to an antivirus engine, where it is disinfected. The cleaned e-mail is then passed through to the mail server, and an alert is sent to the network administrator, the recipient, and the sender.

Most corporations are deeply concerned by the threat of viruses. The best solution is a combination of firewall protection along with installing virus-scanning software at every single computer. McAfee and Symantec are two companies that produce widely recognized virus scanning software. Either product will be useful as long as users continually download the latest updates from the Internet. These updates can be found at either http://www.mcafee.com or http://www.symantec.com depending upon which piece of software you are using. Without updating for the latest virus checks, the software is completely useless against current viruses.

Network Speed

The amount of data being transferred and the frequency of transfers determine the connectivity speed required for your network efficiency. The amount of data refers to size either in kilobytes (KBs), megabytes (MBs), or gigabytes (GBs). Word documents, Excel spreadsheets, and graphic images typically range from less than 100 kilobytes to several megabytes in size. Larger databases are measured in terms of gigabytes. It is essential to determine the size of the files being transferred over your network. This information is the key for determining the specifications of hardware components such as hard-drive size and speed. Today, hard drives range in size from 2.1 gigabytes to 36 gigabytes. If you understand the size of the files being transferred, you can purchase the proper-size hard drives. The size of the data being transferred will help determine the necessary network speed. The majority of networks run at either 10 or 100 MB/sec. If the amount of data being transferred on a daily basis is around 300–400 MB, then it is not necessary to purchase more expensive equipment that allow 100 MB/sec transfer rates. Networks that move a few hundred gigabytes of data need to spend the extra money because it will be much more efficient and cost effective in the long run.

CONFIGURING NETWORK-SERVER OPERATING SYSTEMS

There are three commonly recognized types of LAN-server operating-system software: Windows NT Server, Novell Netware, and Unix. Windows NT Server is a product of Microsoft Corporation. The latest version is 4.0. It is promoted by Microsoft as a "multipurpose server operating system that integrates a variety of network services businesses need today." (http://www.microsoft.com) These services include file sharing, print sharing, security features, and limited-distributed computing features. Microsoft's following is very strong. There are thousands of people holding Microsoft's Certificate in System Engineering (MCSE). Finding support for Microsoft's NT Server will not be a problem. The cost depends on the size and complexity of your network.

Novell's Netware is another option for LAN-server software. Netware is more commonly found in medium and large businesses. Netware offers similar functionality as Microsoft's NT Server and is said to be more stable. Support for Netware is more difficult to find and could cost three times as much as supporting a comparable Microsoft network. Novell has been losing ground to Microsoft because of its higher maintenance expense. A reason could be that the graphical-user interface employed by Netware is not as straightforward as Windows OS. To find out more information on Netware, visit http://www.novell.com/showcase/netware.html.

Unix is the oldest network-operating system. It was developed in 1969 by Bell Laboratories to deliver a simple operating system written in a high-level programming language that allowed for reuse of code. In the eyes of the creators, Unix would serve as a means to connect all computers in a fashion that maximized the collective power of the machines by distributing information and resources across the network. Unix networking support includes remote login, file transfer, electronic mail, and data sharing. Unix's biggest advantage lies in its ability to run on so many different computer systems ranging from small desktops to the largest computers in the world (http://www.hsrl.rutgers.edu/ug/unix_history.html). Once a user has learned UNIX, the skills can be used on many different systems. This ability for a user to work on many different makes of computer systems without retraining is called "user portability." Many users of other operating systems have converted to using UNIX because they felt that UNIX would be the "last" operating system they would have to learn. No other operating system is as easily transferable to different hardware architectures.

There are many different varieties of Unix. Sun bases their Solaris OS on the Unix kernel. Hewlett Packard installs their proprietary version of Unix on large network servers. The licensing fees for both HP and Sun's Unix are astounding. The cost to install and maintain each of these net-work-server packages could cost over $10,000 annually.

LINUX

Linux is a free version of Unix. Linux was originally created by and named after Linus B. Tovald at the University of Helsinki in Finland. Inspired by his interest in Minix, a small Unix operating system, Linus hacked his first kernel in hopes of creating "a better Minix than Minix." Linux aims toward POSIX compliance, a set of standards that show what a Unix should be. It contains all the features you would expect from a Unix and a fully functional operating system. These features include true multitasking, utilizing virtual memory, and multiuser capabilities allowing hundreds of remote users to simultaneously access a single Linux workstation. In addition, Linux contains the world's fastest TCP/IP drivers, making Linux an excellent choice for any server. Benchmarks have shown Linux outperforms traditional servers based on Windows NT, Novell, and other versions of Unix running on similar hardware. This feature can be attributed to the fact that Linux is a child of the Internet. Linux developers utilized the World Wide Web as a means of communication. Speed, therefore, became a necessity. Dr. Mike Holst, a Professor of Mathematics at the University of California at San Diego, views networking and Symmetric Multi-Processing (SMP) support as significantly more developed in Linux than in the Windows NT Server. He based his result by testing performance of both operating systems on his quad processor server.

Linux is the choice for thousands of Internet Service Providers (ISP), university computer laboratories, financial institutions, and software developers. These companies need reliability and stability to run their network, and Linux is becoming the LAN software of choice. Usenet News, e-mail, and File Transfer Protocol (FTP) are supplied with Linux by default. It also comes with an X-Windows interface conforming to the X\Open standard. X-Windows is a Graphical User Interface (GUI) that looks similar to the familiar Microsoft desktop. Redhat's Linux version 6.0 has gone as far to emulate windows as anyone else. Redhat has created a user interface complete with start button (found in the lower left-hand corner), pop-up menus, and even its own version of windows where applications run.

Linux possesses all the features of Unix including interoperability, small size, and portability. Interoperability allows Windows programs to run under Linux through X-Windows with the help of an emulator called "Wine." Windows applications could run up to ten times faster on Linux due to the OS's advanced buffering capabilities. The Linux kernel is extremely small and can be easily transferred to all types of hardware. This means that Linux can be carried around on a floppy disk that could be installed on any machine. This is exactly what Jason Valdry, a computer support consultant at the University of California at Irvine, does. He keeps a portable Linux OS on a floppy drive in his pocket. Imagine the opportunity Linux presents for "Smart Card" technology. A device the size of a credit card could be running a computer application, connecting to the Internet, and databasing all your personal information at the same time.

Linux is a free Unix clone. The Linux kernel is protected under the General Public License (GPL), which states that the source code must be freely distributed and everyone is allowed to make copies for his or her own use or for redistribution. Thousands of FTP servers on the web are available to download the Linux kernel. Linux is available through commercial vendors such as Redhat (http://www.redhat.com), Caldera (http://www.

caldera.com), and Slackware (http://www.slackware.com). The cost is less than $50 for an installation disk and manual. This low cost makes Linux all the more impressive. Sun and HP offer almost identical Unix OSs that cost a minimum of $10,000 annually. This saving is especially important for "financially challenged" companies. Support for Linux is available free over the Internet. Linux user groups, news groups, and chat rooms provide an area where Linux users can post their questions to the world. The quality and reliability of the responses is the Achilles heal of Linux, according to Windows supports. However, the aggregate wealth of knowledge found on the web dwarfs any amount of source code released by Microsoft.

Linux is supported on Personal Computers (PCs) powered by the Intel Pentium and Digital Equipment Alpha processors. Although Linux promotes itself as being supported on a wide variety of architecture, hardware compatibility in your PC is still an issue. Most computer manufacturers offer little or no support for the fledgling operating system. News groups warn people to avoid large computer manufacturers such as Dell and Gateway because of "poor treatment of the Unix community." More knowledgeable companies, such as PSSC Labs (http://www.pssclabs.com) have embraced Linux as a viable alternative to Windows because of its adaptability and powerful networking potential. PSSC Labs has manufactured the Linux-based Aeneas Supercomputer for Dr. Herbert Hamber of the University of California at Irvine. The Aeneas Supercomputer is considered the fastest computer in Orange County with a maximum speed of 20.1 gigaflops. Today's fastest PCs can reach only 0.55 gigaflops. A good source for compatible hardware and available software can be found at Redhat's web site, http://www.redhat.com.

SERVER HARDWARE REQUIREMENTS

At this point you have chosen which network OS server software to power your network. Now you can configure your hardware to meet your needs. We will assume that you have selected either Windows NT Server Version 4.0 or Redhat Linux Version 6.0. Although the functionality of these two competing products are very similar, you need to pay particular attention to the different hardware requirements.

Most people consider the network server the central point of the network. The network server houses the network operating system, stores data from all points on the network, distributes information to clients on the network, and backs up relevant data on a piece of media. If you take a look at any large computer manufacturer's web page, they have a specific line of computers dedicated as servers. In reality a server is simply a computer installed with network-server software. Managers should again examine their speed, power, and backup needs before purchasing any server hardware. Many people believe the more powerful the server, the faster the network. This is not the case. Network speed is limited by many factors other than the server including connection speed and the amount of data being transferred. Let's lift open the case on the typical network server. PSSC Labs (http://www.pssclabs.com) advertises its POWERSERVE as the "ultimate tool for network management." Listed here is the complete configuration for POWERSERVE.

PSSC Labs POWERSERVE includes

Case: Full Tower with 250 Watt UL Power Supply

Motherboard: Dual Processor with Intel 440BX chipset

CPU: (2) Intel Pentium III 500MHz with 512k pb Cache

Memory: 512MB SDRAM PC 100

Floppy: 3.5" 1.44 drive

Hard drive: (2) 18GB Ultra Wide SCSI 7200 rpm, 8.5ms access

HD controller: Adaptec 2940U2W

Video card: ATI Xpert 98 with 8MB AGP

Monitor: Relisys 17"

CD-ROM: 45X

Network: Intel 10/100 Fast PCI

Tape backup: 12/24GB DAT drive

5 pieces of media

Mouse: Logitec 3 Button

Keyboard: Mutsumi 104 Key High Quality

Software: Seagate Back Up Exec Server Edition

O/S: Windows NT Server 4.0

Servers usually come configured with two central processing units. The need for a second processor is not as great as you might think. A second processor benefits only machines that require a constant processing of information. Computers conducting large amounts of calculations, running heavy graphic programs, or managing large databases will show a significant performance increase with the addition of the second processor. Most small-office and small-offices network servers do not require two processors. The role of the server in smaller networks is typically to connect all work-stations and share small amounts of information. Managers can make bet-ter use of financial resources by avoiding the second processor on their network. If you do manage a larger network, it is advisable to add the sec-ond processor.

In the preceding configuration, Intel's Pentium III 500 central pro-cessing unit (CPU) powers the server. Managers need to follow network standards and industry trends. Intel maintains a strong grasp on CPU technology with an over 80% share of the PC market. Software and hard-ware manufacturers test and benchmark their products on computers powered by Intel CPUs. Intel now has several product lines for PC CPUs including the first-generation product known as the Pentium, the second generation called the Pentium II, and the third-generation Pentium III processor. Each of these product lines builds on the technology of the pre-vious generation. Depending on the amount of speed and power the server requires, it is advisable for you to look at the price differences between these processors. If you manage a smaller network where the server is transferring small amounts of data, it is not necessary to purchase the fastest CPU possible. The server's processor speed has very little to do with the overall performance of the network. Again, financial resources can be saved and better utilized on client machines requiring greater processor use.

Managers should not rule out non-Intel-based PC servers. Using less expensive processors by Advanced Micro Devices and Cyrix could cause con-figuration nightmares because of hardware and software incompatibility.

The amount of memory installed on the server is more important than CPU speed to the overall server performance. When you access an applica-tion program or open a file, the data are transferred from the hard drive or CD-ROM and are held in memory while the processor conducts manipula-tions. Servers need to have enough memory to hold all the necessary data. A minimum of 128 MB of memory is standard on most servers. This limited amount of memory could slow down the server's performance by not allow-ing enough space to hold data. It is recommended to use a base of 256 MBs or 512 MBs of memory in your server. Larger network servers hold up to 4.0 GBs of memory. This may be overkill for your network, but you should not cut costs by limiting the server's memory.

The type of memory you use is also extremely important to the server's performance. At the beginning of 1998 Intel released its BX chipset on motherboards. The biggest advantage of this new chipset lies in the ability of memory to transfer data to the processor at 100 MHz. This is a 50% increase over the older TX and HX chipsets, which allowed memory transfer speeds up to 66 MHz. Synchronous Dynamic Random Access Memory (SDRAM) is the memory required for today's fastest workstations and servers. This is a 168-pin memory module that offers the fastest performance for PC memory. SDRAM can come in a parity chip, known as Error Correcting Code (ECC), that tests the accuracy of data as the data move in and out of memory. ECC memory is not a necessity unless you are doing highly computational functions. Small office servers need not use ECC memory.

Hard Drives: SCSI versus IDE

Hard drives offer the greatest degree of variability in the network server. They range in size from 2.1 GB to 36 GB. In addition, there is a fundamental choice between using two different interfaces: Integrated Drive Electronics (IDE) versus Small Computer Systems Interface (SCSI). IDE is a simple path for information stored on the hard drive to be processed using input/output technology. One of the drawbacks of input/ouput technology is it prevents the CPU from accomplishing any other tasks when it is accessing the hard drive for information. This limited multitasking ability greatly reduces the performance of the machine when transferring large data files.

To combat this problem, PC manufacturers turned to Apple for help. Apple first integrated SCSI technology into their Macintosh line of computers. The value of SCSI lies in the increased bandwidth and multitasking abilities it provides. SCSI accomplishes this multitasking function through Direct Memory Access (DMA) technology. DMA allows the CPU to work on other applications while information is being transferred from the hard drive. IDE hard-drive manufacturers are joining the DMA bandwagon and introducing DMA technology into their newer drives.

SCSI comes in a variety of configurations. SCSI drives can be either "Ultra," "Ultra Wide," or "Ultra 2." Ultra SCSI drives transfer data at a maximum of 20 MB/sec. Ultra Wide max out at 40 MB/sec, and Ultra 2 drives peak at 80 MB/sec. This compares favorably to the 33 MB/sec peak performance achieved by IDE drives.

Managers should be aware of the performance of different hard drives. Data-transfer speed is crucial to the performance of network servers. If the server is moving medium to large files, Ultra 2 SCSI hard drives should be used. The time saving allowed by faster data transfer is well within the additional cost for Ultra 2 technology.

FIGURE 8A—1

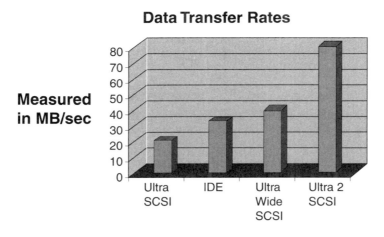

Hard-Disk Mirroring

If you go back to the PowerServe configuration, you will notice that there are two hard drives installed in the computer. The reason for this is not because of a need for greater hard-drive space to store data. All of your data including files, programs, and operating system will reside on a single hard drive. The second hard drive is installed in order to ensure data backup. Windows NT Server 4.0 provides a very useful utility known as "mirroring." Mirroring allows two hard drives on the same system to store the exact information. If you have two mirrored hard drives in your server, you essentially have two hard drives containing the exact information. One hard drive is a mirror of the other. The reason why this is so useful is hard drives do fail. If one of the hard drives fails, the mirrored drive can assume all of the functionality of the original drive. This translates to limited down time for the server and increased network reliability.

Redundant Array of Inexpensive Disks (RAID)

If your data files are extremely large and important, a Redundant Array of Inexpensive Disks (RAID) technology is the best option. RAID systems allow several hard drives to be connected to act as a single drive. The computer recognizes this group of hard drives as just a single drive when it is accessed or written. RAID technology offers much greater fault tolerance than a single drive or two mirrored drives. A common term used in RAID is "striping."

Striping is "a method of connecting multiple drives into one logical storage unit. Striping involves partitioning each drive's storage space into stripes that may be as small as one sector (512 bytes) or as large as several megabytes. These stripes are then interleaved round-robin, so that the combined space is composed alternately of stripes from each drive. In effect, the storage space of the drives is shuffled like a deck of cards. The type of application environment, I/O or data-intensive, determines whether large or small stripes should be used." (http://www.uni-mainz.de/~neuffer/-scsi/what_is_raid.html) There exist six different RAID levels. Following is a brief summary of each level.

RAID-0 is the fastest and most efficient array type but offers no fault-tolerance.

RAID-1 is the array of choice for performance-critical, fault-tolerant environments. In addition, RAID-1 is the only choice for fault-tolerance if no more than two drives are desired.

RAID-2 is seldom used today because Error Correction is embedded in almost all modern disk drives.

RAID-3 can be used in data-intensive or single-user environments that access long sequential records to speed up data transfer. However, RAID-3 does not allow multiple I/O operations to be overlapped and requires synchronized-spindle drives in order to avoid performance degradation with short records.

RAID-4 offers no advantages over RAID-5 and does not support multiple simultaneous write operations.

RAID-5 is the best choice in multiuser environments that are not write-performance sensitive. However, at least three, and more typically five drives are required for RAID-5 arrays.

In order to convert your server to a RAID system, you will need a RAID controller and the software that comes with that controller. Mylex (http://www.mylex.com), DPT (http://www.dpt.com), and Adaptec (http://www.adaptec.com) offer excellent RAID controllers and plenty of technical support. Remember RAID is used only in networks with extremely large data files (10.0 GB or larger).

Using Tape-Backup Devices

To avoid a disastrous loss of data, all network servers need to utilize a tape-backup device. Backup devices along with backup software ensure that your network data is secure even if your server hardware fails. Installing a backup system is the single most important step in any network environment. Backup devices can be as simple as a floppy drive to the most complex Digital Analog Tape device (DAT). Following is a list of several different backup devices along with their backup capacity and estimated cost.

DEVICE	CAPACITY	COST
3.5" Floppy Drive	1.44 MB	$20
Iomega Zip Drive	100 MB or 250 MB	$90 to $165
CD Rewritable Drive	650 MB	$400
Iomega Jazz Drive	2.0 GB	$335
DAT Drive	Up to 24 GB depending on model	$895

Using a floppy drive, zip drive, or CD Rewritable drive is not recommended because of the small capacity allowed by the media. Network managers need to evaluate the capacity of the data that needs to be stored, the frequency of backup, and the speed necessary to complete the backup. By analyzing these three factors, managers can narrow down which backup device will match their network needs. DAT drives are the most reliable and offer the largest capacity for the price.

Simply installing any one of the devices is not enough. Network managers need to install software that will automatically back up the data periodically. Seagate's BackUp Exec is a perfect backup solution for small- to medium-size business. This software works with DAT drives of all capacity and speed. The key to the success of Seagate's product is the ease of use and flexibility it allows. Once this product is installed on the server, it allows network managers to select the specific files that need to be backed up. Most small to midsize offices schedule a backup at the end of every week. All the manager needs to do is schedule the backup and install the tape cartridge.

Seagate's BackUp Exec offers the ability to back up not only data on the server, but data stored on client workstations as well. It is this flexibility that makes BackUp Exec such an effective weapon against network failures. Managers simply need to select the specific files on the server and the clients that they would like to have backed up. This is a very simple process that the backup software walks you through. This process is referred to as "backing up across the network." It is the most efficient way of backing up multiple systems but can be an extremely time-consuming process that could cause significant increases in network traffic.

Managers need to analyze how quickly they would like this job done. Speed will be a determining factor in selecting the proper backup device. Today's DAT drives are considered the fastest backup devices available. There are slower devices that cost less money but it is recommended to use a device that matches your speed requirements.

CONNECTING THE SERVER TO THE NETWORK

In order to connect your server to the network, it needs to contain a Network Interface Card (NIC). The NIC allows a pathway for data transfer in and out of the server. It is a simple insert card that can either be preinstalled in the machine or added at a later date. Selecting the correct NIC can be extremely confusing unless you understand which type of connection you are using. There are two types of connections, which depend on the cabling your network is using. The older type of connection is called BNC, 10Base2, or Coax.

BNC-capable network cards have a cylinder terminal extending from the card. It is here that the cable is connected to your network card. This cable looks very similar to the round, stiff, black copper cable connected to your television. Copper allows data-transfer speeds up to 10 MB/sec. This slow rate of data transfer as well as the stiffness of the BNC cable is limiting.

In order to combat the shortfalls of BNC cables, networks now use network cables based on twisted-pair technology. Twisted-pair—also referred to as 100BaseT, TPO, and RJ45—cable looks similar to telephone cable. It is much more flexible, allowing the cable to be bent in any number of ways without destroying the integrity of the wire. More important, these cables allow 100 MB/sec of data transfer. This provides for a significant increase in network performance.

Notice that there is no protruding cylinder connector similar to the one found in BNC network cards. Instead there is only a gap where the RJ45 cable can be inserted. Today's standard networks utilize 10/100 NICs, but as a manager it is important for you to ask the building supervisor which type of cable is installed in the building.

Uninterruptible Power Supply (UPS)

All too often network managers assume that once they plug their server into the wall, the power will be supplied cleanly and at a constant level. Unfortunately this is not always the case. An uninterruptible power supply (UPS) is not a necessity to all networks but it should be added to networks in environments where there is a risk of power failure. The UPS acts as an automated external power supply that keeps a server running in the event of a power failure. Its job is to run the server for a short period of time and shut down the server in the proper fashion. If the power from the wall outlet fails, users are notified of the failure and the UPS takes over. American Power Conversions (APC), http://www.apc.com, manufactures UPS for all sizes and varieties of networks including Windows based, Unix based, and Novell based. Choosing the correct UPS unit can be confusing, but it is important for managers to ask themselves the following questions:

1. How many components will the UPS need to support?
2. How much time is required to properly shut down the server and clients?
3. How will the UPS unit notify users of a power failure?

The simplest way to purchase the correct UPS is to contact your APC vendor with the answers to these questions. They will tell you the minimum and maximum power requirements for your network.

Now your server hardware is almost completely configured. We will add the standard devices such as a floppy drive, a CD-ROM, a keyboard, and mouse. The video card and monitor do not need to be anything special because most servers are not used as a general workstation with higher video requirements. Most servers come with a 15-inch SVGA monitor and a very simple video card with a maximum of 4 MB of memory.

SELECTING SERVER SOFTWARE

Now that you have selected a network operating system and hardware required for the server, it is time to choose the software required to reach your networking goals. There are three basic server functions mentioned earlier. The first is file-and-print sharing. This is the very basic element of what a server can accomplish. All forms of network operating systems allow this functionality. No additional software is required besides the network operating system.

Most networks want to accomplish much more than this basic level of networking. Database sharing and communications ability are the driving force behind server-based networks. Companies such as Microsoft, Oracle, and Netscape specialize in software suites that allow the functionality your network requires. Let's say you are designing your network to support a large database of customer contacts. As a manager you would like to store this database on the server and allow all of your users to access it. The solution is a product such as Microsoft's Back Office Server. It provides an easy solution to managing customer databases.

CONFIGURING THE CLIENT WORKSTATION

In much the same manner that you selected hardware for the network server, the client workstations should be configured based on the software requirements of the machine. The client operating system is much less robust than the network operating system. Microsoft remains the standard of choice for desktop OS. Microsoft Windows 98 and Windows NT 4.0 Workstation come with user-friendly graphical user interfaces (GUI). More important, these two OSs comprise 96% of the total client operating systems in the world today. This means that the majority of software programs are written specifically for Microsoft protocols. Microsoft recently released Windows 2000, which offers the same easy-to-use interface along with increased functionality. Apple's Mac OS and Linux are available options for client operating systems. However, the lack of available software make it extremely difficult to accomplish your tasks using either of these two operating systems.

Following is a typical client workstation offered by PSSC Labs.

Case: MidTower with 250 Watt UL Power Supply

Motherboard: Single Processor with Intel 440BX chipset

CPU: Intel Pentium III 550 MHz with 512k pb Cache

Memory: 128 MB SDRAM PC 100

Floppy: 3.5" 1.44 drive

Hard drive: 8.4 GB EIDE 33

HD controller: (2) EIDE on motherboard

Video card: Diamond Viper 550 with 16 MB AGP

Monitor: Viewsonic 19" SVGA

CD ROM: 45X

Network: Intel 10/100 Fast PCI

Tape backup: Iomega Zip 250 MB

Mouse: Logitec 3 Button

Keyboard: Mutsumi 104 Key High Quality

O/S: Windows NT 4.0 Workstation

We note the basic differences between the hardware on the client workstations and that required by the server. Client workstations are often relied upon to do more processor-intensive work. For that reason the CPU in client computers should be equal to or more powerful than the CPU found on the server. This is not always necessary; however, most client applications such as Adobe Photoshop and Macromedia Director are extremely processor intensive.

The amount of memory required on the client is usually much less than what is required on the server. The reason is client machines have less data stored in memory. Client workstations typically do not require high-speed SCSI hard drives. A standard IDE hard drive is usually sufficient. Substituting a SCSI hard drive on the client, however, may significantly increase performance if the client workstation is working with very large data files.

Video performance on client workstations is more crucial than on the server. The reason is client machines are required for everyday work functions. Individuals working on client machines prefer the largest monitor possible combined with a video card that is fast enough to smoothly run today's memory-intensive programs. A 17-inch monitor and a video card with at least 8 MB of memory should be your office standard.

Even though you have configured your network server to backup data from client workstations it is still necessary to install some form of tape backup device on your client machines. An Iomega Zip drive or a CD Rewritable drive are perfect solutions for client machines that need to back up small amounts of data. Remember backing up your data as much as possible is essential to prevent the headaches caused by system and network failures.

All of the other hardware components including floppy drive, CD-ROM drive, network card, keyboard, and mouse should be almost exact replicas of the devices installed on your server. This hardware conformity will make it easier to work with machines in case of problems.

CONNECTING THE SERVER AND CLIENTS

Hubs

Now you have configured the hardware and software necessary for the server and all client workstations and assigned IP addresses. The only thing left to do is connect the machines together. In a simple peer-to-peer network, this connection is accomplished via a network card and a cable. The same components are necessary on a server-based network but an additional piece of hardware is required. This piece of hardware is a rectangular box known as a network hub. There are some considerations you need to address before purchasing the hub. First, you need to assess how many machines will be installed on the network. Most hubs today come with ports to connect anywhere from eight to twenty-four computers. If you require more ports, you can purchase a "stackable" hub. Stackable refers to the ability to connect hubs together, thereby doubling or tripling the total number of accessible hub ports.

The next question is how fast do you need to transfer data. Networks are full of speed bottlenecks. One of the major bottlenecks is the network hub. Inexpensive hubs allow you to transfer data at a maximum of 10 MB/sec. Transferring large amounts of data on these hubs can be extremely time consuming. There are hubs that transfer data at 100 MB/sec. Although these hubs are significantly more expensive, they can save large amounts of time because of the increase in data-transfer speed. But what if you have a network consisting of some machines with 10 MB/sec network cards and others with 100 MB/sec network cards? Here you have to be extremely careful in selecting the proper hub. Certain hubs are said to be "switching" hubs, meaning they allow 10 MB/sec and 100 MB/sec connections to the network. However, this can be misleading. Switching hubs will default to the slowest connection speed on the network. This means that even if you have machines using 100 MB/sec connections, they will run only at 10 MB/sec when they are installed on a network with machines running at 10 MB/sec. In this case, the solution is to use a 100 MB/sec switching hub. This type of hub will simultaneously allow data-transfer speeds of 100 MB/sec and 10 MB/sec. These hubs cost significantly more money but, again, the time savings need to be considered when purchasing this equipment.

TROUBLESHOOTING THE NETWORK

Maintaining the network is one of the most difficult jobs for network managers. The key here is to expect the unexpected. Network managers need to be aware of some of the basic problems that arise in networks of all sizes. The following hardware and software troubleshooting hints can help you diffuse most of your basic network problems quickly and efficiently.

When you break down the computer to its most basic hardware components, there are a finite number of hardware failure and conflicts that can occur. Managers must first be able to identify symptoms of hardware problems in order to solve the problem. The computer has suprisingly few moving parts. Only the various drives and cooling fans in the computer possess items with mechanical components. All the other components including memory, central-processing units, motherboards, and insert cards are comprised of stationary circuit boards and silicon chips. This is important because typically only the items with moving parts can actually degrade with use. Hard drives, floppy drives, CD-ROMs, and tape backup devices will fail as time goes along. The stationary components usually will work for the life of the machine. Following is detailed examination of each component, the symptoms of hardware failure, and the corrective action that should be taken.

Hard Drives

These are the components that most often fail in a system. PSSC Labs estimates that 10% of hard drives fail within the first year of a computer's operation. An additional 15% fail the second year, and 15% more fail during the third year. This is unfortunate considering this is the place where all of the data are stored. For this reason it is always necessary to have some form of backup including mirroring, RAID, or a backup device installed in all servers and workstations.

Symptoms of failure: When a hard drive dies the machine will power on. It will go through the process of counting memory and installing the Basic Input Output System (BIOS). Once the BIOS is ready to run the OS residing on the hard drive, the machine will simply stop. The monitor will display a message that reads:

No Hard Disk Found

Solution: Shut down the computer. Remove the case from the machine and detach the hard drive from its housing. Disconnect all the power connections to everything except the hard drive. While holding your ear as close as possible to the hard drive, turn the computer's power back on. If you hear no noise coming from the hard drive, it is "dead." Completely remove the drive and contact your system administrator as soon as possible. If you would like to solve the problem yourself all you need to do is contact the hard-drive manufacturer and obtain a Return Material Authorization (RMA) number. Certain manufacturers, such as Samsung and Maxtor, offer advanced swap policies on their drives where the manufacturer will send you a new drive before you send them the defective product. This is the most efficient technique manufacturers use to replace damaged products. One manufacturer to avoid because of lengthy product replacement time is Western Digital. Whenever possible, avoid buying Western Digital components.

The data on the drive are now lost. There do exist companies specializing in recovering data from dead hard drives. This will cost you thousands of dollars and the effectiveness of this operation is questionable at best.

Floppy Drives and CD-ROMs

These devices are typically more reliable than hard drives. However, because they are comprised of moving parts, there does exist a chance of failure.

Symptoms: A floppy-device failure will become apparent when you turn on the machine. On boot-up the BIOS will check for the presence of a floppy drive. If this BIOS check fails, a message will appear that reads "No floppy device present." A CD-ROM failure does not make itself known until the machine enters Windows. CD-ROM failure is apparent when you insert a piece of media into the drive and Windows cannot access the information. The CD-ROM will continually spin without ever being able to read the media.

Solution: The solution is to follow the same steps as for replacing the hard drive. Floppy drives cost $25 and CD-ROMs $60. It is advisable to keep a few extra CD-ROMs and floppy drives available in case of failure. Once you replace the drive, you can send the defective drive back to the manufacturer.

Video Cards and Monitors

Video cards and monitors work in conjunction with each other. If one of the two devices fails, the other will be affected. It is important to realize this when diagnosing video issues.

Symptoms: Wavy lines, fuzzy picture, or a black screen are all symptoms of a monitor or video-card failure. There is no way to determine which device, the video card or the monitor, is the cause of the problem until you perform the following simple steps.

Solution: While the machine is running, unplug the power and VGA cable on the back of the monitor. Find a replacement monitor on a nearby desk. Attach this new monitor to the machine and plug in the power cable. If the picture returns to normal, the monitor you originally removed is bad. You will need to send the monitor back to the manufacturer and wait for the company to repair or replace their product. Monitor manufacturers are notoriously slow to return a working monitor back to you. The process could take up to six weeks.

If, when you attach the replacement monitor, the problem still persists, you can conclude that the video card is defective. You will have to remove the card from the machine and send it back for repairs. If you do not have a spare video card, the machine is essentially useless. Video cards can be as inexpensive as $25 for an AGP card with 4 MB of memory.

Memory

Luckily, memory will either work right away or it will not work at all. For that reason memory manufacturers offer a lifetime guarantee on their products.

Symptoms: The symptom of a memory problem is continual "crashing" of the operating system. This crash is immediately followed by the "blue screen." The blue screen is exactly what it sounds like. The monitor will display only a blue background as the computer tries to count the memory. Memory problems are probably the most difficult to diagnose because this blue screen can be caused by any number of defects, including a faulty motherboard. If you receive many error messages called "page faults," you can narrow down the cause of the problem to memory. Page faults do not always appear, but if they do, you have bad memory.

Solution: Remove the case. Detach all of the peripheral devices including CD-ROM, sound card, and network card. We are going to use the bare components of the computer. The only items necessary are the power supply, motherboard, CPU, memory, video card, and hard drive. Remove all of the memory except for one piece. Turn the machine on and see if the crashing persists. Continue to add memory one piece at a time until you have narrowed down which piece is the cause of the problems. Now you can return this piece and rebuild the machine to its working condition.

CPU

In ten years PSSC Labs has seen only one defective CPU from Intel. PSSC Labs has built thousands of workstations in that same period. It is safe to assume that the CPU is not going to go bad.

CLIENT/SERVER COMPUTING

In client/server architecture, PCs are considered as "clients" and are linked to specialized, powerful "servers" (databases, communication devices, mainframes, and very powerful PCs), which they share via local or global networks. Such architecture requires telecommunication standards that will allow interconnection of different types of software and hardware. The client/server architecture is used to support the Internet and the intranets. Both clients and servers are connected by LANs and possibly by VANs.

The purpose of client/server architecture is to maximize the use of computer resources. It provides a way for different computing devices to work together, each doing the job for which it is best suited. Another important element is sharing. The clients, which are usually inexpensive PCs, share more expensive devices, the servers.

Client/server architecture gives companies as many access points to data as there are PCs on the network. It also lets companies use more tools to process data and information. Employees can access the databases at will.

CLIENT/SERVER COMPUTING DEFINED

A client is generally viewed as any system or process that can request and utilize data, services, or access to other systems provided by a server. A server is considered to be any system or process that provides data, services, or access to other systems for clients, most often for multiple clients simultaneously. Most servers—mainframes, minicomputers, workstations, and

115

sometimes high-end PCs—are more powerful than individual clients. In the client/server model, servers provide the clients with the data and processing as in a centralized relationship, but the clients themselves are fully capable computer processors that have peer-to-peer relationships among themselves as well. A client can bring locally controlled computing directly to a user's desktop while still sharing computing, devices, and data resources with other users.

Client Process

The client is a process that sends a message to a server process requesting the server to perform a service. Client processes usually manage the user-interface portion of the application, validate data entered by the users, dispatch requests to server processes, and sometimes execute business logic. The client-based process is the front end of the application that the users see and interact with. The client process contains solution-specific logic and provides the interface between the user and the rest of the applications system. The client process also manages the local resources that the user interacts with such as the monitor, keyboard, workstation CPU, and peripherals. One of the key elements of a client workstation is the graphical user interface (GUI). Normally, a part of the operation system manages the windows on the display and displays the data in the windows.

Server Process

A server process fulfills the client request by performing the task requested. The server process generally receives requests from client processes, executes database retrieval and updates, manages data integrity, and dispatches responses to client requests. Sometimes server processes execute common or complex business logic. The server-based process may run on another machine on the network. This server could be the host operating system or network file server; the server is then provided both file system services and application services. The server process acts as a software engine that manages shared resources, such as databases, printers, communication links, or high-powered processors. The server process performs the back-end tasks that are common to similar applications.

Two-Tier Architecture

A two-tier architecture involves a client talking directly to a server. It is usually used in small environments (fewer than fifty users). A common error in client/server development occurs when it prototypes an application in a small, two-tier environment and then scales up by adding more users to the server. This approach will usually result in an ineffective system. It is usually necessary to move to a three-tier architecture to serve more users.

Three-Tier Architecture

A three-tier architecture introduces a server between the client and the server. The role of the server is diverse. It can provide translation services (as in adapting a legacy application on a mainframe to a client/server environment), metering services (as in acting as a transaction monitor to limit the number of simultaneous requests to a given server), or intelligent-agent services (as in mapping a request to a number of different servers, collating the results, and returning a single response to the client).

Middleware

Connectivity allows applications to transparently communicate with other programs or processes regardless of their locations. The key element of connectivity is the network operating system (NOS). NOS provides services such as routing, distribution, messaging, file and print, and network management. NOS depends on communication protocols to provide specific services. The protocols are divided into three groups: media, transport, and client/server protocols. Media protocols determine the type of physical connections used on a network. A transport protocol provides the mechanism to move data from client to server. Once the physical connection has been established, users can access the network services. A client/server protocol indicates the manner in which clients request information and services from a server and how the server replies to that request.

Cooperative Processing

Cooperative processing is computing that requires two or more distinct processors to complete a single transaction. Cooperative processing is related to both distributed and client/server processing. Usually, these programs interact and execute concurrently on different processors. Cooperative processing can also be considered to be a style of client/server processing if communication among processors is performed through a message-passing architecture.

Distributed Processing

Distributed processing implies that processing will occur on more than one processor in order for a transaction to be completed. Processing is distributed across two or more machines and the processes are most likely not running at the same time. Each process performs part of an application in a sequence. Very often the data used in a distributed-processing environment is also distributed across platforms.

Intranet

The explosion of the World Wide Web resulted from the worldwide acceptance of a common transport (TCP/IP), server standard (http), and markup language (HTML). Many corporations have found that these same technologies can be used for internal client/server applications with the same function as when used on the Internet. Therefore, the concept of "Intranet" was introduced to the use of Internet technologies for implementing internal client/server applications. Advantages of web-based Intranets are that the problem of managing code on the client is greatly reduced, and the corporation is already using the Internet so there are no additional code needs to be licensed or installed on client desktops.

CLIENT/SERVER TECHNICAL ISSUES

Characteristics of Client/Server Architecture

First, the basic structure of client/server architecture is a client device and a server device that are distinguishable, but interact with each other. The client process contains solution-specific logic and provides the interface between the user and the rest of the application system. The server process acts as a software engine that manages shared resources, such as databases, printers, modems, or high-powered processors. Second, the

front-end task and back-end task have different requirements for computing resources, such as processor speeds, memory, disk speeds, capacities,
and input/output devices. Third, the environment is typically heterogeneous. The hardware platform and operating system of the client and server
are not usually the same. Client and server processes communicate through
a well-defined set of standard application program interfaces (APIs) and
RPCs. One of the most important characteristics of client/server systems is
scalability. They can be scaled horizontally or vertically. Horizontal scaling
means adding or removing client workstations with only a slight performance impact. Vertical scaling means changing into a larger and faster
server machine or to multiservers.

Types of Servers

The simplest forms of servers are disk servers and file servers. With a
file server, the client passes requests for files or file records over a network
to the file server. This form of data service requires large bandwidth and can
considerably slow down a network with many users. Traditional LAN computing allows users to share resources, such as data files and peripheral
devices, by moving them from stand-alone PCUs onto a networked file
server (NFS).

The more advanced form of servers are database servers, transaction
servers, and application servers. In database servers, clients pass SQL
(Structured Query Language) requests as messages to the server, and the
results of the query are returned over the network. The code processes the
SQL request and the data residing on the server allow the server to use its
own processing power to find the requested data instead of passing all the
records back to a client and letting it find its own data, as was the case for
the file server. In transaction servers, clients invoke remote procedures that
reside on servers that also contain an SQL database engine. There are pro-
cedural statements on the server to execute a group of SQL statements
(transactions), which either all succeed or fail as a unit. The applications
based on transaction servers are called On-line Transaction Processing
(OLTP) and tend to be mission-critical applications that require one-to-
three-second response time 100% of the time and require tight controls
over the security and integrity of the database. The communication overhead in this approach is kept to a minimum as the exchange typically consists of a single request/reply (as opposed to multiple SQL statements in

database servers). Application servers are not necessarily database-centered but are used to meet users' needs, such as downloading capabilities from Dow Jones or regulating an electronic mail process. Using resources on a server allows users to share data, while security and management services, both of which are also based on the server, ensure data integrity and security.

DIFFERENT CLIENT/SERVER MODELS

In a client/sever approach, the components of an application are distributed over the enterprise rather than being centrally controlled. There are three application components that can be distributed. They are the presentation component, the applications logic, and the data-management component. The presentation component is the application interface or how the application appears to the user. The applications logic is created by the business rules of the application. The data-management component consists of the storage and management of the data needed by the application. There are five models of client/server implementation, depending on the partition of the three components between the server and the client. Those five models are distributed presentation, remote presentation, distributed function, remote data management, and distributed data management.

Distributed and Remote Presentation

With distributed presentation, all three components are on the server, but the presentation logic is distributed between the client and the server. With remote presentation, applications logic and database management are on the server and the presentation logic is located on the client.

Remote Data Management

In remote data management, the entire application is on the client while the data management is on a remote server/host. Remote data management is relatively easy to program because there is just one application program. The client communicates with the server through SQL; the server then responds with data that satisfy the query. Workstations support the presentation and function logic and interface with the data server through the data-manipulation language. Distributed data management is an extension of remote data management and uses the distributed facilities of the DBMS to access distributed data in a manner transparent to users. It has all three components on the client, with database management distributed between the client and the server. This is the most relevant for architectures having data spread across several servers.

Distributed Logic and Distributed Database

With distributed logic, data management is on the server and presentation logic is on the client, with application logic distributed between the two. With distributed database, all three components are on the clients, with database management distributed between the client and the server.

Fat Clients and Thin Clients

These models lead to the ideas of "fat clients" and "thin clients." Fat clients have large storage and processing power, and the three components of an application can be processed. Thin clients may have no local storage and limited processing power; therefore, they can handle presentation only.

Open Software Foundation (OSF) and Distributed Computing Environment (DCE)

DCE is the Distributed Computing Environment, from the Open Software Foundation. DCE comprises multiple components that have been integrated to work closely together. They are the Remote Procedure Call (RPC), the Cell and Global Directory Services (CDS and GDS), the Security Service, DCE Threads, Distributed Time Service (DTS), and Distributed File Service (DFS). The Threads, RPC, CDS, Security, and DTS components are commonly referred to as the "secure core" and are the required components of any DCE installation. DFS is an optional component. DCE is called "middleware" or "enabling technology." It is not meant to exist alone; instead, it should be integrated or bundled into a vendor's operating-system offering. DCE's security and distributed file systems, for example, can completely replace their current, non-network, analogs.

Distributed Object Management Systems (DOMS)

DOMS provides a way of putting various components together and managing their communications. They are aimed at addressing the following:

- A single interface to manage the complexities of a heterogeneous environment
- A uniform framework based on standards and extensibility to build, integrate, and deploy open distributed-computing applications
- A method for creating location independence for client applications

Common Object Request Broker Architecture (CORBA)

Common Object Request Broker Architecture is a set of standard mechanisms for naming, locating, and defining objects in a distributed computing environment.

Distributed Application Environment (DAE)

Distributed Application Environment allows people to use IBM's RISC System/6000 and PS/2 computers in a client/server network (or stand-alone) for their business applications. DAE consists of (1) MESSAGING services, (2) DATABASE services, (3) PRESENTATION services, and (4) DEVICE services to capture data and to control a broad category of controllers, devices, equipment, and sensors.

CLIENT/SERVER BUSINESS ISSUES

Client/Server Business-Application Architectures

Traditional applications architectures have been based upon functions. Nowadays, in order to meet the needs of the business, an application architecture should reflect the complete range of business requirements.

Therefore, client/server computing demands a three-layer view of the organization.

1. The user interface layer that implements the functional model
2. The business functionality layer that implements the process model
3. The data layer that implements the information model

Note that this application architecture does not demand multiple hardware platforms. As long as the environment is large and reliable enough and the business is prepared to pay the additional costs associated with workstation and LAN technology, it is good to utilize this kind of technology.

Business Drivers

Client/server computing has arisen because of a change in business needs. Businesses need integrated, flexible, responsive, and comprehensive applications to support the complete range of business processes.

Problems with existing systems include

- Applications were developed to model vertical applications.
- Applications were built in isolation.
- Applications were implemented as monolithic systems.
- Applications were complex.
- The supporting technology was based on a centralized control model.

Information technology, which is an enabling factor in systems building, has almost reached the stage where these systems can be designed and created. Unfortunately, most businesses have existing systems based on older technology, which must be incorporated into the new, integrated environment. The development and implementation of client/server computing is more complex, more difficult, and more expensive than traditional, single-process applications. The reason why client/server applications were built was to meet business's increasing demands and to add more benefits.

Business Benefits

- There is a need for vendor independence. This includes application development methodologies, programming paradigms, products, and architectures.

- Organizations have gone from hierarchies to flatter hierarchies.

- Network management is replacing vertical management.

- There is a change to team-based management.

- The user will perform as much processing as possible during customer-contact time.

- The time required to complete the work will be minimized.

- There is a need for empowerment of staff.

- Multiskilled and multifunction teams need access to multiple applications.

10A

BUILDING AND MANAGING CLIENT-SERVER SYSTEMS

This chapter presents the construction and management of client/server systems. It includes coverage of servers, client/server tools, software evaluation plan, costs, and critical factors.

We discuss in this section the various types of servers and when they are to be used.

SERVERS

Kinds of Servers

Server computers have various uses in client/server systems. The most common uses for server computers are as follows:

File servers

File servers provide centralized disk storage that can be conveniently shared by client computers on the network. The most common use is to store programs and data files. For example, the members of a small work-group can use disk space on a file server to store their word-processing documents.

File servers must ensure that two users don't try to update the same file at the same time. The file servers do this by locking a file while a user updates the file so that other users can't access the file until the first user finishes. For document files (for example, word-processing or spreadsheet files), the whole file is locked. For database files, the lock can be applied just to the portion of the file that contains the record or records being updated.

Most LANs are based on a file server model: Several client computers are connected to a file server to share program and data files. The popular NetWare network operating system from Novell assumes that one or more computers on a network are dedicated file servers.

LAN vendors and consultants sometimes refer to their systems as "client/server" because they use file servers. However, a simple file-server network doesn't qualify as a client/server system because the application workload isn't shared between the client computers and the file server computer. Instead, the client computer does all the work. The file server just acts like a remote disk drive. File servers often double as print servers.

Print servers

One of the main reasons small businesses install networks is to share expensive laser printers. In some cases, a computer is dedicated to function as a print server, whose sole purpose is to collect information being sent to the printer by client computers and print it in an orderly fashion:

- A single computer may double as a file server and a print server, but performance is improved if you use separate print and file server computers.

- With inexpensive laser printers running about $500 each, just giving each user his or her own laser printer rather than messing around with print servers is tempting. But you get what you pay for. Instead of buying five $500 printers for five users, you may be better off buying one $2,500 laser printer and sharing it.

Other resources besides printers can be shared with dedicated servers. Common examples include modems, fax machines, and CD-ROMs.

Database servers

A database server is a server computer that runs a SQL-based database management system (DBMS). SQL is the standard language for accessing relational databases. With a database server, the client passes SQL requests as messages to the database. The results of each SQL command are returned over the network. The code that processes the SQL request and the data reside on the same machine. The server uses its own processing power to find the requested data instead of passing all the records back to a client and then letting it find its own data, as was the case for the file server. The result is a much more efficient use of distributed processing power. With this approach, the DBMS server code is shrink-wrapped by the vendor. However, you must create the SQL tables and populate them with data. The application code resides on the client. So you must either write code for the client application or you can buy a shrink-wrapped query tool. Database servers provide the foundation for decision-support systems that require ad hoc queries and flexible reports. They also play a key role in data warehousing.

Transaction servers

With a transaction server, the client invokes *remote procedures* (or *services*) that reside on the server with an SQL database engine. These remote procedures on the server execute a group of SQL statements. The network exchange consists of a single request/reply message (as opposed to the database server's approach of one request/reply message for each SQL statement in a transaction). The SQL statements either all succeed or fail as a unit. These grouped SQL statements are called *transactions*.

With a transaction server, you create the client/server application by writing the code for both the client and server components. The client component usually includes a Graphical User Interface (GUI). The server component usually consists of SQL transactions against a database. These applications are called *Online Transaction Processing,* or *OLTP.*

Groupware servers

Groupware addresses the management of semi-structured information such as text, image, mail, bulletin boards, and the flow of work. These client/server systems place people in direct contact with other people. Lotus Notes and Microsoft Exchange are the leading examples of such systems, although a number of other applications—including document management, imaging, multiparty applications, and workflow—are addressing some of the same needs. Specialized groupware software can be built on top of a vendor's canned set of client/server APIs. In most cases, applications are created using a scripting language and form-based interfaces provided by the vendor. Typically, the communication middleware between the client and the server is vendor-specific. However, many groupware products now use e-mail as their standard messaging middleware. In addition, the Internet is quickly becoming the middleware platform of choice for groupware. Both Netscape and IBM/Lotus are moving their products in this direction.

Object application servers

With an object server, the client/server application is written as a set of communicating objects. Client objects communicate with server objects using an *Object Request Broker (ORB)*. The client invokes a method on a remote object. The ORB locates an instance of that object server class, invokes the requested method, and returns the results to the client object. Server objects must provide support for concurrency and sharing. The ORB and a new generation of CORBA *application servers* bring it all together. After years of incubation, "real life" commercial ORBs are now in production. Examples of commercial ORBs that comply with the Object Management Group's CORBA standard include Iona's *Orbix,* Inprise's *VisiBroker,* ICL's *DMS,* JavaSoft's *Java IDL,* BEA's *ObjectBroker,* IBM's *SOM,* and Expersoft's *PowerBroker.*

CORBA is also the foundation technology for the *Enterprise JavaBeans* component model. A new generation of CORBA application servers—also called *Object Transaction Monitors* (OTMs)—provide server-side component coordination services. Examples of CORBA application servers are BEA's *M3,* IBM's *Component Broker,* Oracle's *Application Server 4.0,* GemStone's *GemStone/J,* Persistence's *PowerTier for EJB,* Sun's *NetDynamics 4.0,* Sybase's *Jaguar CTS,* and Inprise's forthcoming *Application Server.* However, CORBA is not the only game in town. Microsoft has its own ORB called the *Distributed Component Object Model (DCOM).* DCOM is the foundation technology for Microsoft's enterprise software and also its *ActiveX* component model. The *Microsoft Transaction Server (MTS)* is the application server for ActiveX components. Also note that the latest name for this technology is *COM+* (Microsoft also calls it *DNA).*

Applications servers

An application server is a server computer that actually runs application programs. Application servers are sometimes used when mainframe-based applications are downsized. For example, you may use an AS/400 minicomputer to run programs that were previously run on a mainframe.

Web servers

With the growing popularity of the World Wide Web and corporate Intranets, a new type of server computer has emerged: the Web server. A Web server is simply a server computer equipped with software that enables it to run Web applications. Typically, the server runs either the Windows NT or UNIX operating system and has Web server software from Microsoft or Netscape. The World Wide Web is the first truly intergalactic client/server application. This new model of client/server consists of thin, portable, "universal" clients that talk to superfat servers. In its simplest incarnation, a Web server returns documents when clients ask for them by name. The clients and servers communicate using an RPC-like protocol called HTTP. This protocol defines a simple set of commands; parameters are passed as strings, with no provision for typed data. The Web client/server model is evolving. More specifically, the Web and distributed objects are starting to come together to provide a very interactive form of client/server computing. We call this new convergence the *Object Web.*

CLIENT/SERVER TOOLS

To help IT managers deal with a complex web of client/server hardware and software components, various hardware and software specialized components and tools are used. A client may need a special operating system, a special hardware network connection card, and other components to participate in the client/server architecture. The server may likewise need a special operating system, special hardware networking features, and other components to participate in the client/server architecture. These added layers of capability come at a cost and must be monitored and maintained in order to ensure ongoing functioning of the client/server setup.

In order to help ensure the proper interaction between clients and servers, a new type of software has been developed that is often called "middleware." *Middleware* can translate client requests into a form that certain servers can better understand and translate server responses into a form a client can better understand. Middleware can monitor system performance, alerting system operators to problems or realigning processing responsibilities on its own. Middleware can aid application software developers and maintainers to plan, document, and code software for clients and servers. In effect, middleware is in a gray area between doing work that a client or a server should do and work that some sort of system "overseer" should do. Again, it is part of the continuum of roles between clients and servers and the fact that there is no single master controlling slaves. A given client/server setup, however, may not have any distinguishable middleware at all. The clients and servers may deal with any necessary translation themselves. In general, however, most client/server systems do use some sort of middleware.

The following are the most prevalent types of client/server tools used to develop or support client/server applications:

Query and Reporting Tools. These tools are used to create basic data access applications and reports quickly with little or no coding. They can reduce the cost of IS operations by off-loading some of the development to the end user, provide ad hoc access to business data, and provide strong links to other personal productivity products such as spreadsheets, word processors, and charting applications.

Eis/Dss Tools. Similar to query and reporting tools, executive information and decision support system tools provide strong support for legacy and on-line data sources—especially for strategic applications. These tools allow knowledge workers to traverse large amounts of data easily looking for trends or other unexplored relationships, thus converting data into information. Some others contain sophisticated graphic functions.

Frontware. Frontware tools allow developers to create appealing graphical user interfaces (GUI) for existing mainframe programs, without the much greater expense of having to change the mainframe code. They can provide a good bridge between a client/server system and a centralized system or help acclimate users to the eventual migration to client/server.

Client/Server Development. These tools are cross-platform development environments for creating high performance client/server applications. Some can be used for object-oriented and object-relational databases. They are also useful for porting programs across platforms or downsizing legacy systems.

CASE Tools. These tools, either component CASE (computer-aided software engineering) tools or fully integrated CASE tools, support the rapid generation and maintenance of applications. CASE tools guide analysts and programmers through development and maintenance cycles, support automated documentation, and even write code based on documented requirements and development designs.

THE SOFTWARE EVALUATION WORKPLAN

As a first step, businesses usually form a project team to evaluate and select the financial software. The project team uses a workplan outlining these high-level tasks:

- Define the requirements.
- Obtain information on the software's functionality.
- Compare the software's functionality to the requirements.
- Select the software that best satisfies the requirements.
- Check references to verify that the vendor is acceptable.

Many project teams use a Request for Proposals (RFP) to document their requirements and obtain information from the vendors. They ask the vendors to compare the functionality of their software to the business's requirements. Because vendors have a tendency to say "yes" to all requirements, they must answer another question: Is the requirement satisfied with a standard feature, or is a custom modification necessary?

There are many variations to this classic software evaluation workplan, but the basic premise never changes. *The critical factor in software evaluation is the software's ability to satisfy the requirements.* Software is selected based on its ability to satisfy most requirements with a minimum of programming modifications.

What happens most frequently today is that most vendors say they satisfy all of the requirements in the RFP with no modifications. Not likely. But it isn't feasible to evaluate the software of 30 to 40 vendors. Team members might ask: "Evaluating the software's functionality worked the last time we selected financial software. Why isn't it working this time?" The answer is that client/server software is different.

CLIENT/SERVER FINANCIAL SOFTWARE
IS DIFFERENT

The classic software evaluation workplan no longer is effective because client/server financial software is different in three major ways:

- Functionality of the software exceeds the requirements of most businesses.
- The software is flexible, so programming modifications are eliminated.
- Client/server software is designed to run on networks of open systems.

Each of these three are discussed below.

Functionality Exceeds the Requirements. Under the classic workplan, every time a vendor said "no" to a requirement, it was eliminated. Client/server financial software is designed so a vendor will never have to say "no" to a functional requirement. In fact, the software's functionality exceeds the requirements of even the largest businesses. Financial software vendors have been responding to requests for proposals, developing software, and supporting their installed base of customers for more than 25 years. Essentially, they know how to satisfy functional requirements.

Programming Modifications Are Eliminated. The software is flexible. Every business has unique requirements such as existing forms, reports, and even processing logic, so packaged software always must be tailored to satisfy these requirements. Client/server software, however, is designed to satisfy them without programming modifications. Instead, it incorporates user-defined parameters and any number of customization tools to address a company's unique requirements. Although the software still has to be tailored using parameters and customization tools, there are no programming modifications. Client/server software may not have to be modified, but it will be customized.

Client/Server Software Is Designed to Run on a Network of Open Systems. The software's technical design determines the type of computer required to run the software. Before client/server, when a company specified a type of computer to use, the list of financial software vendors that fit was short. For example, specifying that the software must run on a mainframe meant that only vendors with mainframe financial software were acceptable. With client/server, any vendor designing software for networks of open systems is acceptable. There are more than 40 of these vendors.

EVALUATING VENDORS AND CLIENT/SERVER SOFTWARE

Evaluating the vendor as an acceptable business partner is now more important than evaluating the software. What good is the software if the vendor goes out of business or is acquired by another vendor? No longer is a vendor successful just because it has good software. With the competition in client/server financial software, a vendor needs a sound management team, a great team of software developers, effective business strategies, financing, effective marketing and sales, strategic alliances, and excellent software.

When the challenge was finding the software to match the requirements, it made sense to evaluate the software's functionality first. The challenge in evaluating client/server is identifying a vendor that is an acceptable business partner. A buyer still needs to make sure the software satisfies the requirements—but only after it has been determined that the vendor is a suitable party. The vendor must be reliable and known for a high quality product and service.

Information about the vendors and their software is readily available, usually through their marketing staffs, who will send you company and software brochures upon your request. Many vendors are publicly traded, so be sure to ask for their published annual reports. All critical information can be obtained from company brochures, software brochures, and financial statements. Using the information requires a predefined set of "critical" evaluation factors, which are the few absolutely essential requirements that have to be met. (See Table 10A-1 for a quick overview of vendor and software critical factors.)

VENDOR CRITICAL FACTORS

The purpose of defining vendor critical factors is to develop a set of evaluation criteria that are quantifiable measures of an acceptable business partner. The biggest risk in selecting client/server software is the long-term viability of the vendor. The vendor critical factors help to quantify the

TABLE 10A-1
VENDOR/SOFTWARE CRITICAL FACTORS

Evaluation Objective—Identify software vendors that are acceptable business partners.

Transition or start-up vendor	Quantifying acceptable risk.
Size of vendor	Quantifying acceptable risk.
Financial stability	Quantifying acceptable risk.
Sales channel	Identifying software vender preference.
Implementation services	Identifying implementation service vender preference.

Evaluation Objective—Determine at a high level that the software can satisfy the requirements.

Functionality integration	Assessing current software and/or defining requirements.
Parameter-driven flexibility	Assessing current software and/or defining requirements. Identifying single vendor or best-of-breed preference.
Customization tools	Assigning responsibilities for implementing and maintaining the software.
Client/server specifications	Developing technical specifications for client, network, and server.

amount of risk your business is willing to take. Use the vendor's company brochure and disclosed financial information to compile vendor critical factor information:

- *Transition or start-up vendor.* Define your business's preference for either a transition or start-up software vendor. All vendors that offer client/server software are either in transition or a start-up. Transition vendors were successful selling software that runs on local area networks (LAN), minicomputers, or mainframes. Now they are in transition to client/server. Start-ups don't have to make such a transition because they started as a client/server vendor.

- *Size of vendor.* Define in terms of revenue, number of employees, and number of customers.

- *Financial stability.* Define in terms of number of customers that have implemented the client/server software. Financial measures include future earnings, future growth, and financial ratios.

- *Sales channels.* Define preference to buy directly from the vendor or from an authorized sales agent.

- *Implementation services.* Define preference to use the vendor's staff or use third-party implementation services or implement the software yourself.

SOFTWARE CRITICAL REQUIREMENTS

There are three categories of software critical requirements: functionality, flexibility, and *client/server* specifications. These are fully discussed below.

Functionality Requirements. The two functional critical requirements are the sophistication and integration of the financial software. Sophistication is the measure of functionality, and vendors are using functionality to position their software to meet the requirements of different sized businesses. We have identified three categories of functionality:

- *Phase 1 functionality.* Software is positioned to satisfy the requirements of small businesses. Phase 1 runs on a single PC and/or a LAN. These software products are Windows products, but they are not client/server software. PCs and LANs lack the multi-user capabilities needed by larger businesses.

- *Phase 2 functionality.* Software is positioned to satisfy the requirements of mid-sized businesses that are migrating to client/server by upgrading LANs or replacing small to medium-sized minicomputers.

- *Phase 3 functionality.* Software is positioned to satisfy the requirements of large businesses that are migrating to client/server from a mainframe or large minicomputers.

Define the functionality critical requirement based on the requirements of the business. Most businesses know without detailed requirement studies whether they need Phase 1, 2, or 3 functionality. If they have any questions about what they need, they should define at least high-level requirements. The other alternative is to select Phase 3 functionality, even though the business doesn't need it right now, so the business can grow into Phase 3 functionality without having to replace the software.

Software integration is determined by the breadth of the vendor's product line. Integration categories are:

- Integrated financials—accounts payable, accounts receivable, fixed assets, budgets, and financial reporting integrated to the general ledger.

- Integrated financials and human resources—integrated financials plus payroll, human resources, and benefits.

- Integrated financials, human resources, and operational (for example, manufacturing or distribution)—all software for the business from a single vendor.

Define critical integration requirements by looking at the problems with your company's current financial software. For example, if the business doesn't have integrated financial and manufacturing software and wants better integration, the critical integration requirement is integrated financials and manufacturing software. Integrated software means single vendor solutions. The critical integration requirement also is defined by how much software the business is willing to buy from a single vendor.

The opening paragraph in a vendor's company brochure usually describes the vendor's functional positioning. For example, vendors offering Phase 3 functionality will claim that they sell to Fortune 1,000 companies and multinationals. The second paragraph usually defines the breadth of the product line. It will include the software products offered and their level of integration. The software brochure provides more details on the software's functionality and integration.

Flexibility Requirements. Software vendors have known for years that some requirements cannot be satisfied with "off the shelf" or packaged software. A good example is the general ledger chart of accounts. Every business has a chart of accounts, but every one is different. If a software vendor designs its software for one chart of accounts, it won't satisfy the requirements of most businesses. Vendors address this type of requirement through user-defined parameters so that a chart of accounts is defined by parameters set up during the software implementation stage.

The greater the number of parameters, the more flexible the software. Many client/server products have unlimited flexibility. That is, every functional requirement that can be unique to a business is driven by parameters.

The second flexibility factor is customization tool sets. Tools are used to customize forms, reports, queries, and even the processing logic. Every client/server product integrates with a desktop tool set such as Microsoft Office, which allows the user to access and manipulate information.

Customization tools are the second set of tools and are used to tailor the software during implementation and to maintain the software once it is in operation. There are three alternatives to categories of customization tools used by the financial software vendors.

- Microsoft's desktop tools, plus Microsoft's software development tools.
- Purchased software development tools. They are purchased from either a vendor that specializes in software development tools or from a relational database management system vendor.
- Vendor-developed software development tools. Some financial software vendors have crafted their own tool set that they sell with their software.

The flexibility critical requirement is defined by assigning responsibilities for software setup and maintenance. The individuals who will be responsible for these tasks have to decide how much parameter-driven flexibility is desired and determine the best customization tools set for the company.

Information on user-defined parameters and customization tool sets is available in the software brochure. Look for the words "user-defined" and "unlimited number." The greater the number of times these words appear, the more flexible the software.

Client/Server Specifications. Client/server software is designed to run on networks of open systems. The critical client/server specifications are the vendors and products that comprise the client, the network, and the server.

Client specifications include:

- Operating system, such as Microsoft's MS/DOS, Apple's Macintosh, IBM's OS/2.

- Graphical user interface (GUI), such as Microsoft's Windows, Apple's Macintosh, IBM's Warp.
- Tool set, such as Microsoft Office, Lotus Notes Suite, WordPerfect Office, or best-of-breed tool set.

Network specifications include:

- Network operating system, such as Novell's Netware or Microsoft's LAN Manager or Windows NT.

Server specifications include:

- Server operating system, such as proprietary operating systems, one of the many UNIX variations, or Microsoft's Windows/NT.
- Relational database management system, such as Oracle, Sybase, Informix, or Microsoft SQL Server.

In many businesses the information systems (IS) staff already has developed the client/server specifications. If the specifications have not been defined, you can work with the IS staff to do so.

EVALUATE THE SHORT LIST

Acceptable business partners are the vendors who satisfy the critical factors and critical requirements. They will be your "short list." In most cases, there are two or three vendors that make it. Now the evaluation team can focus on this short list, confident that no acceptable vendor was overlooked.

Evaluate the Software's Functionality and Flexibility Short List Tasks. Software on the short list can satisfy a business's functionality and flexibility critical requirements. Now the objective is to find out *how* the software does it. The best way is to get an evaluation copy of the software and install it. Businesses that have a network installed probably already have the computing resources necessary to run the software. If the in-house evaluation copy doesn't work, then demonstrations are the other alternative. Instead of watching a canned demonstration, however, ask the vendor to walk through the implementation workplan and show every user-defined parameter that has to be set up. This demonstration will take a lot of time and probably will be boring, but it is the most effective way for a buyer to understand how the requirements are satisfied.

Document the number of user-defined parameters that have to be set up and the extent of tailoring using the customization tools. This information will be useful for estimating the software training and implementation effort. The more parameters and customization, the greater the implementation effort.

Evaluate the Software's Response Time and Network Performance. Software on the short list has met the critical client/server specifications. Now the objective is to verify how the software performs on your network.

All vendors believe that their software has the best client/server technical design. But it is difficult to explain a technical design effectively, so the vendors use simple adjectives to describe why theirs is best. Thus, "true client/server" is a vendor's belief that its technical design is best. The truth is there are many different approaches to client/server technical designs, and each runs best with certain clients, networks, and servers.

The best way to verify the software's performance is to see it in action. Schedule site visits to businesses that have a similar network configuration, number of users, and number of transactions. If it works in their environment, it probably will work in your company's environment. Client/server response time also is a factor of network management. Verify that your business has the skills to manage a network running client/server financial software.

Evaluate the Vendor's Support Staff and Services. The next objective is to find the best vendor. You can do this by meeting with the vendor's representatives during the evaluation process. A visit to the local or regional support office is a good way to meet the vendor's staff that will be supporting your business after the sale.

Check references to verify the quality of software releases, support for complying with changing rules and regulations, training, and hotline support. Also check references to verify the implementation complexity and quality of the vendor's support and service. If you plan to use a third party for implementation services, then check the third party's references. One good reference is a user group CEO.

Evaluate the Vendor's Management Team. It is a good idea to meet the senior management team. Don't be afraid to ask difficult questions:

- How does the company plan on becoming successful in the client/server market?
- How is the company financing the development of the client/server software?
- What are management's forecasts for growth and financial stability?
- Is the company making the forecasted numbers?
- What are the contingency plans?

WHAT ABOUT COSTS?

The critical vendor factors determine the cost of the software. The most expensive client/server software comes from large vendors offering Phase 3 functionality. Phase 3 functionality from a small vendor costs much less.

Software pricing has to cover all the vendor's costs. Large vendors have many offices, large sales and marketing staffs, implementation specialists, and a group of software developers. Smaller vendors have one office, no sales staff, small marketing staff, and a small group of software developers. Small vendors rely on third parties to handle sales and implementation services. You are determining the cost of the software as you define your critical vendor factors.

PLANNING THE PROJECT

Building an effective software evaluation workplan is the first step to choosing the right software. Divide the project into two stages. The first stage includes defining critical vendor factors, defining critical software requirements, identifying the short list of vendors, and selecting the software by evaluating the short list. The second stage is software implementation. The key to a successful implementation is having one project team responsible for both software selection and implementation.

The selection and implementation of client/server financial software is a major investment. Therefore, the software selection decision has to be the right decision. Define your vendor critical factors and software critical requirements. Compile the vendor and software information. Categorize the information using your critical factors and requirements. Then focus on a comprehensive evaluation of the short list. Using this workplan, you can be assured you have made an informed client/server financial software selection decision.

AUDITING INFORMATION TECHNOLOGY

Understanding the role and function of auditors is important for information systems management. Information Systems (IS) managers frequently interact with auditors. By understanding the auditing functions, IS managers can make effective use of the audit function. Managers will obtain a better understanding of why auditors are making certain recommendations and how the recommendations will affect the IS function.

The purpose of information technology audits is to

- Provide management with reasonable assurance that control objectives are being met.
- Identify significant weaknesses in control.
- Assess the risks related to weaknesses in control.
- Report on the status of controls and actions that should be taken.

Information systems auditors can perform a variety of audits to enhance the efficiency and effectiveness of operations. Auditors generally spend a significant part of an audit in examining controls. If controls are working effectively, there is greater assurance about the accuracy, completeness, and integrity of the data.

Audit steps typically include

- Obtaining an understanding of the business needs and risk exposures
- Determining the control objectives

- Identifying the control measures
- Reviewing organizational policies and procedures
- Interviewing staff and management to gain an understanding of the process
- Evaluating the appropriateness of the controls
- Performing tests of compliance to determine if the stated controls are working
- Documenting the controls and activities affected by IT
- Assessing the risk related to control objectives not being met by using analytical procedures and other techniques

PERFORMING OPERATIONAL AUDITS

In an operational audit, auditors may examine the various functions of the information systems department to determine weaknesses and recommend improvements. Recommendations may be made about

- Improving customer service
- Contingency planning and disaster recovery
- Staffing and personnel needs
- Outsourcing certain IS functions
- Contracting needs
- Workload planning
- System- and hardware-capacity management
- Hardware and software maintenance and upgrade
- Systems maintenance
- Documentation and procedures
- Security considerations

CONDUCTING INFORMATION AUDITS

Information-technology auditors can evaluate if appropriate procedures are used to record, store, and maintain information. For instance, an organization may be wasting resources keeping the same information in multiple departments. An audit may reveal unnecessary redundancies in information management and if critical information is not being appropriately backed up. An information audit helps an organization manage strategic business information.

CONDUCTING SECURITY AUDITS

A security audit is used to identify vulnerabilities. The use of network computers and the Internet makes an organization more vulnerable to security threats. A security audit will typically examine the following:

- Access security
- Backup policies
- Common Gateway Interface (CGI) scripting
- Cryptographic methods and techniques
- Dialup networking and remote access
- E-mail
- Firewalls
- Network protocols
- Password policies and maintenance
- Processing controls
- Virus protection
- Web site

CONDUCTING SOFTWARE AUDITS

There are several types of software-related problems that should be examined by IT auditors. Software-testing techniques should be used to detect problems in software applications and systems.

For example, the auditor should test software for vulnerabilities due to buffer overflow. Essentially, the software program tries to copy data from one object to another object without checking to ensure that the destination object is large enough to contain the source object. Vulnerabilities in software can have unexpected effects. Software failure may cause the computer system or network to crash. Further, hackers frequently take advantage of such vulnerabilities to gain access to the computer system or network.

ESTABLISHING A CONTROL ENVIRONMENT

Controls may be classified as either general controls or application controls. General controls are used to ensure that an organization's

- Transactions are recorded accurately, completely, and in a timely manner in accordance with management's general or specific authorization.
- Assets are safeguarded.

General controls affect all applications. Their purpose is to provide a reasonable level of assurance that the organization's control objectives (safeguarding assets and data integrity) are met.

Application controls, on the other hand, are specific to individual applications. Their purpose is to provide reasonable assurance that specific procedures in a software application are recorded and processed fully, accurately, and on a timely basis based on management's authorization.

The following factors should be considered in evaluating the control environment of the IS department:

- Do a large number of positions in the IS department remain unfilled?
- Do the users of the IS department have a good perception of the department and its performance?
- Does the IS staff appear to be motivated?
- Is the IS staff adequately trained?
- Is there a rapid turnover of the IS staff?
- Is there accountability and responsibility at the senior-management level for the IS department?
- Is there an excessive backlog of work within the IS department?
- Is there excessive dependence on certain key individuals within the IS department?
- Is there segregation of duties within the IS department (e.g., among operators, programmers, librarians, systems development, technical support, etc.)?

- Are operating instructions up-to-date?
- Are operating instructions being followed by personnel?
- Are backup files frequently needed for recovery?
- Have backup files repeatedly been found to have errors or be corrupted?
- Are performance levels specified in facilities management contracts?
- Are there adequate statistics on performance levels and failure rates?
- Are physical and software-access controls used to restrict access?
- Are user identifications set up for each person, and not by department or job title?
- Are password files encrypted?
- Are security violation reports from the security software followed up by appropriate individuals?
- Are users prohibited from downloading or using unauthorized public-domain or shareware software (to reduce the likelihood of virus infections)?
- Is dial-in access to systems controlled?
- Does the organization have a security policy?
- Is access to data files, computer terminals, and documentation restricted to authorized users?
- Are terminals automatically logged off when left unattended or kept on a certain period of time?
- Are failures of hardware or software logged and investigated? Is a report of the failures provided to senior management?

SETTING CONTROL OBJECTIVES FOR INFORMATION AND TECHNOLOGY

Control Objectives for Information and Technology (COBIT) is a major research project completed and published by the Information Systems Audit and Control Foundation (ISACF). It is based upon technical standards from several organizations including

- Government Accounting Office (GAO)
- Institute for Internal Auditors (IIA)
- American Institute for Certified Public Accountants (AICPA)
- International Standards Organization (ISO)
- Codes of Conduct issued by the Council of Europe

COBIT provides standards for controls in information technology. COBIT is an authoritative source on IT control objectives and IT audits. Its standards may be used on an enterprise-wide basis for all types of information systems. COBIT is being used within the United States and internationally by auditors, security professionals, governmental entities, and academics.

COBIT may be used as a benchmark for security and control purposes. It can help auditors in evaluating internal controls and in advising on IT controls. The COBIT framework serves the industry by enabling the development of effective IT policy and procedures.

COBIT classifies human resources, such as the skill and productivity of employees, to be one of the primary resources to be managed by the IT processes. COBIT classifies the IT processes into four domains:

- Planning and organization
- Acquisition and implementation
- Delivery and support
- Monitoring

Internal controls provide only reasonable assurance that the organization's objectives will be met. There are inherent limitations to internal controls. For example, management may be able to override controls. It is possible to override controls through collusion; two or more personnel may collude to perpetrate fraud. It is essential to consider the cost/benefit of implementing controls.

The control environment is affected by a host of factors, including the

- Integrity of senior management
- Operating philosophy of management
- Training, competence, and integrity of personnel
- Oversight function of the board of directors

Risk assessment is an important part of evaluating the internal-control structure. COBIT considers risk assessment in the information-technology environment, including

- Business-risk assessment
- Risk identification and measurement
- Risk acceptance

Risks specific to information technology, such as security and technology risks, are examined from a global as well as a system perspective. Management's responsibility to monitor the IT process is discussed in COBIT. It emphasizes the need to obtain independent assurance on controls.

COBIT provides guidance for more than 250 control objectives. It provides navigation aids, which allow users to implement, organize, and categorize control objectives according to IT needs.

SOFTWARE DEVELOPMENT

Creating and modifying information systems quickly, reliably, and efficiently is essential for every organization. The software product must

- Meet user needs.
- Be developed within a reasonable time period.
- Be reliable and stable (bug free).
- Satisfy budgetary constraints.

Information-system auditors should look for signs that signal weakness in software-development controls. Controls are likely to be weaker if senior management does not actively participate in the development of projects. If management is uninvolved and is not kept up-to-date, auditors should be concerned. Significant pressure to complete the project on time and within budget can signal trouble. Historically, if projects are frequently not completed on time or within budget, the auditors should consider it a serious weakness.

The demand to develop a system quickly and within a limited budget can result in serious errors. Controls should be in place to minimize the probability of errors in systems development. Factors to consider include

- What will be the effect on the organization if the system fails?
- Is there a history of failure of new systems?
- Is there a lack of user involvement in the development process?
- What are the qualifications of the project manager and the project team? Does the project team have sufficient training and experience?
- What types of quality-assurance procedures are in place?
- Is the main development project divided into multiple short segments for monitoring purposes? Have budgetary allocations been made for each segment of the project?
- Is variance analysis performed at periodic intervals to ensure adherence with standards?
- What types of review procedures are in place?
- Is senior management closely monitoring the projects?
  - Is reporting to senior management comprehensive?
  - Does reporting accurately reflect the project's progress as well as the problems encountered?
- Are major projects formally scrutinized to assess their necessity?
- Are specifications for a new system (or significant modifications to an existing system) formally reviewed and accepted by users?
- Have security needs been considered?
- Is there division of responsibilities among incompatible functions (such as programmers and librarians)?
- Is the system capable of maintaining an audit trail?
- Is there a high inherent risk that makes the system vulnerable to fraud (either by programmers at the coding stage or by the users or hackers at the production stage)?
- What special precautions or security features are used to minimize potential fraudulent activities?

- Is the system formally tested to ensure adherence with user specifications?

  - How is the system tested?

  - What testing tools were used?

  - How are the test results documented?

  - Do users formally review the test results and acknowledge that the results are satisfactory or acceptable?

- What procedures are used to ensure that only the fully tested and authorized version of the software is used with live data?

  - How is the transfer from the development environment to production environment controlled?

  - Is access to the software denied to the programmers after the software has been developed, but before it has been tested, to ensure that unauthorized modifications are not made?

- Is the system well documented?

  - Does the documentation adequately describe the user interface and provide detailed instructions on operating and maintaining the system?

  - Is there adequate documentation concerning the data structures?

  - Is the source code adequately documented with remark statements?

  - Have the programmers adhered to the organization's coding policies?

- What procedures are used for version control in the development stage?

  - Are procedures in place to ensure programmers/developers are working on the correct version of the software and its documentation?

  - How are a software application's components managed as new releases are created and distributed to users? How are older releases uninstalled and removed from production?

  - Is an audit trail maintained for each change or modification? For example:

    - Who authorized the modification?

- What modifications were authorized?
- How was the priority of the modifications determined?
- When were the modifications made?
- Who coded the modifications?
- Who reviewed the modifications?

SOFTWARE MODIFICATION

Procedures should be in place to ensure system modifications are based on business need. All change requests should be recorded, typically by maintaining a change-request register. All requests for modifications should go through a formal process. Usually, the user department will initiate the request for modification. The need for modifications should be justified based on cost-benefit analysis. Change requests should be prioritized considering importance, the availability of technical expertise, and costs.

Most of the controls used for modifying software are the same as those for software development. The designing, programming, and testing procedures are essentially the same as when designing a new system. Similarly, standard procedures should be followed even for "emergency" modifications. The following is a list of factors auditors should consider in evaluating controls for software modification:

- Is there a history of erroneous modifications? In other words, the modified software does not do what it was supposed to do. This could be due to program-coding errors or because specifications were not followed.
- Is there a backlog of software-modification requests?
- Are there frequent "emergency" modifications to software?
- Are users unsatisfied with modification response time?
- Do users attempt to modify or develop software themselves?
- Is a large amount of time spent on modifications and maintenance and very little time spent on developing new systems?
- Is the documentation up-to-date? Are quality-control-review procedures in place to ensure that documentation has been adequately updated?

SOFTWARE ACQUISITION

Before creating or developing software, an organization should consider using prepackaged software. The most important issues to consider in making an acquisition decision is whether the software

- Meets the business needs of the organization
- Has quality and is reliable
- Comes from a reputable supplier

Users should be asked to specify the functions needed in a software package. It is essential to ensure that the package satisfies the security and control requirements, including error reporting and maintenance of an audit trail. The software acquisition contract should specify the

- Functional requirements
- Security and control features
- Performance standards
- User documentation
- Maintenance and support service
- Availability of source-code and custom modifications
- Licenses and ownership requirements
- Availability of major and minor software updates
- Warranties

Using a single vendor for the entire system, including hardware, software, training, and maintenance services, allows the organization to place full responsibility on the single vendor. It helps avoid disputes over who is responsible when problems arise. Vendors should be asked to provide references of other organizations using their hardware and software systems.

The prepackaged software should be adequately tested before using real data to ensure that the software meets the organizational needs and is stable and reliable. The level of testing will vary with the type of software package, its vendor, and the organization's prior experience with such packages.

13A

WORLD WIDE WEB AND ELECTRONIC COMMERCE

It seems almost ironic that technology spawned from the military and political minds wrapped up in the Cold War became arguably the single greatest advance in the business world in the twentieth century. Originally designed as a channel through which the Unites States government could share postapocalyptic information, the Internet, and its spin-off network, the World Wide Web, have become an integral part of day-to-day business around the world. Since the National Science Foundation lifted its ban on commercial use of the Internet in 1991, this advanced computer network has rapidly become much more important to today's business world than it ever was as part of the government infrastructure.

With the transformation of the Internet and the World Wide Web into much more user-friendly business models, the resulting explosion in their popularity spurred the development of a radically new method of conducting business transactions. The revolution of electronic commerce (e-commerce) has since completely reshaped the business world's approach to consumer interaction and business transaction. As more businesses and consumers turn to the Internet and the "web" for their day-to-day business and operations, e-commerce will certainly prove to be much more than just a passing fad.

THE RISE OF THE INTERNET AND WORLD WIDE WEB

The theory behind the Internet has its roots in the Cold War of the early 1960s and the perceived need for a decentralized computer network that would enable the United States government to maintain open lines of communication in a postnuclear apocalyptic society.

Researchers felt that a decentralized computer network consisting of multiple-location computer nodes connected to one another via a backbone of high-traffic telephone lines would present too many targets for the Soviet Union to take out in the event of a nuclear war. This network, dubbed the ARPANET, would survive through its collection of nodes even in the event that several of the nodes were destroyed. From this initial concept, it is not difficult to foresee the numerous ways in which a computer network connecting businesses and consumers in much the same way would be invaluable to business communication and sales.

By the end of the decade, advances in the ARPANET would spawn what has become the Internet. The new system was designed as crude newswire to handle the transfer of news articles between nodes. The year 1972 proved to be a monumental year in the development of the ARPANET and specifically the spawning of the Internet. In that one year the first computer-to-computer chat took place, the first electronic mail program was developed, and the first public demonstration of ARPANET using Internet protocols took place in San Francisco (May, 1998). The following year the system went international as additional nodes were set up in Europe.

Over the next decade, advances in Internet technology enabled businesses to begin to take advantage of this new network. The development of an Electronic Data Interchange (EDI) allowed businesses to communicate via proprietary networks among manufacturers, suppliers, and sellers. The EDI presented the first case of business using the Internet to open up better lines of interoffice communication. Business was now online, and in time over 100,000 companies developed some level of EDI (Booker, 1996). While EDI empowered business partners to share information on sales, inventory, shipping, and other project information, developing these proprietary networks proved to be tremendously expensive and therefore available and cost-effective only to the largest of companies. This, however, was all about to change in 1984.

In 1984 the National Science Foundation, which was the administrator of the nation's network backbone, developed a new network separate from the Internet. The new NSFNET backbone marked the beginning of what would become the World Wide Web. By the end of the decade the first relays between a commercial electronic mail carrier and the Internet had taken place. The year 1990 proved to be another landmark year in the development of the Internet and the World Wide Web as "The World" became the first commercial provider of dial-up access, and later the same year the first remotely operated machine was hooked to the Internet. The "Internet Toaster" was to be the ancestor of the present server-based system that the World Wide Web is now based on (Zakon, 1998). Despite these tremendous developments in the World Wide Web and Internet technology, the NSF still maintained complete control of the two fledgling networks. Up until 1991 the NSF had implemented a commercial ban on Internet use. The lifting of the commercial ban on the Internet was like opening the flood gates to the Internet. The Internet was now ready for the revolution.

Developing separately from the Internet, the NSFNET backbone created a new network over which computers were able to communicate. In 1991 Tim Berner-Lee developed a new set of protocols, including "http," URL, and "html," separate from the Internet and designed to run on the NSFNET backbone. It was the development of these protocols that created the interface of today's World Wide Web. By 1993 the World Wide Web was growing 341,634% annually, and estimates have placed the current number of registered domains worldwide at over seven million (Zakon, 1998; NetNames, Ltd., 1999).

The year 1993 was marked by the development of the first mainstream web-browser software, Mosaic. The web was now poised for the development of today's rich content that makes the web so dynamic. The advent of the web protocols and the browser enabled the World Wide Web to separate itself from the Internet according to the rich graphical interface that was now possible on the web. Corporations had a new and exciting medium to display their corporate messages as well as to achieve a level of consumer interactivity that was never before possible.

It was not long after the advent of the Internet, and later the World Wide Web, that network administrators began to fear that traffic was approaching self-destructive levels. The Internet was originally designed to handle the transfer of two articles per day between nodes, and data traffic quickly began to push the limit of the new networks (Winstein, 1996). The same year that Tim Berner-Lee developed the World Wide Web protocols, NSFNET upgraded the congested backbone to new T-3-bundled telephone lines. With the new backbone in place the Internet and the web were now ready for the unprecedented growth witnessed in the mid 1990s to the present. The backbone was now in place to handle the individual dial-up access that has expanded the Internet and the World Wide Web from a handful of large corporations and researchers at various universities to the individual consumers, businesses, and computer enthusiasts.

INTERNET AND WORLD WIDE WEB ACCESS

In 1990 "The World" became the first ever provider of commercial dial-up access. This marked a huge turning point in the history of the Internet and the World Wide Web as these networks were now available to individuals and business. What had previously been accessible by only a handful of researchers and government agencies was now available to the world. This was one of the biggest steps in bringing the Internet and the World Wide Web to the forefront of business. Until individual consumers and businesses were able to access these networks, there was no commercial value to the Internet and the web. In 1995 several new dial-up companies appeared and began providing access to the Internet and the World Wide Web. America Online, CompuServe, and Prodigy quickly developed the infrastructure to bring the Internet and the web to the masses. These companies positioned themselves as the telephone companies of the Internet and the World Wide Web. The rise of these Internet Service Providers and their ability to provide affordable access to the Internet and the web has been one of the single biggest steps to the commercialization of these networks.

WORLD WIDE WEB AND ELECTRONIC COMMERCE

With the World Wide Web in the homes and businesses of tens of millions of people worldwide, businesses now have a new and exciting method of conveying their corporate messages. Companies began to shift resources away from traditional advertising methods and into web campaigns. Forward-thinking companies were quick to take advantage of the unique advantages that the World Wide Web presented. Here was a totally revolutionary way for companies to achieve a level of interactivity and intimacy with consumers that marketers had never before dreamed possible. Additionally, instead of trying to capture the attention of potential consumers as with radio, television, and newspaper advertisements, here was a system in which consumers were actually seeking out product/service information from the company.

Businesses were now able to present corporate information to consumers at the point of sale. Companies no longer had to sit and hope that consumers would follow an advertisement to the store. Consumers could now be exposed to an advertisement and then immediately make a purchase. Fortune 500 companies quickly began to compile web budgets and most were spending between $840,000 and $1.5 million just to get their web sites up and running. Many Fortune 500 companies have continued to spend as much as several hundred thousand dollars per year to maintain and market their web sites (*Internet World*, 1996).

As the web continued to grow, web sites began to move beyond just an online brochure. Companies quickly began to build not only sites with appealing graphical content and informative copy, but sites that implemented secured credit systems to accept online purchases and entire databases to compile consumer information and manage products online as well. This new point-of-purchase situation that was created as the World Wide Web continued to develop enabled sellers to generate revenue from additional sources. Manufacturers could now sell directly to consumers, smaller domestic companies could now sell internationally, and an entire niche of new businesses began to pop up seemingly daily. This new method of electronic commerce quickly enabled the web to become an even more powerful business resource.

With the development of this new way to shop for and buy products came new challenges for businesses to overcome, however. First and foremost, how were consumers going to pay for their purchases? Second, with past experiences with individuals gaining uninvited access to computer networks (see Vladimir Levin, pp. 10–11), security issues began to be raised as it became apparent that large amounts of money would now be changing hands daily over this new network. Finally, businesses needed to address the subtle challenges that arose from e-commerce such as new methods for organizing products online and maximizing consumer convenience, as well as completely new marketing strategies and techniques.

As companies began to sell on the Internet in ever increasing sales volumes, it became increasingly important to develop, or integrate, a monetary system that would be compatible with this new medium. Myriad currency systems quickly popped up on the web. However, it has been the integration of credit-card processing via the web that has come to dominate e-commerce transactions (Lang, 1999). As credit transactions over the web became the preferred method for purchasing goods, many of the initial online currency systems have vanished. There still exist, however, several alternatives to paying with credit cards. These few, viable payment methods, while not as popular as credit transactions, still remain an important means to giving consumers and sellers flexibility in e-commerce.

Online check systems and online cyberbank accounts are two of the most popular alternatives to electronic payment. Systems such as the Online Check System and CyberCash enable the consumer to send an electronic check directly from the consumer's bank account much as the consumer would do if he or she were to write a traditional check in a mall. Other services such as CyBank and CyberCents allow consumers to set up online bank accounts to disperse payments for products and services over the web. These online accounts are set up through deposits from the consumer's credit card. While these systems may provide important payment options, they require sellers to implement these systems into the seller's online store, which in some cases may increase the initial set-up costs for e-commerce systems. Additionally, the online bank-account system such as those offered by CyBank and CyberCents may present a perceived dual security issue in the minds of potential consumers. With the negative portrayal of web security in the media, potential consumers may be fearful of storing their money online and then conducting business transactions online. With credit card processing and CyberCash systems, there is only a single security issue.

Despite the few advantages presented by a CyberCash system, straight-credit transactions using the consumer's credit card of choice has been the most convenient and the most popular method for purchasing products and services online. These systems are easy to set up and do not require the seller to implement any special purchasing systems other than encrypting any web transactions. Additionally, credit transactions enjoy another distinct advantage over these other systems that is particularly important to web consumers. Credit companies, in the rare event of fraud or system malfunction, will traditionally reimburse all or at least part of a consumer's purchase (Lang, 1999). This is an advantage that electronic checking and online account systems often cannot match.

TYPES OF ELECTRONIC COMMERCE

There are three distinct general classes of electronic-commerce applications: interorganizational (business-to-business), intraorganizational (within business), and customer-to-business. From the interorganizational perspective, electronic commerce facilitates the following business applications:

1. *Supplier management:* Electronic applications help companies reduce the number of suppliers and facilitate business partnerships by reducing purchase-order (PO) processing costs and cycle times and by increasing the number of POs processed with fewer people.

2. *Inventory management:* Electronic applications shorten the order-ship-bill cycle.

3. *Distribution management:* Electronic applications facilitate the transmission of shipping documents such as bills of lading, purchase orders, advanced-ship notices, and manifest claims, and enable better resource management by ensuring that the documents themselves contain more accurate data.

4. *Channel management:* Electronic applications quickly disseminate information about changing operational conditions to trading partners. By electronically linking production-related information with international-distributor and reseller networks, companies can eliminate thousands of labor hours and ensure accurate information sharing.

5. *Payment management:* Electronic applications link companies with suppliers and distributors so the payments can be sent and received electronically. Electronic payment reduces clerical error, increases the speed at which companies compute invoices, and lowers transaction fees and costs.

The purpose of intraorganizational applications is to help a company maintain the relationships that are critical to delivering superior customer value. How is this accomplished? By paying close attention to integrating various functions in the organization. From this perspective intraorganizational electronic commerce facilitates the business applications for workgroup communications, electronic publishing, and sales-force productivity.

In electronically facilitated consumer-to-business transactions, customers learn about products through electronic publishing, buy products with electronic cash and other secure payment systems, and even have information goods delivered over the network. From the consumer's perspective, electronic commerce facilitates economic transactions in social interaction, personal financial management, and purchasing products and information. Consumers consistently demand greater convenience and lower prices. Electronic commerce facilitates factory orders by eliminating many intermediary steps, thereby lowering manufacturers' inventory and distribution costs and indirectly providing consumers with lower prices. Intermediaries are economic agents that stand between the parties of a contract (or transaction), namely buyers and sellers, and perform functions necessary to the fulfillment of a contract. Most firms in the financial-service sector, including banks, insurance companies, mutual funds, and venture-capital firms, are intermediaries. The results are more efficient production and distribution and lower prices. Whether strict, general, or electronic interpretations are adopted, it's clear that intermediaries comprise a significant portion of the online economy. Therefore, understanding the forces that give rise to the demand for intermediaries, as well as the characteristics and structure of intermediate online markets, is crucial to understanding the operations of electronic markets.

HOW THE INTERNET IS AFFECTING DIFFERENT INDUSTRIES

The Internet is affecting all businesses in similar ways. Every industry, for example, has suddenly become part of a global network where all companies are equally easy to reach. However, even though the forces affecting them are the same, the consequences for each industry are very different.

Financial Services

Universal access to information is hitting hard in the financial services industry. This is a classic example of how the Internet can open up an existing infrastructure. In the past, brokers have justified their high fees by pointing to the quality of their advice, but now knowledgeable amateurs and industry experts can trade stock for no charge in popular personal investing sites such as the Motley Fool. Investors can get advice and market information from many sources other than from full-service brokers, so they are less willing to pay a premium just to trade. Assets worth $111 billion are already managed online, and that figure will rise to over $600 billion by 2002. The challenge here is to survive on thin margins or to find some way to add value. There are currently some 140 banks on the web from 26 different countries.

Travel and Airlines

Over a hundred airlines throughout the globe have created web sites, and a number are not only taking queries, but are actually receiving orders for tickets. Travel agents are another group that has survived on exclusive access to information. Most travelers prefer using travel agents to checking every airline and figuring out how to work the flight-booking services on commercial online services, especially since using an agent costs them nothing. However, the Internet is giving the airlines an opportunity to eliminate the place of the middleman and cut the cost. They are doing this in two ways. The first is by selling seats on their own web sites and together on Sabre's Travelocity, American Airlines' booking service. The second, led by Northwest and Continental, is by cutting the fees they pay to online travel agencies to 5%, because customers find and book by themselves on the net, so the costs are far lower than in the physical world. Still, online sales make up less than 1% of total airline-ticket sales. As long as the airlines are prohibited by law from offering online bookers a price advantage, most independent travelers will prefer a quick call to their travel agent.

Retailing

The advantage of online shops are that their costs are lower and they are less constrained for space than their physical counterparts. Yet, less than a third of online marketers are making money today. The reason is that most of their offerings are distinctly unimpressive. Even big mail-order retailers such as JC Penney and J. Crew offer only a small fraction of their print catalog online. Plus, those items are hard to find, slow to download, and hard to see on-screen. Building an online shopping site that is attractive to buyers takes longer and costs more than most retailers thought.

Perhaps one of the most famous examples of marketing on the web comes from Van den Bergh Foods—otherwise known as Ragu. Hundreds of recipes and an online soap opera fill this site! Interflora is another great example of adding value to existing services.

Music

In comparison with the book industry, the music industry is controlled by just a few labels. They therefore have the power to stifle any online venture that offers serious competition. Several online music stores have had trouble getting record companies' permission to offer album samples, and their prices are typically a little lower than those of physical music stores. As a result, most are losing money. Still, good online music stores such as Firefly are showing their sites built around a thriving community of music fans. They have the potential to outdo their physical competitors such as Amazon, which beats its book-trade rivals. But, it could be slow going. Online music sales will increase to $250 million by 2002.

Books

This market is no longer a one-horse race. America's two largest booksellers, Barnes & Noble and Borders, have opened their sites online. Optimists think online book sales will reach 8% of the market by 2002. Pessimists think there will be a struggle for just the bottom 1–2%.

Cars

It seemed like a foolish idea to buy a car on the Internet, but more customers are shifting to online shopping instead of spending a long afternoon with a salesperson. Customers report prices up to 10% lower than their best face-to face negotiation. The reason is that it costs a dealer only about $25 to respond to an Auto-By-Tel lead, instead of hundreds of dollars to advertise and sell a car in the conventional way. Chrysler, which puts its Internet sales in 1996 at just 1.5% of the total, thinks that the figure will be increased by 40% by 2002. Manufacturers are thrilled by this trend. They generally consider dealers a necessary evil, just as airlines do travel agents. But a creative dealership, which can set up its own web site, can also use the Internet to expand its franchise.

Advertising and Marketing

Although these two industries are not strictly in the category of electronic commerce themselves, they are being profoundly changed by it, because the Internet is an interactive medium and completely customizable for each viewer, unlike any advertising vehicle before. In today's world, reaching twelve people is easy by using telephone. Reaching twelve million people is also easy by taking an ad during the Super Bowl. However, reaching the middle 10,000 people is hard. The best tool is direct mail, which is expensive and inefficient. The Internet makes it easier both to target potentially interested consumers and to communicate with them. Another advantage of an Internet ad is an immediate response. It provides a direct link to the advertiser's site, offering interested consumers an easy way to go there for more information or for an opportunity to buy. Total Internet advertising revenues were just $267 million in 1996, compared with $33 million spent on television advertising in America alone. However, the possibility is huge. America Online with sixteen million subscribers (and adding even more subscribers), which is the biggest Internet service provider, has more viewers than any cable television network or newspaper, and all but the world's most popular magazine. It is just that the market is too new for advertisers to be sure that they will get their money's worth, but it will be a matter of time. Many publishing houses have developed web versions of traditional print media.

ADVANTAGES OF ELECTRONIC COMMERCE

Ability to Conduct Business Twenty-four Hours a Day/Seven Days a Week

Keeping a retail establishment open twenty-four hours a day and seven days a week can be a very costly decision. To begin with, there are certain variable costs to deal with in a normal retail store. The largest variable expense most likely is the cost of labor. In addition, high turnover rates for those employees working the "graveyard" shift can be expensive.

Depending on your business, another consideration is security. Installing items such as security cameras and bulletproof glass can be a significant expense. Armed security can cost a great deal. In addition, other variable expenses such as electricity can add up.

Of course, one reason why most businesses do not stay open around the clock is the idea of diminishing returns. At certain times of the day it may cost more to keep a business open than the business makes by being open. Businesses are turning away from the profit of the few customers who want to shop after normal business hours due to other commitments.

Electronic commerce is a great way to get the business of these "off-peak" shoppers. A company can put a web site up for a very small amount of money and have its "cyber-shop" open twenty-four hours a day and seven days a week.

Save Money on Customer-Service Staff

When customers had questions about a product in the past, especially from a mail-order company, the customer had to call one of the company's customer-service staff. In a company that deals with a variety of products, it can be difficult if not impossible to expect the customer-service staff to know every detail about every product the company sells.

To best serve the customer, Internet web pages can be utilized. A detailed description of each product can be put on the web page. Such product descriptions can include details such as price, dimensions, test results, pictures, and even virtual reality files that will allow the customer to look at the object in three dimensions.

Save Money on Telephone Operators and Salespeople

Every customer making a purchase online is one fewer customer using the company's telephone operators and salespeople. The more customers use electronic commerce to purchase products from a particular company, the less need for telephone operators and salespeople. While doing away with these employees entirely is not practical, a reduction in the number of employees needed and therefore a reduction in variable selling and admin-istrative expenses ensue.

Update Catalogs and Prices Instantly

When selling items that change price frequently, printed catalogs can be inaccurate before they reach the customer. This problem can be elimi-nated by electronic commerce. When the customer is shopping online, he or she knows the current price of the item. When a price change is needed, a simple change of the web page will correct it. This saves money on catalog printing.

In addition to price, products can change often. With printed catalogs, if a product is added to inventory, the business must wait for the next catalog printing before customers will know about it. Likewise with a discontinued product. With web-based commerce, products can instantly be added or deleted.

Product Targeting

Product targeting can be accomplished actively or passively on the Internet.

Active Targeting One way to target products to a particular customer is to ask what interests him or her. For example, in order to shop on some web sites you must first get a cyber shopping cart. In order to do this, the shopper must create an account. As part of the account creation, the customer is asked questions that will allow for the web site to target products to the customer.

For example, after-market car parts retailers such as Jegs and Summit will ask the shopper what car he or she owns. This allows the company to target products made for the customer's car(s) to that customer when he or she is shopping online.

In addition, obtaining a customer's e-mail address from him or her at the time of purchase can be used in the future for advertisements. For example, when a new product is added to the inventory, potential interested customers (based on past buying history) can be contacted via e-mail. Since e-mails are often free, there is no cost.

There are two disadvantages to active targeting. One is that the system requires the user to enter the information into the web page. If this process is too long or involves too many questions, this may discourage the customer from shopping at the site.

Another disadvantage is reliability of the responses. With the news stories lately creating concerns about individual privacy in the information age, some customers may be prone to give purposely inaccurate responses to the questions.

Passive Targeting Another form of targeting is passive targeting. This does not rely on the customer filling out a questionnaire or opening an account. The process is transparent to the user. Here is how it works: A customer goes to a site that sells bicycle equipment. He purchases some mountain-bike tires and some mountain-biking shoes and looks at some mountain-bike pedals. It can be assumed that the customer owns a mountain bike. The information about the items he purchased and the items he looked at can be stored on the user's computer in what is known as a "cookie." The next time the user goes to the site, the site looks for any existing cookies. The site reads the information from the cookie. It sees that the person who is browsing the web site is interested in mountain biking. Now the web page can suggest products to the user that might be of interest. It can also target advertisements to the user, either advertisements from the company or from third parties.

Better Overhead and Inventory Control

Using Internet-based purchasing, inventory control can be made simple. When a shipment of a product is received, the quantity is entered into a computer database. As customers order the products and the products are shipped to the customers, the computer can track the number of remaining items in stock.

Small Company Can Operate and Advertise Worldwide

With the Internet being *worldwide,* it is economically possible for even the smallest business to engage in global trade. Also, small companies can now advertise globally for a very small price.

Customers Do Not Need to Go to the Store, Helpful for Disabled Individuals

Online shopping appeals to the person who doesn't like actually to shop. However, online shopping enables some people who wouldn't otherwise be able to shop in an actual store. This includes anyone disabled in any way.

DISADVANTAGES OF ELECTRONIC COMMERCE

Credit-Card Fraud

Credit-card numbers can be stolen by the disgruntled or criminal employee who has legitimate or illegitimate access to the electronic commerce system of the company. These employees can either use the credit-card numbers to purchase goods for themselves or sell the credit-card numbers to others. (Note: An employee of a catalog company can do the same.) This can put the company at great liability when it is discovered.

Another means of credit-card fraud on the Internet is when a consumer gives a credit-card number for a card that does not belong to him or her. With current technologies, it is very difficult, if not impossible, to verify if the person at the keyboard is the legitimate owner of the credit-card number. There are ongoing developments in electronic signatures to reduce fraud in electronic commerce. Credit-card theft and fraud are a great concern when doing business overseas. There is a much higher rate of stolen credit-card-number usage overseas, particularly in Eastern Europe (Radosevich, 1999).

Consumer Can't Touch Product or Ask Questions

The company involved in electronic commerce usually has very descriptive web pages on the product or products it is selling. Such descriptions can include dimensions, pictures, specifications, and even virtual-reality clips. Despite all this, there are items that are very difficult to sell effectively over the Internet. An example is diamonds. It is impossible to show the beauty of a diamond on the Internet. In this instance, electronic commerce may not be practical or possible.

Not Everyone on the Net

Although the number of people on the Internet is increasing at an amazing rate, the simple fact is that not everyone is on the Internet. Stores that operate strictly on the Internet such as Amazon.com are missing the non-Internet user. Some are not on the Internet by choice, but others may not be on because of geographical or governmental restrictions.

Small Companies Not Prepared for Worldwide Commerce

Even though the smallest businesses can put up a web site and start engaging in electronic commerce around the globe, they may not have the experience or knowledge that worldwide trade requires. To begin with, doing business worldwide means having a web page that considers cultural differences. U.S. web designers tend to like designing web pages with black backgrounds. However, black has a sinister connotation in other countries, including Asia, Latin America, and Europe (Radosevich, 1999).

Another problem with worldwide commerce is worldwide currencies. Most small companies are not set up to handle other countries' currency. The easiest way is to use credit cards since the conversion rates and other hassles are handled by the credit-card company. However, one needs to be aware of the problems with stolen and fraudulent credit cards as mentioned earlier (Radosevich, 1999).

Finally, getting the product overseas to the customer may be a chore in itself. In the case of a small company that sells a relatively small product, an international shipping company such as DHL may be the easiest and quickest way to get a product overseas. These companies will deal with the logistical problems such as shipping. Larger items may require other shipping means.

DEVELOPING AN E-COMMERCE STRATEGY

Successful e-commerce business strategies must address an entirely new set of challenges unique to the World Wide Web. As with all new business ventures, intense research is vital to the success of e-commerce systems. Research will not only uncover what it takes to get started, but will also expose potential markets. The Internet has been thought of as the perfect environment for "niche" projects. Because of the access the World Wide Web offers to potential consumers across various geographic and demographic sectors, niche e-commerce systems have been particularly successful. While it is not necessarily a prerequisite for e-commerce, developing a niche market will give any potential e-commerce project an immediate advantage.

In addition to uncovering certain niche markets, research will also provide potential web entrepreneurs with the information to implement the proper systems required for successful e-commerce. These systems include encryption of transmissions, shopping-cart or product database features, and types of payment to accept. Implementing the proper, convenient product-management systems as well as encrypting any confidential transactions will result in increased sales. Likewise, it is important to choose the best method for purchasing products. Peter Lang (The Internet Marketing Center, 1999) recommends that any e-commerce purchasing system be based on credit-card transactions.

With the appropriate back-end systems in place, it is crucial that any successful e-commerce site provide a good HTML interface to the consumer. Appearances on the World Wide Web are very important. With many niche e-commerce sites, the appearance of the web site will be the first contact a business will have with a consumer. Because of this fact it is exceedingly important that e-commerce sites provide a good HTML interface. This HTML interface is what makes the first impression to the consumer. The appearance of successful e-commerce web sites will belie a clean, professional appearance that is easy to read and move through.

While a good HTML interface is crucial, it may be completely ineffective if consumers are not coming to an e-commerce site. To overcome this, successful e-commerce systems will take an aggressive, tireless approach to marketing the e-commerce site. Search-engine listing and relisting, conducting banner and link exchanges, issuance of press releases, and mass electronic-mail campaigns will generate the exposure that is vital to the success of the e-commerce site. Additional value-added content features such as pre- and post-sales support, testimonials, and personalized customer support should be included in any e-commerce web site (Lang, 1999). Other features including multilingual capabilities, contests, multiple methods for ordering (i.e., via facsimile or 800 numbers) will increase sales. It is especially important to allow consumers to order multiple ways, as many consumers are still leery of providing credit-card information over the web. The providing of multiple methods for ordering will allow sellers to receive orders from consumers who would not have otherwise made a purchase over the web.

ESTABLISHING ONLINE SECURITY

With personal credit information being transferred across networks as well as other confidential information, security has always been a major concern of both businesses and consumers. To provide a viable e-commerce system, businesses must address the issue of security. Businesses now protect themselves and their consumers by encrypting transmissions of credit information and other confidential data. Secure Server Lockout system, as well as firewall systems to protect online accounting, billing, product management, and electronic-mail databases, help provide the encryption necessary to protect the seller and the consumer. In order to ensure secured transmissions, e-commerce systems must obtain secure certification from the site host to publicize that site as secure.

While e-commerce sites design systems to protect themselves and their consumers, consumers may take an active role in ensuring the security of their transmissions. *ZDNet On-line Magazine* urges consumers to buy only from secured sites and to educate themselves on an e-commerce site's privacy policies. Watchdog organizations such as the "Truste" have been formed to police the privacy policies of e-commerce sites for consumers. Consumers should provide only that information required to process the order and to always order with credit cards. Ordering via credit card, as opposed to alternative payment methods, provides an extra layer of security as credit-card companies will reimburse consumers for fraud perpetrated by e-commerce merchants (Lang, 1999). Finally, the Office of the United States Attorney General recommends that consumers use an 800-number to place orders whenever possible. Finally, consumers may educate themselves on the various online scams through nonprofit groups such as the U.S. Consumer Gateway, the FTC, and the Internet Fraud Watch.

THE FUTURE OF E-COMMERCE

In 1998 e-commerce revenue exceeded $32 million USD (IDC, 1998). Forecasters are expecting the e-commerce industry to top $3 trillion dollars by the year 2003 (Forrester Research Group, 1998). The future of e-commerce is so attractive to business that by 2002 70% of all U.S. firms are expected to have some level of e-commerce system in place (Financial Executives Institute, 2001). The e-commerce projections have proven to be staggering. However, as more businesses begin to take advantage of this seemingly fail-safe gold rush, less than 5% of all e-commerce enterprises are expected to actually generate a profit in the first twelve to eighteen months of operation. While this may be a sobering thought in the craze to sell online, lower overhead, decreased capital investment requirements, and the ability to sell globally are factors that will continue to make e-commerce attractive.

On the seller side of e-commerce, declining web development costs, advanced security, better product management, and inventory-, sales-, and accounting-systems integration will pull more businesses to e-commerce into the future. As businesses continue to enjoy increasing success through their e-commerce sites, it will become increasing important for competitors to develop some level of e-commerce or they will lose market share. In fact, e-commerce has become so important to today's business world that companies that have been slow to adopt some level of e-commerce have suffered lagging stock performance on Wall Street. Market analysts are demanding to know what plans companies are making for incorporating e-commerce systems. From a consumer standpoint, decreasing computer costs and dial-up costs, as well as dramatically increased connection speeds, will make buying on the web ever more attractive. E-commerce will continue to offer consumers increased selection, convenience, and in many cases better deals as it is easier than ever for manufacturers to sell directly to the consumer, thus eliminating the costs of wholesalers and retailers.

Connectivity issues and the development of new proprietary business networks via the web promise to have a dramatic effect on the future of e-commerce. The implementation of cable lines and modems as well as recent DSL technology offered by companies such as Verizon have led to a tremendous increase in the speeds with which people may connect to the web. These increased connection speeds have made shopping online much more convenient because it is easy to browse e-commerce sites online, and these increased connection speeds have enabled e-commerce systems to process sales faster than ever.

The new proprietary networks that businesses are now developing online are based on the Electronic Data Interchange networks. The new eXtensible Markup Language (XML) promises to bring the same business principles available only to the largest companies via EDI to small businesses. Small businesses will now be able to share proprietary information among sellers, wholesalers, and manufacturers using the web backbone. By using the web backbone, small businesses will be spared the costs of setting up their own proprietary networks among additional complementary companies. Sharing this information electronically will enable e-commerce systems to run much more efficiently as companies may now share inventory, sales, and fulfillment information directly from their e-commerce sites.

According to *InternetWorld OnLine Magazine*, the next great areas of e-commerce expansion will be in financial and institutional services, travel, entertainment and sports, and groceries with seven million households expected to be purchasing grocery products online in the year 2002.

CONCLUSION

Businesses rely on the Internet and the World Wide Web as an invaluable advertising and marketing medium. In fact, IBM had announced that their e-commerce revenue is now topping over $1 billion per month (www.nua.ie.com, 1999), and Dell Computers announced a single e-commerce transaction of $7 million (www.nua.ie.com, 1999). In addition to comprising an ever increasing portion of total sales, e-commerce sites are beginning to integrate inventory, accounting, and fulfillment software platforms into the web. As transactions are made, sales are becoming automated, inventory and accounts are updated, and orders are processed to fulfillment areas.

As business begins the new millennium and e-commerce becomes a multitrillion-dollar economy, more operations and traditional business software platforms will become integrated into a web platform. Advances in connectivity and the downward trend in computer prices will bring more people worldwide onto the Internet and the web. In this millennium, e-commerce may become the way that international business is conducted. A global economy developed over the World Wide Web network may very likely become the future of business.

13B

THE INTERNET AND THE ACCESS-PROVIDER INDUSTRY

Whether you are a seasoned Internet user who has been online for years, or you have yet to send your first e-mail message, a key aspect of the Internet that you should understand is the role of the Internet Service Provider, better known by the acronym ISP.

An Internet Service Provider provides your physical connection to the Internet. To understand the importance of the ISP and its role, a useful analogy is in order. Think of the driveway leading from your front door down to the street in front of your house. Your ISP supplies the driveway connecting your home or business to the rest of the Internet. Then consider the vast network of streets, thoroughfares, local freeways, and major interstate highways spread across the landscape. That is the rest of the Internet, a network connecting everyone and everything attached to it. From your driveway, you can travel to anywhere you want to go. But just as there are limits on how fast you can drive the roadways based on their size, traffic conditions, and quality, your Internet Service Provider controls how fast you travel on the Internet. And as anyone who begins to use the Internet soon learns, the speed of your Internet connection quickly becomes a vital concern once the novelty of the medium wears off. For business users, there are also strategic, and increasingly, mission-critical reliability, scalability, and security concerns to consider as well.

INTERNET BASICS

It is useful at this point to understand the makeup of the Internet. A "web" of high-speed fiber-optic cables, buried underground, connects the major metropolitan areas of the United States. These large bundles of cables are called the "backbones" of the Internet and are principally owned by the large telecommunications companies such as MCIWorldcom, Sprint, and AT&T. There are also fiber-optic cables strung under the major oceans of the world, connecting the United States to similar types of networks in every major country and continent. Networks of progressively smaller cable bundles connect smaller cities and regions to the high-speed backbones. This is how the term "World Wide Web" originated. At each physical location where the "web" intersects, there are special computers called routers and switches, receiving packets of digital data, reading the "address" on each packet, and routing them on to their final destination.

To see how this works, consider the transfer of a web page to your computer over the Internet. You send a request for the web page by clicking on a special word, phrase, or graphic on your computer screen containing a link to the address of the web page you want. A packet of data requesting the page travels from your computer to your ISP. Your ISP's router reads the address and sends your packet on to the next closest router to its final destination. It speeds along from router to router, point to point until the packet arrives at a computer called a server located at the address on your packet. The server then sends the web page you requested back to you in the same fashion.* How fast your connection is to your ISP and how your ISP connects to the backbones of the Internet are the key to understanding the ISP market.

The Need for Speed

According to Forester Research, the number of online accounts will grow from 28.7 million in 1999 to 77.6 million in 2002. At the same time, many people will use the Internet for videoconferencing, telephony, telecommuting, and online gaming.** As more and more companies and individuals embrace the Internet, each ISP's ability to handle the ever larger volumes of traffic will be challenged. How your ISP handles the increased demand for speed and volume will determine whether it survives or is gobbled up by the competition. ISPs have to supply you with a fast connection from your computer to their network, and then they have to connect their

---

*Available at <http://www.infoworld.com/cgi-bin/displayArchive.pl?/97/18/e01-18.71.htm>
**_PC World,_ March 1999, p. 164

network to the high-speed backbones of the Internet. We'll discuss the computer-to-ISP connection first.

Referred to in the ISP industry as "the last mile," the connection from your computer to your ISP can be fast or slow. The six most common connections today are listed here, along with price ranges, speeds, pros and cons. Most connections download information to your computer faster than they receive uploaded information from you. Connection speed is measured in thousands of bits-per-second, Kbps, and millions of bits-per-second, or Mbps.

Dial-up

Telephone dial-up service is the universally available method to connect to ISPs. Using a 56Kbps modem and a phone line, your maximum performance range is from 56Kbps downloading to 33.6Kbps uploading. Typical monthly cost is $20. Today, dial-up access is cheap, easy to install, and available everywhere. It is slow, however, and it ties up a phone line. It is recommended for people who can't get other types of connections and for notebook-using travelers. Travelers can dial into their ISP's network via modem from anywhere.

ISDN

Integrated Services Digital Network, or ISDN, is a service from your local phone company. At 128Kbps, it is about twice as fast as a standard 56Kbps modem connection.* The cost of ISDN is between $50 and $130 a month and is more complicated to set up than dial-up. The speed is relatively slow, although the availability of ISDN is widespread. It is recommended for the home business user who needs better than dial-up speed, but can't get other faster connections.**

Satellite

The next fastest connection type is satellite, which is available to anyone with a view of the southern sky. At 400Kbps download speed, it is about

---

*Available at <http://www.isdn.ocn.com/general/index.html#what is ISDN>
**PC World, March 1999, p. 110

three times as fast as ISDN. However, to upload, you must use a ground-based connection, that is, a standard telephone modem at 33.6–56Kbps. The satellite sends high-speed data in only one direction. The cost is about $50 for 100 hours, and installation is complex. This connection is recommended for business and home users who can't get other high-speed connections, especially in rural areas.

Cable

Where available, cable is currently the least expensive way to get a continuous high-speed connection to the Internet. At between 1 and 5Mbps downloading and 33.6Kbps–2.5Mbps uploading, it is very fast, and you stay connected to the Internet continuously. At $30–$65 per month it is relatively cheap. Its drawbacks are that its availability is not widespread yet, and you can't currently choose your ISP. You must use your cable provider as your ISP. Also, most businesses are not wired for cable today, so home users will benefit the most from this service.

DSL

Digital Subscriber Line connection, or DSL, is another high-speed route to the Internet that is beginning to hit the marketplace. The availability is limited, but analysts project up to 1,000% growth for both cable and DSL for the next few years. DSL uses the standard copper telephone wire already in your home or office and converts it to a high speed digital data carrier. With upload and download speeds of up to 8Mbps, it converts your ordinary telephone line into a fast connection that is always on. The cost is high, however, ranging from $49 to $1,200 per month. DSL will be used by small offices that can't afford frame relay/T1 connections, and for home users who can't get cable.*

Frame Relay/T1/T3

The current method of connection to the Internet for medium- and large-size businesses is frame relay and T1/T3 connections. These connec-

---

PC World, March 1999, p. 110

tions are widespread, business-oriented services and come with speed guarantees and quick repair service. Upload and download speeds reach 45Mbps because you are paying for a fiber-optic-cable connection much closer to the Internet backbones than the preceding connection types. The cost, at $300–$3,000 per month, limits this connection primarily to serious business users.*

Future Connection Technology

A new type of Internet connection called Broadband wireless is in the beginning stages of introduction. Two companies, Virginia-based Teligent and New York-based Winstar, plan to traverse the last mile using wireless radio frequencies instead of congested copper phone lines. They place a small dish on the roof of your building and transmit voice and data to a local central office connected to your ISP. Designed primarily for urban areas, this arrangement is much cheaper than laying underground fiber optic cable, with connection speeds up to 622Mbps.

Sprint rolled out a new connection service called ION®, or Integrated On-Demand Network in mid-1999. It will deliver voice, data, and video at speeds up to 620Mbps. Businesses and home users alike will be able to buy an ION hub at a local retailer for $200–$300 and connect it to a standard phone jack. Then, by connecting your computer to the ION hub via a standard Ethernet network card in your computer, you will have a persistent high-speed Internet connection, video conferencing, local calling with caller ID, and virtually unlimited long-distance calling, with service and support from Sprint.**

A SAMPLING OF U.S. INTERNET SERVICE PROVIDERS

The advent of the Internet has spawned an explosion of ISPs worldwide. There are now more than 7,000 individual ISPs in the United States alone.† While the ISP market is still growing at a fast pace, it is expected that once the growth begins to slow, many local and regional ISPs will merge or be acquired by larger, better capitalized ISPs. The reason is that as technology

---

PC World, March 1999, p. 110
**PC World*, March 1999, p. 165
†The Internet Service Provider List; available at <http://thelist.internet.com>

advances, many small ISPs will not upgrade their networks and equipment fast enough to retain their customer bases. As a result, they will be acquired by the remaining larger players. However, there will always be a niche for ISPs who cater to markets either too small or too distant from major cities to be economically viable to the major ISPs.

Currently, the Internet Service Provider market is divided into three tiers: the large national ISPs, midsize regional ISPs, and small regional and local ISPs. We will focus this analysis of the ISP market on the national ISPs and some of the large regional ISPs. The vast majority of the 7,000 ISPs are small local and regional companies who contract with the larger ISPs for access to their networks and backbones. The pros for using a smaller ISP include the possibility of more direct contact and service support from the provider. The cons are that they are more distant from the backbones of the Internet, and therefore data has farther to travel through more switches and routers on its path to the broader Internet. They may also not offer the value-added Internet services that the larger, business-oriented providers do.

The large national ISPs such as AT&T, MCIWorldcom, and Earth-link/Sprint boast of direct access to their own fiber-optic networks and the benefits of contracting with a large provider who can offer businesses value-added services and fast physical networks.

When choosing an ISP, you must consider what level of service your company will need in the future as well as the present. An ISP Finder service is available on *PC World Online* at http://www.pcworld.com/top400, which allows you to fill in the type of service you require and your telephone area code, and it brings up a list of the local ISPs in your area. Following is a sampling of the product and service offerings of the largest national ISPs. The large regional ISPs offer many of the same services, but have to contract with the larger ISPs for network access.

America Online (http://www.aol.com)

America Online (AOL) is the largest Internet Service Provider in the world. With over fourteen million subscribers, mostly individuals, it easily dwarfs its next largest competitor. AOL makes it easy to get started on the Internet for beginners; however, AOL is not well-suited for business subscribers. Its proprietary software interface is not designed for business use, though if simple e-mail and World Wide Web access is all you need, it may suffice. Its network speeds are rated the slowest of the major ISPs.*

AT&T (http://www.ipservices.att.com/products/index.html)

As an Internet Service Provider, AT&T is now one of the largest in the United States, with a customer base of more than three million corporate and consumer users. AT&T has been rated consistently as one of the top ISPs by Inverse Network Technology, which performs monthly tests of the thirteen top national ISPs in the United States, measuring call-success rate, download time, and other service metrics.

The company said it offers the world's premier single-source, global remote-access service, enabling users to easily access the Internet, Intranets, and Extranets from nearly sixty countries, by simply selecting a local calling number in the AT&T dialer client.

The span of AT&T's world-class networking capabilities now extends to more than 850 cities in nearly 60 countries with more than 2,000 local points of presence, giving AT&T the ability to provide national, regional, and global connectivity to businesses in those countries.**

AT&T Solutions Group provides customers the broadest range of managed-network services, advanced IP solutions, and custom network outsourcing available worldwide. In addition to the former IBM Global Network business, the group consists of the existing AT&T Solutions outsourcing and professional services business and AT&T Solutions Information Technology Services, which handles AT&T's internal information technology and communications needs around the world.

AT&T WorldNet® Virtual Private Network Service combines the best of the Internet technologies with the advantages of private networking. They have created a single, end-to-end, state-of-the-art solution with security features that allows controlled access to employees, business partners, and customers. Using AT&T's world-class, high-performance IP backbone, they now offer a platform that enables you to create Extranets, Intranets, and provide remote access to LANs.

For global-business customer support, AT&T now has more than 700 in-language Help Desk professionals in fifty countries.

---

*PC World, March 1999, p. 128
**Available at <http://www.ibm.com/services/pressrel/PRESSREL_30061.html>

Earthlink (http://www.earthlink.net)

EarthLink Sprint TotalAccess is an Internet Service Provider committed to delivering all the access, service, and tools you need to get the most out of the Internet. And with high-speed local access from more than 1,200 locations nationwide, they are in your neighborhood. They offer fast, nationwide 56K Internet access from more than 1,200 local dial-up numbers, as well as Sprint's Integrated Online Network and an extensive array of business connection services.

MCI WorldCom (http://www.us.uu.net/about/)

UUNET, the Internet services division of MCI WorldCom, is a global leader in Internet communications solutions offering a comprehensive range of Internet services to business customers worldwide. Providing Internet access, web hosting, remote access, and other value-added services, UUNET offers service in 114 countries, to more than 70,000 businesses, and owns and operates a global network in thousands of cities throughout North America, Europe, and Asia Pacific.

Internet, Intranet, and Extranet Business Solutions Today, UUNET offers a complete line of high-quality, high-performance Internet, Intranet, and Extranet solutions enabling customers to increase productivity and profitability through Internet technology. Through its comprehensive service offerings, UUNET is meeting the requirements of businesses, online service providers, and telecommunications firms. Customers can choose from in-house deployment to end-to-end, fully managed, Internet services all backed by unparalleled technical resources, people, and experience.

Products and Services UUNET's product portfolio contains cost-effective *IP-based services* including:

- Internet access—dial-up and dedicated access from 56Kbps to OC–3 speeds, and wholesale Internet access provisioned for Internet and online service providers

- Other communications services—including Internet fax services and multicast-based services (currently only available in the United States)

Value-added Internet services available include:

- Virtual Private Networking (VPNs)
- Remote access
- Managed security
- Hosting and electronic commerce—including core hosting, electronic-commerce solutions, extended enterprise, colocation, integrated application, and custom and complex hosting

Ensuring seamless service for the customer, UUNET offers businesses a comprehensive range of customized programs including end-user billing support, customer premise equipment (CPE) purchasing/leasing options, end-user help-desk support, and end-user implementation services.

Service and Support UUNET is committed to worldwide customer service and support, demonstrated by its outstanding customer service record, 24/7 coverage, and local service and support. UUNET's Network Operations Centers and technical support staff offer customers individualized support for their business-critical Internet solutions and provide network monitoring 24 hours per day, 365 days per year. Supporting customers locally through 52 offices worldwide, including local operations in Belgium, Canada, Denmark, France, Germany, Hong Kong, Italy, Japan, Luxembourg, the Netherlands, Sweden, Switzerland, the United Kingdom, and the United States, UUNET's field integration teams develop unique solutions by working with customers to evaluate applications and business requirements.

The UUNET Global Network For more than 10 years, UUNET has built its reputation on constructing one of the most rigorously engineered and widely deployed IP networks in the world—delivering high-quality, innovative services to businesses. The UUNET network spans more than 1,000 Points of Presence around the globe, and UUNET offers connectivity in 114 countries.*

---

*Available at <http://www.us.uu.net/about/>

IBM Internet Connection (http://www.ibm.net)

While AT&T recently acquired the IBM Global Network, IBM continues to offer Internet access and a broad array of business Internet services. IBM offers three service levels for businesses to access the Internet.

Business Dial Service This connection will allow a business to use services such as the World Wide Web, e-mail, and newsgroups. The dial service is available nationally and in many countries around the world. Connection speeds are 56Kbps and ISDN. IBM supplies you with their integrated Internet Access Kit, which includes your choice of Internet browser software and the IBM Global Network Dialer. With this service, you receive 12MB of e-mail storage space, and your e-mail addresses can be customized to allow meaningful e-mail addresses. They have over 1,300 IBM Global Network dial-in numbers in 52 countries worldwide, including over 500 V.90- and x2-capable dial numbers in the United States and Canada. They also provide over 600 ISDN connection numbers worldwide for a $1 extra surcharge per hour. Toll-based 800 access numbers are available in the United States and Canada for roaming access at $6-an-hour surcharge. IBM has a 24 hours, 7-day-a-week toll-free technical help desk available free for their subscribers. Personal web storage space of 10MB is available for an additional monthly charge as well.

LAN Internetworking Service The next level of Internet connection from IBM is the LAN internetworking service, which comes with firewall security. This is important if you are connecting your business's local area network to the Internet via one single connection.

Leased Line Service (Frame relay, T1/T3) Direct Leased Line Internet access provides an open two-way traffic between the customer's site and the Internet. No security is available. Customers may choose to implement any Internet protocol on their own, but no security is provided by IBM. Currently, e-mail and newsgroup support are not available through the Leased Line service, but customers may implement their own software.

IBM can be contacted at www.ibm.net for ISP service information, or at www.ibm.com/services about e-commerce consulting services.

ISDN FastPack MindSpring, which is now part of Earthlink.net, along with Eicon Technology and Nortel Networks, offers digital Internet access, The ISDN FastPack. The ISDN FastPack is ideal for the Internet user who needs faster Internet access—today.

Advantages of using ISDN for Internet Access include

- *Speed:* Faster than traditional phone lines and analog modems.
- *High-Performance Connection:* ISDN means fewer errors when sending or receiving files. The dependable digital connection means no telephone-line interference or distortion.
- *Versatility:* Data transfer speeds up to 128Kbps. Two lines in one, for voice data, fax, or video.

LAN on Demand LAN on Demand allows a small business to connect all of its computers to the Internet with a single ISDN line. Toshiba and Nortel Networks, is offering this convenient package: Provide Internet access for all the computers in your office with MindSpring's LAN on Demand account. Using an ISDN line and an ISDN Router recommended by MindSpring, you can have a have a high-speed connection to the Internet whenever you need it. Simple to set up and maintain and backed by MindSpring's top-notch Tech Support team, LAN on Demand is ideal for businesses that need Internet access but can't afford an expensive dedicated connection.

A LAN on Demand account with MindSpring requires an ISDN line and an ISDN Router (they specifically recommend two). The router has a built-in DHCP server so it can be used to network several computers together if they aren't already connected, or it can be added to an existing network. Once the router is on the network, any Internet application (such as a web browser, mail client, or news reader) that makes a call for information on the Internet causes the router to connect to your MindSpring account to handle the request. The router stays connected as long as there is activity and disconnects when activity stops. Because of the speed of ISDN, the router can connect in a matter of seconds. Because it all happens in the background, it's like having a dedicated connection without the expense.

The DirectConnect dedicated services enhance your company's efficiency and effectiveness. They're designed to give you a dedicated port, which only you can use, giving your business a direct, full-time connection to the Internet. You get the scalability, flexibility, and security critical to success.

The DirectConnect product line is supported by an expansive high-speed network and high-quality, responsive support. Plus, DirectConnect 56K, Frame Relay, Flex T1, and Full T1 services are backed by the industry-leading Service Level Agreement (SLA), which provides a 99.5 percent uptime guarantee.

There are six DirectConnect solutions to choose from. All include 24/7 toll-free technical support and allow you to use critical business applications such as e-mail and web hosting, file transfer, multimedia presentation, and video conferencing. They order your line with the local telephone company or carrier, register domain names and IP addresses, provide domain name services (DNS), and configure and test the equipment purchased from MinuSpring.

Concentric Network (http://www.concentric.net)

Concentric Network offers a full range of "always on" access solutions to fit your business needs. With services ranging from 144Kbps IDSL to full OC–3 connections, they have the bandwidth to meet your current needs and the capacity to grow as your bandwidth needs expand.

DSL Services ConcentricDSL provides high-speed, "always-on" Internet access over standard telephone lines, at prices lower than comparable ISDN service.

Speed At speeds ranging from 144Kbps to 1.5Mbps, ConcentricDSL is a good access solution for small businesses, SOHO, telecommuting, or high-speed personal Internet connectivity. All speeds are symmetric, which means that they operate at the same speed in both directions, except for the 1.5Mbps/384Kbps ADSL service, which offers the faster 1.5Mbps speed in the download direction.

Wireless Services ConcentricWireless provides high-speed "always-on" Internet access to businesses at speeds faster than ISDN but without many of the distance limitations of DSL and at a fraction of the cost of T1 services.

Speed At speeds ranging from 384Kbps to 1.5Mbps, ConcentricWireless is a good access solution for small business, SOHO, telecommuting, or high-speed personal Internet connectivity. ConcentricWireless offers business class Internet access with the ideal combination of speed, availability, and reliability. ConcentricWireless's unique wireless distribution system provides sustained speeds up to 1.5 Mbps. That's 50 times faster than analog modems that use ordinary telephone lines and 10 times faster than an ISDN line. Even with all this speed, ConcentricWireless is competitively priced with ISDN and DSL, and costs significantly less than T-1 services.

Dedicated Access Concentric's Dedicated Access Services allow your enterprise to communicate with its elements without the high cost of point-to-point dedicated circuits and without the security risks and poor performance associated with carrying wide-area-network and Intranet traffic over the Internet. It is fast, offering connectivity at speeds ranging from 56Kbps through OC–3 (155Mbps). Concentric's Dedicated Access Service utilizes its own private IP network to connect enterprises to remote offices, business partners, and to the Internet via a high-capacity, nationwide backbone that is rigorously engineered for business-critical operations. All SuperPOPs are housed in hardened telco-grade facilities.

A staff of technical experts monitors network performance 24 hours a day, 365 days a year from the Network Operations Center (NOC), where they will handle everything to get a business up and running. This may include primary Domain Name Service (DNS), CPE configuration, on-site installation, and end-to-end circuit testing to ensure successful implementation. Concentric's Dedicated Access service is seamlessly integrated into your LAN environment.

A SAMPLING OF MAJOR U.S. REGIONAL ISPS

- *Ameritech* (Midwest U.S. region) http://www.ameritech.net

  Nimble performer, clearly the Midwest choice, excels at everything but support quality and ease of use.*

- *SBC/Pacific Bell Internet Services* (Southwest U.S. region)http://public. pacbell.net/business.html

  Hard to set up, but its great performance—the best after AT&T's— makes it a great choice.*

- *BellSouth* (Southern U.S. region) http://www.bellsouth.net

  Good performance over its main competitor in the South, Cybergate.*

- *RCN* (Northeast U.S. region) http://www.rcn.com

  Solid, all-around service, especially for those who want to upgrade to new high-speed technologies.*

- *Rocky Mountain Internet* (Rocky Mountain region) http://www.rmi.net

  Limited support hours, but reliable service give it the edge over US WEST in this coverage area.*

THE FUTURE OF THE INTERNET-SERVICE-PROVIDER MARKET

With the continuing fast-paced growth of the Internet, the Internet-Service-Provider market has been growing right along with it. However, industry consolidation has already begun, as small ISPs have been taken over by larger ISPs desiring larger customer bases and increased revenues. The largest long-distance company, AT&T, purchased two of the largest cable companies, Tele-Communications, Inc., and Media One, Inc., giving it access to nearly 60% of homes with cable. AT&T intends to be the market leader in Internet access to both consumers and businesses.

Because the technology of the Internet is in a state of constant transition, it is recommended that you choose an ISP with whom you have culti-

---

*PC World, March 1999, p. 128

vated a business relationship. As your company and its needs grow, the ISP should be able to scale their connection speeds and bandwidth up without disruption to your enterprise. Outsourcing some or all of your information technology needs through your ISP will allow you to focus your internal resources on the products or services that you do best, while your ISP keeps you current and supplied with the best, most competitive technology the ever changing Information Age has to offer.

INTERNET MARKETING

The Internet allows us to see the world as a single market. Companies can effectively and inexpensively build a global presence even if the company has only a small office in Laguna Niguel, California. But it is the Internet's broad reach that makes it such a difficult medium to advertise in. Internet Software Consortium (ISC) has been tracking the number of "domain names" registered on line. This survey is conducted by querying the domain system for any name assigned to every possible Internet Protocol (IP) address. Think of the IP address as the equivalent of your home's street address. Every IP address is unique to that web site. The ISC survey checks to see if anything is residing on a particular IP address by sending a packet of information, or "ping," and waiting for a response. The graph in Figure 13C–1 represents the ISC survey.

FIGURE 13C—1

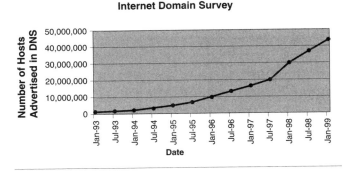

The Internet explosion is clearly visible. The survey estimates that there are close to 45,000,000 web sites today. If the Internet continues to grow at this rate there should be one billion registered web sites during the year 2001.

This brings us to the hottest marketing question of the day. With so many online stores available, how do you attract customers to your web site? It is important to differentiate customers from "traffic." Traffic refers to the total number of people visiting your web site. It does not reflect the effectiveness or profitability of a site. Generating traffic is essential to building an online customer base. But traffic can also be seen as lost opportunity if it does not translate into revenue. We assist web marketers in not just generating traffic, but by turning that traffic into customers. We will explain how to do this by using a few of the well-known methods such as improving search-engine rankings and some not so well-known methods such as using direct e-mail to interact with your target market.

ATTRACTING NEW CUSTOMERS ON THE WEB

"Traffic means everything right now: It impacts advertising dollars, impacts investment in a company, and it impacts strategic partnerships," says Chris Charron, media analyst at Forrester Research Inc., in Cambridge, Massachusetts. http://www.zdnet.com/zdnn/stories/zdnn smgraph dis play/0,3441,2124838, 00.html

Imagine owning retail clothes stores. How would you attract customers? Find the best location possible, advertise in local newspapers, and offer special promotions to bring people in. Advertising on the Internet does not exactly follow these traditional techniques. The most important difference is the "bricks-and-mortar" storefront has been replaced by digital technology and Internet addresses.

Location on the Internet refers to a web site's Universal Resource Locator (URL). Network Solutions will register any URL if it is still available. The cost is $200 for a two-year registration. Network Solutions allows you to query its database of registered URLs in order to determine availability. If the URL is already registered, Network Solutions will provide you with information about the person who registered the URL. Many times people just register a URL in order to sell it to the highest bidder. One time an author attempted to register Thelibrary.com. To the author's dismay, the URL was already registered. The owner of the Thelibrary.com wanted to sell the URL for $2,000. That is a great profit for doing almost nothing.

Selecting the Right Name and Location

A web site's name is as important as the content. For some companies, selecting a URL is very simple. Software developer Microsoft wants people to easily locate their web site. Therefore their URL is Microsoft.com. But what if you are starting a small, not so well-known company that needs to attract people quickly? Your name, or URL, can bring people in. Companies such as Buy.com and Etoys.com attract traffic simply because their URL is easy to recognize and remember.

Very often smaller companies will purchase a URL that is similar to the URL of their market leader. Microsoft owns a monopoly of the Operating System (OS) market. People from all over the world are collaborating to create a new, free OS. It is called LINUX. One of the major LINUX distributors, Redhat, attracts people to their site by registering a URL that is just a misspelling of Microsoft.com. Redhat owns microsotf.com. If anyone incorrectly spells Microsoft, they are immediately transferred to Redhat.com.

Registering a URL is just as important as finding the perfect bricks-and-mortar store location. Use a name that is easily recognizable and informs people what you do. Be as creative as possible. If the URL is already registered, try something else. Do not overpay for a URL unless absolutely necessary.

USING SEARCH ENGINES

Finding the right web site for a product or service oftentimes depends on the creativeness and determination of the person searching. Most people have accepted search engines as the best way to find the information they need online. There are several hundred search engines, and each engine provides a unique set of results. Search engines can be categorized according to the techniques they employee to index the web. There are two mechanisms. The first type is similar to a directory. These search engines possess a database of web sites indexed according to the information on those web sites and the number of visitors it attracts (see Figure 13C–2).

FIGURE 13C—2

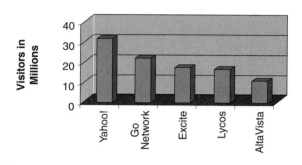

Search Engine Traffic

Today Yahoo indexes several million web sites. Thirty-one million visitors query their directory every month. This makes Yahoo the most accessed search engine today.

Yahoo's search engine "looks" for matches with category names, web-site titles and comments (as they appear in the Yahoo directory), content from individual web pages (a service provided by Inktomi), Yahoo News stories, and Yahoo Net Events. Matches are presented on the "search results" page in this same order: Yahoo categories first, then web sites, then individual web pages scanned by Inktomi, followed by news stories and Net Events. Keyword matches are organized by "relevancy," depending on a couple of factors, such as

1. *Multiple keyword matches*—sites, categories, or documents with more keyword matches are ranked higher than those with fewer keyword matches.

2. *Document-section weighting*—sites and categories with keyword matches found in the title are ranked higher than those found in the comment, body, or URL.

3. *Generality of category*—matching categories that are listed higher up in the "Yahoo hierarchy" are ranked higher than specific categories listed deeper within the hierarchy. http://help.yahoo.com/help/search/search-02.html

The complete rules for registering with Yahoo's directory can be found at http://www.yahoo.com/info/suggest/. This page describes in detail the correct method to submit your site with Yahoo free of charge. You will need to provide your site's title, URL, and a brief description. Be as specific as possible when registering your site. This will help improve search-engine rankings.

One search-engine directory, <u>GoTo.com</u>, allows search terms to be purchased in order to improve a web site's ranking. According to the creators of the site, "<u>GoTo.com</u> is the most cost-effective way to drive targeted traffic to your web site. You select the search terms that are relevant to your site. Then you determine how much you are willing to pay on a per-click basis for each of those search terms. The higher your 'bid,' the higher in the search results your site will appear. It's targeted, cost-per-click advertising and you set the cost per click!" Sounds great, so where's the catch? <u>GoTo.com</u> does not improve the exposure of everyone who registers. <u>GoTo.com</u> is a directory where large companies with more marketing resources will always win out over smaller companies with less marketing resources. GoTo's search model boils down search ranking to one factor: The amount of money invested. It does not account for any of the other methods for improving search rankings (these methods will be discussed later). In the opinion of the authors <u>GoTo.com</u> is not a search engine at all. It is a portal site designed to enhance exposure of companies willing to spend money. Companies listed in the <u>GoTo.com</u> directory are just buying exposure. It is more similar to an advertising network than a search engine.

Robot Search Engines

The second type of search engines scan the web using software "robots." Robots, also referred to as "spiders" and "ants," conduct a text query of as many web sites as possible. The software agents then pull out the words they believe are significant. Some robots extract specific words or phrases. Others index every word on every page. Once the robot extracts the information, it compiles a database that can be queried. According to recent studies, these "spiders" cover only about 25 percent of all web sites. Information search engines that utilize spiders include Excite, Infoseek Ultra, and AltaVista.

Excite uses "artificial intelligence" to extract a site's general purpose. Excite's Intelligent Concept Extraction (ICE) "assumes that words found near each other are conceptually related. Working from this conceptual relationship, ICE generates a site's dominant theme, which becomes the standard against which searchers' queries are measured to match and rank the site. ICE is the major criteria for ranking on Excite. Excite does not support keywords, meta tags, or page popularity" (*Getting Hits*, Sellers, 1998). In order to rank high on Excite, use concise, descriptive sentences at the top of your pages. Avoid any unnecessary information such as jokes.

Infoseek Ultra is considered the model for next-generation spider indexes. Fast submission times, quick search times, and searches that include nonessential terms such as "a" and "and" make Infoseek Ultra the future of spider engines. If you submit your site on Infoseek's URL link, your site will be available on the search within minutes. In comparison, the majority of search engines take anywhere from two to six weeks to enter your site once you register. Infoseek monitors how often your site changes and adjusts the frequency of visits by the spiders based on that information. Meta tags and keywords are supported by Infoseek Ultra. Higher rankings are awarded to sites containing more terms used in the query and uncommon terms indexed on the site.

AltaVista is considered the granddaddy of big, fast search engines. AltaVista is a creation of Digital Equipment Corporation (DEC) and offers one of the largest databases of any search engine. AltaVista's spider, known as "Scooter," varies how often it returns to a web site depending upon the observations of how often information on the web site changes. AltaVista does support meta tags and keywords but page popularity is not considered in ranking.

Unfortunately, software robots are not very intelligent. Very often the robots will extract unimportant information. In addition, these robots cannot differentiate between multiple word meanings. A site dealing with "Rock Music" appears in the same index as a site about "Prehistoric Rocks." Thankfully, there is a technique to educate these robots or at least point them in the right direction. "Meta Tags" specify relevant information about a site within the language used to write web pages, hypertext markup language (HTML). This information is found in the head (<HEAD>) portion of the HTML page.

The next time you are looking at your favorite web page, take a minute to view the HTML used to generate that page. You can do this by clicking on the "View" tab and selecting "View Page Source." Here you will see how a web page is generated. HTML consists of two main components: the "head" and the "body." The body portion contains all the information you actually see on your computer monitor. The body includes text, images, tables, and links.

It is the head portion of the web page that can make or break a site's ranking in the search engine. Within the <HEAD> </HEAD> tags reside the "meta tags" for your page. There are two types of meta tags: keyword and description. Keywords meta tags list words that emphasize the important points about your web site. When generating a list of keywords think of words people could use to find your site through a search engine. Description meta tags consist of a short sentence that summarizes what your site is about. Not all search engines scan both types of meta tags, but it is a good rule of thumb to include the keyword and description tags in at least the index page of your web site. Here is the head portion of my company, PSSC Labs, index page.

<head>

<meta name="description" content="PSSC Labs is the answer to your computing needs in your laboratory, office, and home. We can help you simplify your work by providing cost effective solutions to every problem">

<meta name="keywords" content="computer, reseller, computer reseller, hardware, Alpha, Intel, Servers, Processors, Nodes, Beowulf, RedHat, Dual-Boot, Dual Boot, Scanners, CD-burners inexpensive, affordable, cost-effective, Microsoft, Linux, Super-Computer, University, Universities, Southern California, Internet Orange County, custom configurations, custom, Dell, Gateway Micron, UCI, UCLA, University of California, University Computing, Professor, Student, Office Networks, Modems, Monitors, Network Hubs, 3-Com">

<no frames>
<title>PSSC Labs, your computer experts.</title>
</head>

Notice that the description is written in sentence format and keywords consist of single words and short paraphrases. Certain search engines like Infoseek and AltaVista will include the meta tag description sentence in their listings of search results. When I search Infoseek for PSSC Labs my site is listed as:

PSSC Labs: All of the leading brands from people you can trust. PSSC Labs is the answer to your computing needs in your laboratory, office, and home. We can help you simplify your work by providing cost effective solutions to every problem. PSSC Labs is . . . 22% Date: 9 Nov 1998, Size 1.3K, http://www.pssclabs.com/

This could be people's first contact with your web site. Be certain to carefully plan what you want to say in your description meta tag.

PAYING FOR SEARCH-ENGINE EXPOSURE

Search engines offer methods to make it easier for people to find you. These techniques are not free, but they can greatly increase your web site's exposure. Several engines allow you to purchase specific words that people may enter in their search. When someone enters a term you have purchased, your promotional banner will appear at the top of the page. (I will go into greater detail about banners in a later section.) Buying keywords does not improve your site's ranking in the search engine. This is a common misconception. Buying keywords guarantees only that your banner will be displayed. There are directory services, such as GoTo.com mentioned earlier, that will improve directory search rankings when people invest more money in GoTo.com's service.

AltaVista offers three keyword-rate programs: "Premium & Exclusive," "Standard," and "Run of Site." The premium and exclusive service allows you to own a search term outright. Anytime someone enters that keyword, your banner and only your banner will appear. Buying standard words is similar to the premium service except other people can buy those same words. Therefore your banner appears in a rotation with other banners. Run-of-site words will randomly display your banner anywhere on AltaVista. People do not need to enter a specific term to see your banner. It is displayed at anytime and anywhere on the site. The rates for these different services are listed in Figure 13C–3.

These rates are based on cost-per-1,000 impressions. Impressions is the term web advertisers use to define the number of times your banner advertisement is displayed. If we visit a search engine and type in a specific term

FIGURE 13C—3.
ALTAVISTA KEYWORD CATEGORIES AND RATES

Premium and Exclusive	$85 per 1,000 Impressions
Standard Words	$70 per 1,000 Impressions
Run of Site	$20 per 1,000 Impressions

Source: http://www.doubleclick.net/advertisers/altavista/rate_card.htm

that someone purchased, a banner for that person's web site is displayed. One impression has been used. Considering the large number of visitors popular search engines attract, 1,000 impressions could last less than two days. Sites with heavy traffic will accept orders only for a minimum of 50,000 impressions.

Purchasing keywords is not only expensive but requires you to use a little psychology. The goal with keywords is selecting words people will use to find your product or service using a search engine. It is important to select generic terms that specifically target what you are providing. For PSSC Labs, we use keywords such as rackmount computer, beowulf supercomputer, and lunchbox computer. These are all generic terms people could use to fulfill a specific computer need.

Doorway pages are another method you could use to better direct search engines. These are pages designed specifically with search engines in mind. Take a look at the webpage

http://www.pssclabs.com//harpua/linuxpages.htm

for Linux. This is a doorway page created to help you find our web site.

Click on the links and linked images to enter. This is a doorway page created to help you find our web site. Click on the links and linked images to enter.

And here is the HTML used to generate the page.

<html><head>

<title>Linux. Click here to enter this site now. Thank you for visiting . . </title>

<meta name="keywords" content="Linux, here, click here now">

<meta name="description" content="Linux. Click here to enter this site now. Thank you for visiting. Click here to enter this site now. Thank you for visiting. Click here to enter . . ">

</head>

<body bgcolor="#FFFFFF" text="#000000" link="#0000FF" vlink="#0000FF" alink="#0000FF">

<small><a href="http://www.pssclabs.com"><img src="http://www.pssclabs.com/gif/circle1.jpg" border="2"></a></small>

<h1><small><small>Linux. This is a doorway page created to help you find us . . computer. Operating System. OS.</small></small></h1>

</body></html>

Notice how simple and straightforward this page is. No image maps. No background images. No frames. No embedded sounds. No Java. No JavaScript. No banners. No counters. No redirect pages. Doorway pages are not complicated or intricate. Doorway pages are visible only to the search engines; someone browsing the Internet will never see your doorway pages. These pages use Server Side Inclusion (SSI) technology to "serve" the main page of your site when the doorway page is called upon. SSI technology accomplishes this by allowing the server to scan the web-page request for information that will direct the server about any special instructions. In the case of the doorway pages, SSI technology forces a request for the doorway page to redirect to the web site's index page. http://bignosebird.com/ssi.shtml

Several services exist to create doorway pages for you. An example of this service is provided by Superior Software Solutions. This company offers a piece of software called "The Agent Delivery Solution." The promoters of this software claim, "The Agent Delivery Solution is the answer to what is needed to get your web site ranked high in the search engines and to out-rank your competitors. It is the web master's companion for pushing a web site to the top of the search engines by feeding the search engine Spiders, Robots, Ants and Crawlers with what you want them to see while allowing the web browsers to see your full content!" Each search engine uses differ-ent robots that look for specific doorway-page characteristics. Some require a specific number of words on the doorway page, others do not allow images, and some do not index pages that contain frames. The Agent Delivery Solution takes the guesswork out of designing a doorway page. The software includes templates and outlined tips for creating the perfect door-way page for different search-engine robots. All you need to do is follow the directions and input the proper information. The software generates and submits the doorway page to the specified search engines.

This service is not free. The Agent Delivery Solution claims to be the least expensive on the market and costs $300. The level of return on invest-ment is questionable. One of the authors submitted several PSSC Labs door-way pages to AltaVista and Infoseek. Four weeks after registering the doorway pages we checked our site's search-engine ranking. On both engines our site did increase slightly in rank when we entered specific key-word search terms associated with our doorway pages. However, this rank-ing increase is not significant enough to justify spending hundreds of dollars for our doorway pages.

SEARCHING EMBEDDED LINKS

The search engines' job is to display sites that match your request. Chances are you are not the first person making that request. Search engines moni-tor the "embededness" or popularity of a site. This popularity is determined by analyzing how many links there are to the web page from other web pages. A very embedded web page will possess several hundred links to other pages and could have thousands of links to it from other web pages.

DebbieFerrari.com is the web site for Southern California Real Estate Agent Debbie Ferrari and is a perfect example of a well-embedded page. William Kolzer manages the page. He believes that including any link on your page, even links that have nothing to do with what you are offering, benefits your search-engine ranking. DebbieFerrari.com has links to every-thing from stock quotes to tips on reducing junk e-mail. Of course, you don't want to list a million links on your web page, but you can strategically place links that may be interesting to your web-page visitors. For PSSC Labs, there is an entire section devoted to Community Links. This section includes links to Linux resources, customers' web sites, and basketball such as NBA.com.

Placing links on your page is simple enough, but, more important, you need to have links to your site from other web sites. To accomplish this effectively you need to utilize a variety of methods. Free techniques to exchanging links are extremely time consuming. You can spend days finding sites that may be interesting to your target audience. You can then contact the administrator of those sites, usually via e-mail, and ask if he or she would be interested in exchanging links. Typically, most people are willing to take part in a link exchange with you. This process will help embed your site deeper into the Internet.

Link-exchange programs are similar to the preceding technique except they already possess a database of people willing to exchange links. There is no need for you to spend precious time looking for interested parties on the web. Stop by TheLinkexchange.com to see one of the best resources for embedding your site. This free service will place a link on several hundred sites if you agree to place links on your site. All you have to do is submit general information such as the type of site (business versus non-business), target audience, and the amount of traffic you expect from your site. There are link-exchange programs that cost money, but there is no guarantee that these are any more effective than the free services. Spend time communicating with people in the web community and try the free link-exchange services first. If your site is not generating any traffic, then consider joining one of the pay services.

There is one surefire way to increase your web site's search rank. *Register, register, register!* You can do this any number of ways. RegisterIt!.com will automatically register your site with up to 400 search engines and monitor that registration for future reference. Monitoring registration is key because search engines can lose your site if it is infrequently referenced. Register-It! costs $40 per year for a single web-site address.

If you absolutely must keep costs down, you can manually register your web site with every single search engine. Each search engine will ask you a number of different questions and automatically submit your information. The amount of time and energy this takes is definitely worth more than $40. We have used Register-It! and are very satisfied with the results. Unlike with using doorway pages, we see a significant increase in the PSSC Labs ranking on almost every search engine. Even better, our web site's ranking improved as time went on.

USING ADVERTISEMENTS AND BANNERS

Did you know blank space on your web page can be used to pay your bills? *Banner advertising is the Internet's version of a commercial.* You see banners on almost every heavily trafficked search engine, commerce site, or information resource.

Just like a commercial, a banner is designed to immediately catch the attention of the web-page viewer. Flashy images, movement, bright colors, and interesting product offers can be effective in banners. *Your banner should say "Hey! Forget why you came to this site. Click ME!"*

Each site has specific guidelines for inserting a banner. A layout of 460 pixels in length x 60 pixels in height is the generally accepted large-banner format. Small banners are 150 pixels x 100 pixels. Most sites do not limit the size of the banner. Size refers to the amount of data the banner consumes. Banner size is where you can use your knowledge of technology to obtain an advantage. Because banners are transmitted over digital lines, there is a delay period between when the banner is called up and when it actually appears. You want to limit this period of time as much as possible The smaller the banner size, the faster it will reach the web viewer. Banners have less than a third of a nanosecond, to attract the web viewer's attention. If your banner does not appear in that one-third nanosecond you wasted precious advertising dollars. To limit banner size, use as little color as possible. Don't detract from the look of the banner but if you can substitute black or white in place of really heavy bright colors your banner will display much faster. Also try using only 16 bits of color in your design rather than the heavier 256 bits.

Most sites accept banners only in the .GIF or .JPG format. We recommend using the .GIF format because it compresses your image without losing much of the quality. When sites accept banners created with a program called Flash, the problem of banner size will disappear. An 11K Flash file looks more like an animated movie than a simple banner. For now, keep your banners as light as possible.

Banners are the most expensive Internet advertising technique. Advertising rates significantly vary depending on the amount of site traffic.

Heavily trafficked sites charge premium rates. We now show you an example of banner-advertising cost based on the number of impressions. PSSC Labs manufactures computers with Redhat's LINUX operating system. We scour the web to find heavily trafficked LINUX-specific web sites that accept banners. Several Linux resources exist that allow advertising, such as the official Redhat site, the official site for the LINUX organization, LinuxHardware.net and SearchLinux.com. Figure 13C–4 is a table comparing the amount of traffic and advertising rates for each site. CPM stands for Cost Per 1,000 impressions.

FIGURE 13C–4
TRAFFIC AND ADVERTISING RATES

	Visitors per day	CPM on Frontpage	CPM on Target Pages
REDHAT.com	60,000	$70.00	$80.00
LINUX.org	17,000	30.00	45.00
SEARCHLINUX.com	3,000	19.00	18.00
LINUXHARDWARE.net	1,000	8.00	12.00

As you can see, banner ad rates directly depend upon web-site traffic. Sites require you to purchase minimum blocks of impressions. For example, Redhat.com will sell advertising only in blocks of 50,000 impressions. Linux.org will sell advertising in blocks of 15,000 impressions or more. You can usually specify where you would like your banner to appear on a site. Sites offer different rates for banners that appear on their home page or on pages deeper in the site. Target pages are certain pages on a site that best correlate to the product you are advertising. Linux.org offers target advertising programs. Being a hardware vendor, Michael McLagan from Linux.org recommends that we advertise the PSSC Labs banner on the following target pages:

Hardware Vendors:	http://www.linux.org/hardware/index.html
Complete Systems:	http://www.linux.org/vendors/systems.html
Hardware Components:	http://www.linux.org/hardware/components.html
Homepage:	http://www.linux.org/

It is clear that there is no definitive banner advertising rate. Many of the companies compare their traffic numbers to other sites in order to create the CPM. Banner rates can easily cost you over $1,000 per month per site. We chose to advertise with <u>Linux.org</u>. We purchased 10,000 impressions on target pages for a total of $300. Our results are not incredibly promising. Traffic to <u>PSSCLabs.com</u> did increase when our banner first appeared on <u>Linux.org</u>. Unfortunately, the ads generated just two new customers. Some doubt the benefit of banner advertising. According to an article in the *Los Angeles Times* Advertising and Marketing section, "some advertisers have become so discouraged by the poor response to their online banners that they have signed off advertising over the Internet." The problem is that advertisers have not figured out how to attract the web viewer's attention. "As marketers, we really don't know how to use the web effectively," says Denis Beasejour, Procter & Gamble's vice president of worldwide advertising. Kevin McSpaden, director of electronic commerce and retail marketing at Levi Strauss Direct, estimates that he is "spending from $56 to $120 per paying customer to get them to come by. From a business and e-commerce standpoint, it doesn't pay."

Despite these negative testimonials, Internet advertising is growing rapidly. A recent survey of advertising dollars spent on the Internet is shown in Figure 13C–5. This survey covers all forms of Internet advertising including banners, spam, and direct e-mail. Banners account for around 52% of online advertising dollars in 1998. With the number of people online growing rapidly, advertisers believe it is important to build a brand name now. Their hope is to turn that brand-name recognition into a profitable web store.

FIGURE 13C—5

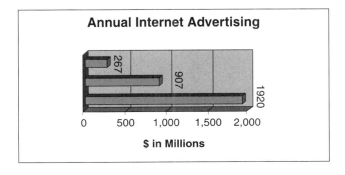

DEALING WITH UNWANTED ADVERTISEMENTS

California law AB-1629 "establishes somewhat 'keep off the grass' situation for Internet Service Providers (ISP) and e-mail domains. It proposes strong language which clearly allows mail internet service providers to establish rules for their users regarding sending unsolicited advertising mail. It also clearly allows for an ISP to publish a prohibition against use of their facilities for reception of such mail, and establishes civil right of action against violators to the tune of $50 per message up to $15,000 per day." http://www.tigerden.com/junkmail/laws.html
    Spamming appears to have worn out its welcome in the web community. It consumes time, bandwidth, and money without any significant benefit. Spam is considered successful if 0.0001% of total-sent e-mails result in an actual sale. But to be fair, spam has influenced the way advertising is conducted over the web. Internet users are constantly bombarded by offers to earn up to $50,000 per month or coerced into clicking on a link to see "a thousand girls in their string bikini." Spam allows advertisers to reach hundreds of thousands of people for almost no cost. Even more significant is the ability of advertisers to actively communicate with web users. These spam e-mails ask people for feedback, including participating in a survey and signing up for services. Spam opens the world to the entrepreneurs armed with only an idea and an Internet Service Provider (ISP).
    E-mail lists are easily accessible over the web. You can buy a list, compile this list yourself, or have someone take care of the entire spamming process for you. Buying a list is not expensive. Vantage Mall offers two million e-mail addresses every month for a one-time payment of $50. The people who own these e-mail addresses are completely unaware that their identities have been sold.
    Don't want to spend the $50? You can amass a list of e-mail addresses yourself. Visit any newsgroup on DejaNews and join a discussion group. This discussion group contains thousands of e-mail addresses that are instantly added to your e-mail program when you join the group. You can spam any message you want over this discussion group without any significant consequences. Leverage the power of the Internet to help you succeed.
    What if you have a specific target audience in mind, say all of the people that work at CSULB. Go to CSULB's homepage and you will find a tab for people search. Type in any name. Make it generic as possible. CSULB's server will display all of the possible matches including name, e-mail

address, position, and phone number. This will take some time and you may not collect the complete list of e-mails you are interested in. There is a solution. You can write a program to extract e-mail addresses from any server on the Internet based on its domain name. The domain name is what you encounter after the "@" symbol in the e-mail address. For example, one e-mail address is alex@pssclabs.com. The domain name is PSSCLABS. Eager to test our friends' programs we ask for a list of UCI e-mail addresses. Within twelve hours, we receive a Microsoft Excel spreadsheet with over 2,000 e-mail addresses ending in "@uci.edu."

If you don't feel comfortable sending spam mail, then maybe it would be easier if someone else could do it for you. There are hundreds of services that will send spam mail on your behalf. Some spam services claim "e-mail advertising usually gets a much better response rate than bulk postal mail advertising," and they even "guarantee response." These services ask for a one-time payment or a small commission every time someone signs up. We recently received an e-mail solicitation from a spamming service. The e-mail made the following offer:

We send your ad, no limit to the size, at the following rates:

$100/200,000

$575/million

$2,000/5 million

We guarantee response, you create the ad, we send it.

Yes! We can target ads by region.

Only over the Internet can you reach 5 million people for $2,000.

USING E-MAIL LIST MARKETING

"Opt-In" marketing is the practice of sending commercial e-mail to people registered to receive commercial e-mail. Net Creations claims to be the leader in Opt-In marketing. They manage PostMasterDirect.com, a web site offering e-mail lists of people who would like to receive specific information. We contacted Michael Mayor at PostMasterDirect to find out more about his company's services. According to Mayor, PostMasterDirect rents and manages distribution of e-mails to several thousand people. You can rent a list of people for a specified fee. Renting a list refers to PostMasterDirect's policy of not distributing actual e-mail addresses to its customers. Instead, PostMasterDirect manages all e-mail distribution. The reasoning for this, according to Mayor, is to prevent illegal list distribution that could lead to spamming.

PostMasterDirect offers 170 different lists. Lists are compiled by third-party companies that guarantee 100% of e-mail addresses come from people who have "voluntarily signed up to receive commercial e-mail on topics of interest." (PostMasterDirect.com) The cost is ten cents to thirty cents per name (CPM) depending on the list you select. Mayor explains that the higher-cost CPM lists are technology and computer related. After informing Mayor of the products and services offered by PSSC Labs, he responds with the following recommendations:

Computer Software-Linux by AllFreebies (#34830)-
1037 subscribers @ $.25 an e-mail address

Mail to qualified prospects interested in Linux software, tips and techniques. Subscribers have qualified themselves by specifically selecting this topic from among 300 available.

Reach those interested in Linux.

Computer Software-Linux by CDROM_Guide (#14110)-
10448 subscribers @ $.20 an e-mail address

Computer Software-Linux by CMPnet (#8644)-
5951 subscribers @ $.30 an e-mail address

Computer Software-Linux by Windows_Magazine (#36221)-
211 subscribers @ $.30 an e-mail address

Operating Systems: Linux by NetCent_Communications (#14746)-
1806 subscribers @ $.20 an e-mail address

Total Count: 19,166 Unique Names

We want to target even further. We asked Mayor, "Do you have any list oriented to government buyers or subcontractors, like Parker Hannifin, General Dynamics, Army, Navy, and college campuses? Linux users tend to be do-it-theirself types and build their workstations on their own. We have great relationships with many Fortune 500 and government agencies. We would like to go in that direction." Unfortunately, PostMasterDirect cannot target by company or company domain.

Mayor estimates 10–15% of sent e-mails result in someone "clicking through" to the advertised site. This is significantly more effective than the 0.5% of click-through generated via the best banner advertisements.

CASE STUDY

Direct E-mail: Today's Best Internet-Marketing Technique

In our experience, the most successful technique to attract people to your web site is to entice them with free information. *"Direct e-mailing"* refers to sending individuals personal e-mail messages every time you have new information that may be beneficial to them. Much like traditional direct mailing, direct e-mailing can generate interest in your company simply by keeping people aware of your products and services.

Direct e-mailing is not spamming. Direct e-mail provides people with important information. Spamming is considered successful if 0.0001% of sent e-mails result in sales; direct e-mailing can be one thousand times more effective. Direct e-mailing builds relationships with customers. It can be used to start conversations that result in actual sales.

At PSSC Labs we generate innovative methods for marketing and bringing in new customers. Being a custom manufacturer of personal computers, we compete directly with Dell, Gateway, Compaq, and Micron as well as thousands of "white-box" manufacturers. Our niche is providing machines that other manufacturers cannot build. Our clients include the University of California at Irvine (UCI), Northrop Grumman, the United States Army, General Dynamics, and Lucent Technologies.

Building a web presence is essential in today's business environment. Competitors already have established themselves as reliable brand names with full-service web sites. Not having the marketing resources available to our larger competitors, we generate interest in our web site and company by providing people with information they need when buying a computer. We created "University Computing," a newsletter dealing with the latest advancements in computer hardware and software. Our goal is to assist busy professionals and professors with their computer-buying decisions.

There is another free technique to build a target list of e-mail addresses. If you go to most large corporate, university, and government web sites, they possess directories of employee e-mail addresses. With a little determination and a lot of time you can gather thousands of e-mail addresses without spending a single dollar.

Effective direct e-mailing builds a relationship with your customers. This is direct e-mailing's major advantage over spamming. You can become personal with your audience, making it significantly easier to foster a relationship. Tell your audience who you are, why you are sending them the e-mail, and the benefits of the information you are sending. This is the most important distinction between spamming and direct e-mailing. Because the list you compile will consist of current customers and a specific target market, you can communicate with them in a manner not available through spamming. Nobody wants to feel as if they have been placed on a general e-mail list for distribution. Most people would rather read a personal message or something that is directed to their interests.

How can you determine if your marketing strategy is working? Web-hosting companies, such as Valueweb, provide statistical information on the amount of traffic coming to your site. Typically, these companies track the total amount of data transferred from your site, the total number of pages accessed on your site, and the pages on your site that are viewed most often and least often.

The true measurement of the Internet marketing success is not just generating traffic but turning traffic into sales.

Direct e-mail can be the most influential technique used to generate sales over the Internet. From our experiences direct e-mailing offers the most return for the time and money invested in your web site. Personalizing your message is essential, and anything you discuss must generate interest in your products and services. Be persistent. The more you communicate with your audience, the greater the chance they will become a customer.

Using Giveaways and Other Enticements

Companies can draw people in using that great four-letter F word, "Free." Free computers, free subscription, and free passwords are just some of the things offered online. Giveaways are a great way not only to pull people in, but also to make them loyal customers. Computer companies are now offering free personal computers to anyone who signs up for three years of Internet access. This strategy is similar to cell phones. Give away the hardware and make money on providing access.

Using Other Promotions

The Internet does not exist in a vacuum. People are directed to specific sites through more traditional advertising mediums such as television, radio, and print. You just have to watch a single half-hour television program to see how prevalent the Internet has become. Who hasn't heard William Shatner, a.k.a. James Tiberius Kirk of the USS *Enterprise,* preach about the benefits of Priceline.com? Almost every advertisement now includes some reference to the company's web page and e-mail address. Calvin Klein posts only its model's picture and e-mail address on CK One billboards. Everyone from the Big Three in the U.S. automotive industry to brand-new Internet startups are placing their web sites in front of the public. .COM fever is in full swing, and people are investing heavily in it.

Let's say you don't have half a million dollars for a thirty-second spot on the NFL Super Bowl. Don't worry, people want to give you money to become the next Amazon.com. Established companies such as Disney and Oracle as well as obscure venture-capital firms are investing heavily on people who have nothing except an idea in their head and a snazzy name followed by .COM. Disney and Earthlink Network came together to create ECompanies, an Internet incubator that provides financing, resources, and expertise to entrepreneurs in Southern California. ECompanies "expects entrepreneurs with nascent companies to apply for space in their incubator."

Oracle wants to lend a helping hand to anyone who will "promote innovation by companies developing products and services based on Oracle 8i." http://www.uk.oracle.com/info/news/jan99venture.html Oracle's helping hand amounts to a $100-million venture fund. According to Lawrence J. Ellison, Oracle chairman and CEO, "The next generation of business applications will be designed for and run on the Internet. Oracle plans to invest in and work closely with software companies that share this vision."

Offering What the Customer Needs

Great, now you know how to woo people to your site, but what are you going to do now that you have them there? Are you going to sell them a product or offer a service? How are you going to support these customers when there is a problem? This is where most Internet based companies fail. In the June 28, 1999 edition of the *Los Angeles Times* Business Section, Charles

Piller makes the point that "Most net retailers are all sale, no service." Piller is correct. He points out that "Web merchants have concentrated on capturing new customers rather than on satisfying them once they log on." He points out several high-profile e-companies that inadequately serve their customers. Buy.com is developing a reputation for not being able to deliver products and for changing advertised prices. Another example is eBay, the Internet's leading auction site. The site enrages users because of periodic system failures.

Most of these large e-commerce sites are based on the ideas of entrepreneurs with limited retailing experience. In certain instances it is fair to say that e-companies cannot handle the amount of business they generate. "Why not grow a site only when it can actually handle more traffic," asks Piller. He further points out the need for good communication. "Communicating with the customer is fundamental to retailing, and on the Internet people expect instantaneous responses." The *Industry Standard* surveys Internet users on behalf of e-commerce sites. According to their surveys of the top ten e-commerce sites, the average wait time for a response to an e-mail is a day and a half. Amazon.com responds the fastest with a blazing thirty-four minutes.

Like most people, we believe it is easier if you can have someone walk you through a new process such as buying a product online. Unfortunately most e-commerce sites want you to find the answer on your own by digging deeper into the web site. If you need information quickly and would like to call one of these companies, good luck finding a phone number. The reason is that the cost of employing customer-service agents is too expensive.

Poor service and even poorer communication leads to lost customers. In a recent Forrester study, Piller discovered that "more than half the consumers who had bad online buying experiences said that they abandoned the offending merchant, and fully half abandoned e-commerce altogether." An e-commerce site must first be a successful company. This includes providing superior service, good lines of communication, and high-quality products. Even if a company can generate one million hits a day, if it fails to deliver on any of these services it will not succeed.

Customer-Profile Data Collection

"You rarely see a site that learns customer sensibilities as a consumer," Charles Piller continues.

The Internet offers companies the ability to learn about their customers' desires. Companies can interact with customers by asking questions, recording answers, and developing new products to fit customer needs. For some reason the vast majority of companies completely ignore this opportunity. Nobody knows how to retrieve customer data effectively. That is not to say that these sites are not learning anything about customers. Sites use all sorts of data collection techniques such as

Textfield: <input type="text" name="textfield">

Buttons: <input type="submit" name="Submit" value="Submit">

Checkboxes: <input type="checkbox" name="checkbox" value="checkbox">

Radiobuttons: <input type="radio" name="radiobutton" value="radiobutton">

List menus: <select name="select"></select>

File fields: <input type="file" name="file" enctype="multipart/form-data">

These methods of data collection are best used for credit-card and shipping information. Sites are designed to get you in and out as soon as possible. On average most people visit three pages on a site. That translates into less than sixty seconds of time spent per web-page visitor. Data lines can handle thousands of people at a single site if necessary. What bricks and mortar store can make that claim? Web sites need to keep people in the site as long as possible.

Companies are beginning to understand the potential of the Internet by tapping its information-rich underbelly. The Internet moves consumer-information data. That data can be stored, databased, queried, analyzed, and interpreted. Java Cookies has a common technique for utilizing data over the Internet. Java Cookies, according to the popular Internet information source Webmonkey, are "bits of information that slip onto your hard drive, essentially without your knowledge, and track where and what you've done on a particular web site." Java is a program language developed by Sun Microsystems that can place a small "applet" of information onto the hard drive of someone visiting a web site. These applets can be extremely useful to store passwords, monitor page views, and establish user preferences. Most sites use applets today. If you would like to see which sites install these applets, you can set your browser to prompt you every time a web site is attempting to install an applet.

Applets will not destroy data on your hard drive. They can perform only two functions: read and write. The read function of applets allows you to record information on the user hard drive. If you go to your Windows Explorer there is a file buried in the "Programs Directory" called "Cookies." Here you can see all of the cookies that reside on your hard drive as a simple text file. Here's an example of a cookie.

"Netscape HTTP Cookie File
http://www.netscape.com/newsref/std/cookie_spec.html
This is a generated file! Do not edit.
www FALSE / FALSE 1293753600
        NETSCAPE_LIVEWIRE.CAPABILITIES 2:2::2::4::871::7::2::8
www FALSE / FALSE 1293753600
        NETSCAPE_LIVEWIRE.CAPABILITIES 2:2::2::4::885::7::2::8"

Under all of this exists information about the pages that the web-page viewer visited. The read function allows web pages to interpret these text files and make changes to their browser. Java cookies are extremely limited as to what they can accomplish. Reading and writing information is a step but not a complete solution.

Active Server Pages (ASP) is a new technology that promises to deliver more information about web-page visitors than ever before. It represents Microsoft's futurist approach to the Internet. Active Server Pages push dynamic information depending on the manipulations conducted by the server. In simple terms ASP allows the web server to change information that is sent to a web user. This can be extremely useful when targeting repeat visitors. If you visit a web site with a .asp extension in the URL you are at an Active Server Page. You can change your address in a database residing on the server by simply answering a few questions. For business, ASP promises to build user profiles that can be databased, queried, and interpreted. And the best part of ASP is the web visitors are the ones doing all of the work.

Building Relationships over Digital Lines by Offering Superior Service

"One thing I can tell you about [Internet retailing] is that customer loyalty is nonexistent," says Seymour Merrin, an industry consultant based in Santa Fe, New Mexico.

Customers are flocking to the Internet for one reason: to save money. Products online can be anywhere from 5% to 70% less expensive than in retail stores. Web retailers pass along savings to consumers by eliminating distribution channels and "bricks-and-mortar" outlets.

Comparison shopping online is as easy as clicking your mouse. The Internet allows people to easily compare prices at different stores. In the material world, this type of comparison shopping is time consuming and annoying. Combine this shopping ease with competitive price wars and the power has shifted into the hands of the consumer.

The Internet is already the most competitive business environment we have seen. Buy.com, Amazon.com, and thousands of other web retailers admit to huge financial losses. They believe it is essential to build a strong brand-name web presence right now. However, this strategy can easily backfire due to the incredible price wars and lack of customer loyalty.

Building a loyal customer base online requires the same steps as building a loyal customer base in the bricks-and-mortar world. Offering superior service will keep people coming back even if you are not the low-cost leader.

On-time delivery is only part of what it means to provide superior service. Business involves solving problems. Companies that can effectively solve these problems usually succeed. Online merchants need to treat web customers with even more care than businesses treat normal customers. If a customer registers a problem or complaint, the company needs to respond immediately to his or her needs.

CONCLUSION

No one is completely certain how to draw people to your site. It is a combination of many factors, all of which are not under your control. Here are our ten essential steps to Internet marketing.

1. Learn about your customers through software agents such as cookies and active server pages.
2. Register your web site with as many search engines as possible.
3. Reregister your web site with as many search engines as possible.
4. Integrate into the Internet community through chat rooms, newsgroups, and banner-exchange programs.
5. Target a specific market.
6. Devise a direct e-mail program.

7. Provide superior service by responding to your customers, meeting customer demands, and solving customer problems.

8. Raise capital for off-line advertising.

9. Continually update your site with new information.

10. Make it "free."

13D

ELECTRONIC BANKING AND PAYMENTS

Electronic banking and payments are an integral part of electronic commerce, which covers a wide area of business. Automation of business transactions is the primary goal of electronic commerce. Business-to-business and individual-to-business transactions, online payments for services and goods, electronic bills' payment, personal banking, and delivery of information are among the many other features of electronic commerce. Electronic commerce covers improving the quality of service for online selling of products and information via the Internet, the telephone, and private digital networks.

The most fundamental view of electronic commerce for business is effectively interacting customers and business partners. Businesses have been using private networks for business-to-business transactions. However, individual consumers are recent additions to the picture. Not only does the Internet enable businesses to reach out to their individual consumers, but it is also making the business-to-business transactions less expensive. Electronic commerce offers a number of long-term and short-term benefits—easier and faster servicing of the existing customer base, reduced paperwork, better tracking of customer needs and satisfaction, and feedback from customers. All these enable a business to expand into new markets quickly and service them efficiently, in addition to satisfying current customer needs.

UNDERSTANDING ELECTRONIC COMMERCE

Electronic commerce on the Internet is a relatively new area in the commerce arena. New systems are constantly being proposed and tried with varying levels of success. Many different companies, such as Microsoft (www.microsoft.com), IBM (www.ibm.com), Hewlett Packard (www.hp.com), Sun Microsystems (www.sun.com), Netscape (www.netscape.com), Cybercash (www.cybercash.com), and Verifone (www.verifone.com) are developing software that allow use of a web browser for electronic-commerce applications. Companies such as Intuit (www.intuit.com) in the area of personal finance and Charles Schwab (www.eschwab.com), Datek Online (www.datek.com), and E Trade (www.etrade.com) in the area of online stock trading are also contributing to the advancement of electronic commerce. Volume of stock traded online is growing, and online stockbrokers are offering better and faster service for a lesser price compared to traditional stock traders.

Another area of interest is the Secured Electronic Transaction (SET) protocol. Companies such as Visa (www.visa.com) and MasterCard (www.mastercard.com), in collaboration with software vendors, are proposing encrypted electronic transactions that protect the identity of the customer and prevent fraudulent usage.

Electronic Data Interchange (EDI), a protocol for business-to-business transactions over private networks, has been in use for some time. EDI is secure, and the transactions are real-time. However, the nature of EDI and the fact that it is used over private networks makes it expensive. The Internet, on the other hand, is far less expensive and can be used to reach a bigger audience.

THE BASICS OF ELECTRONIC BANKING

Electronic banking involves the gamut of financial transactions among financial institutions, individuals, corporations, and government. Among banking businesses, retail and investment businesses stand to benefit most from electronic commerce. In order to improve profitability, banking organizations are trying to control costs and reduce operating expenses. Technology and innovation are being used as the tools to achieve results. Computer networking, Internet, and business-analysis solutions are lowering service costs while still providing good customer service. Other factors for the change are computer literacy among consumers, consumer awareness, and explosion in PCs.

Large businesses have traditionally used computers for financial operations within and outside their organizations. However, with advances in technology even medium and small businesses are demanding electronic service from banking institutions previously enjoyed by large business only.

Proliferation of PCs in households is spawning another revolution in the personal- and home-banking area. The main services offered by any home banking system are access to the customer account, ability to transfer funds, pay bills, and download personal-account information. Proprietary bank dialup service lets customers connect to their banks over dial-up private connections. Use of off-the-shelf software to manage personal finances has increased in recent years. Web-based banking allows customers to connect to their banks over the Internet. Almost all major banks, for example, Bank of America (www.bofa.com) and Wells Fargo (www.wellsfargo.com), allow their customers to connect online and conduct their transactions.

ELECTRONIC PAYMENT

Electronic payment is an online financial exchange that takes place between a buyer and seller. An electronic payment is in many ways similar to a conventional physical payment. The exchange is usually a digital financial instrument that is backed by a bank or an intermediary. Financial transactions are expected to grow to 150 billion by 2002—an average annual growth rate of 12%. In comparison, paper transactions show an average annual growth of 2.5% for the same duration. The growth in electronic banking and commerce is fueled by

- Increase in number of Internet users
- Reduction in operational and processing cost due to improvements in technology
- Affordability of high-performance technology

Traditionally, businesses have made electronic payments with EDI or Electronic Fund Transfer (EFT). However, these have been limited to big players because of high administrative and technology costs forcing smaller operators to contend with conventional physical-payment methods. One other limiting factor has been the inability of the systems and protocols to handle small amounts of money. With lower technology cost and the advent of the Internet, these issues have been resolved. It is now possible to make small, immediate (real-time) payments for goods and services using a web browser.

One of the most important issues in all of electronic commerce is the security of transactions for customers and businesses. Many different techniques are being used currently to ensure that transactions and customers are protected. *Public-key cryptography, cipher text, symmetric encryption, digital signature, digital certificates,* and *spoofing* are some of the various methods used for protecting communication among different entities. *Firewalls, secure web servers,* and *virtual private networks* reduce the risks of outside attack on our systems.

Other Areas

Other areas of technology, such as *transactional commerce* and *web portals,* aid and enhance electronic commerce. Transactional commerce is the application of customer-specific information to guide transactions in real-time. It is the integration of real-time interactions of customers with their profile databases. Companies such as Amazon.com (www.amazon.com) integrate customer-specific information to track shipments dispatched through United Parcel Service and post information on real-time to customers.

FINANCIAL INTERMEDIARIES

Financial intermediaries are economic agents that stand between the parties of a contract and perform functions necessary to the fulfillment of a contract. Various intermediaries such as the *merchant server, payment-acquiring bank, issuing bank, credit-card processor, third-party processors, brokers, agents, traders,* and *mediators* are economic agents. A second category of intermediaries that are not economic agents but participate in e-commerce activities are *equipment providers, network-access providers, information-access providers,* and *web portals.*

A financial intermediary provides financial services toward the successful completion of an economic transaction. In the absence of an intermediary, a seller will be forced to identify and serve individual buyers resulting in decreased efficiency. Intermediaries play a vital role in e-commerce. They are as follows:

- Provide information to buyers on the existence and availability of products and services.
- Help buyers in identifying sellers.
- Provide an efficient means of exchanging information between buyers and sellers.
- Conduct and/or assist in the execution of electronic transactions.
- Provide after-sale support.

With an intermediary the process of identification of a service provider (financial or nonfinancial) becomes very easy. Intermediaries serve an integration function that provides value to both buyers and sellers. The need for an intermediary becomes pronounced when business is conducted over the Internet. Because of the spread and disparity of buyers and sellers, it becomes essential that intermediaries be used. As buyers we need to identify possible suppliers or service providers within our budget, satisfying our quality requirement and at our preferred location. We need to ensure that the financial transactions are secure and accurate. We want value for our money. On the other hand, sellers need to identify possible customers, offer quality service at reasonable cost, and ensure that transactions are secure and accurate. It is these critical intermediate functions of electronic commerce that intermediaries provide best.

IDENTIFYING BUYERS AND SELLERS

Web portals are search sites that contain a database of generic information on all subjects. Sites such as Netscape (www.netscape.com), Yahoo (www.yahoo.com), Infoseek (www.infoseek.com), Microsoft (www.msn.com), Excite (www.excite.com), Alta Vista (www.digital.altavista.com), and Lycos (www.lycos.com) provide these search services. These sites help identify products, services, articles, and web sites, among many others. By using these portal sites a customer can not only identify product and service providers, but also get information on the quality and cost of those products. Microsoft sites such as Car-Point (www.carpoint.msn.com) and Expedia (www.expedia.msn.com) offer quality information for specific types of products and services. At Carpoint a customer can view all kinds of information on different cars, vans, and SUVs (sports utility vehicles) based on search criteria. At Expedia customers can plan and make reservations for their next vacation.

Customers truly benefit when they quote the price they want to pay and the sellers decide if they want to provide the requested product or service at that price. Priceline (www.priceline.com), for purchasing air travel tickets and for buying cars online, offers such a service. Customers quote the price they want to pay, and depending on the availability they can get cheaper air-travel tickets.

EXECUTION OF TRANSACTIONS

Financial intermediaries execute economic transactions. They are responsible for *transaction management, chargeback and return, capture and settlement, inventory, accounting, fulfillment and authorization,* and *settlement.*

Intermediaries based on systems from First Virtual (www.firstvirtual.com), CyberCash, and Verifone are used for protection against merchant fraud. Some intermediaries issue digital certificates to firms that they use in identifying themselves. Figure 13D–1 shows the relationship between the bank and the customer.

CONVENTIONAL PAYMENTS SYSTEM

Payment is a financial exchange that takes place between a customer and a business entity. The instruments of these financial exchanges in a conven-

FIGURE 13D–1

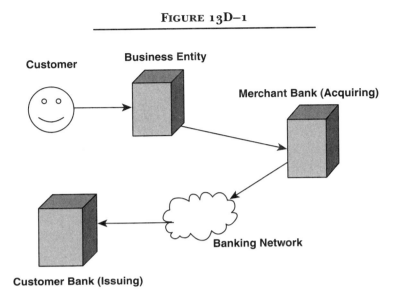

tional payment system are *cash, cashier's check, checks,* and *credit-card payment* over the counter or over the telephone. Although cash, cashier's check, and regular checks are the safest (in terms of safety of the financial exchange itself and not counting the physical safety of individuals involved), other means of conventional payments are by far less secure. Further, the payments themselves will not be real-time and there exists an inherent delay in the processing of the payment. This introduces a financial risk for the business entity. The sense of security that conventional payment systems have generated over time is very high. Offline-payment systems that demand physical presence are by far the safest. However, there are many problems with the traditional payment system.

Some of the issues are

- *Lack of convenience:* The need for physical presence—either in person or on the telephone—for both parties limit transactional freedom. For customers this translates into a delay in acquiring the product or service and results in higher cost, whereas for the seller the limiting factor introduces a loss of revenue (due to reduced or lost sales).

- *Non real-time payments:* Conventional payments are not real-time. The delay in actual realization depends on the type of payment. (For example, check payments may take anywhere up to one week, for credit-card payments it could be a couple of weeks.)

- *Lack of security:* Offline payments are less secure. Signatures can be forged, credit card numbers could be stolen, or merchants can commit fraud.

- *Higher cost of payments:* Each transaction costs a certain fixed amount of money. For smaller payments these costs barely cover the expenses and therefore make it unattractive.

After having said all these things about offline payments, we should realize that these payments are here to remain. The convenience offered by traditional payment systems for physical transactions will always be unmatched. We have seen some shifts in the introduction and use of check cards (debit cards) and electronic payment by traditional methods such as the use of credit cards over the telephone.

ELECTRONIC PAYMENT SYSTEM

Many modern-day payments are electronic in nature. *Automated-teller machines, online transactions—secure and nonsecure—electronic-fund transfer, credit-card authorizations and payments, check-card authorizations and payments,* and *electronic-check verification* use some form of electronic communication.

Electronic payments emerged with the simple concepts of wire-transfer. Human operators conducted these transfers with minimal verification and acknowledgments over private voice networks. Over time EFT graduated to using private digital networks and enabled banks and other organizations to reduce the fund-transfer time. Development of electronic payment mechanisms have concentrated on the following major areas:

- Minimizing banking cost
- Speeding up payment
- Minimizing fraud
- Improving customer satisfaction

The most notable feature of the modern-day electronic-payment system is user interaction. Earlier electronic-payment systems did not (and could not) allow end-user interaction, thereby increasing the cost of payment and the time for payment completion. With increasing user-interaction, the cost of making payments is coming down. This makes payment of smaller amounts, appropriately called micropayments, possible.

Consumers can use credit cards, digital cash, microcash, and electronic checks for making payments electronically.

CREDIT CARDS

Electronic payments with a credit card follow the same procedure as conventional credit-card payments. Customers present their credit-card number to the merchant. The merchant verifies the ability of the customer to make the payment with the bank or credit-card issuer and creates a purchase slip for endorsement. Eventually, the merchant uses this purchase slip to collect the payment for goods or services offered.

Now, however, the process is online and automated to a large extent. In an online scenario, the customer uses the web browser to fill in the transaction on an online order form. This form is processed by the web server, which forwards the authorization request to the bank. The bank then makes the payment to the merchant.

FIGURE 13D–2

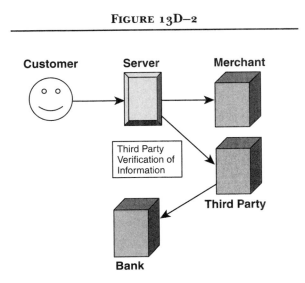

In a nonsecure transaction, all the data communication is plain text, and anyone snooping on the line can read the information. In a secure environment, all or parts of the information are encrypted—most important, the credit-card information. In order to protect the customers from possible credit-card fraud by everyone including merchants, we use a trusted third-party decryption of the credit-card numbers.

These third-party systems are available from First Virtual, CyberCash, or Verifone. CyberCash and Verifone both use helper applications called *Wallet* for the web browser. A wallet essentially encrypts the credit-card number and passes the encrypted number to a third-party server for verification. The merchant does not see the number at all. This is depicted in Figure 13D–2.

First Virtual issues a *VirtualPIN* to the customer, who then uses the PIN instead of the credit-card number. When FirstVirtual receives the PIN, it converts it to a credit-card number to clear the purchase.

ELECTRONIC CHECKING

Two firms—Financial Services Technology Corporation (FSTC) and CyberCash—have developed systems for letting customers use electronic checks to pay merchants. FSTC uses a format similar to the paper check. Electronically initiated, these checks are signed using a digital signature. FSTC allows different instruction mechanisms such as certified-check and electronic-charge slip that the customer specifies at the time of making the purchase. CyberCash uses an extension of their Wallet application. Unlike the credit-card processing, CyberCash does not handle the check payment itself; instead these are passed on to an electronic-payments handler.

In both cases, electronic checks are handled by an electronic-payments handler and distributed by the appropriate network. An electronic-payments handler could be a bank, clearinghouse, or any other financial agency authorized to process the payments.

DIGITAL CASH

Digital Cash, also called *e-cash,* is best suited for making real-time payments over the net. Setting-up and using digital cash is more complicated than using conventional cash. Banks issue what are called *tokens* to their customers. A token is an electronic object—much like a payment advice—with a unique serial number. Customers then use these tokens at the time of making purchases. Merchants present these tokens to the customer's bank for processing and payment. The bank handles these tokens as they would a physical check. The bank prevents reuse of these tokens by comparing the unique serial numbers.

The addition of *blind signature* (developed by DigiCash) to e-cash makes it look more like actual cash. The person holding the cash is not identified with the cash. E-cash with a blind signature attached has to be honored by the issuing bank as it has no knowledge of who tendered the payment.

A major advantage of digital cash, also called *microcash,* is the removal of financial intermediaries from smaller transactions. Merchants can make payment with digital cash for purchases or services over the net. Once merchants have enough digital cash (collected from customers), they can pay for purchases or services over the net using them. Or they can elect to convert their digital cash to regular cash by presenting it to the bank.

Some areas of using microcash could be the purchase of small online items such as an image, a sound clip, documents, and game sessions.

LEGAL AND BUSINESS ISSUES

It is important that we address the legal and business issues of electronic-banking and payments. Banking is a mature industry, closely monitored by the government. However, electronic payment is in the hands of consumers. Some of the issues are record keeping, proof of purchase, and privacy.

Record keeping and proof of purchase are the easiest to manage in an electronic environment. All transactions follow a series of stages and pass through a number of computers. It is possible to keep records at each significant processing computer and never delete these records. In the event of a lost record, it will be fairly simple to reconstruct the entire transaction and fill in the missing link.

In an electronic-transactions environment, it will be easy to invade the privacy of consumers. Since we can reconstruct transactions, purchases, spending, and receipts, privacy will have been given a great deal of thought. Privacy must also be maintained against eavesdropping on the wire.

As technology evolves and consumers become confident in the system, we should see an increase in electronic commerce. Legal and business issues will play a major role in the acceptance of these systems. For e-commerce to be successful, consumers must feel comfortable about privacy issues and be confident of their control over their finances. Ultimately, success of e-commerce is dependent on consumer satisfaction.

13F

INTRANETS AND EXTRANETS

Intranet utilization in corporate America is rapidly growing. Because Intranets use Internet technology, there is ready access to external data. In effect, Intranets are internal web sites. An Intranet is an important tool to use in business and is developed and used by the company itself. An Intranet is easy to install and flexible (what is developed for one platform may be used for others).

Corporate managers must have a knowledge of Intranet structure and organization because it relates to accounting, tax, audit, control, and security issues. Managers, customers, employees, stockholders, potential investors, creditors, loan officers, government-agencies representatives (SEC, IRS), and other interested parties can access the database or information in a company through web browsers (interfaces) such as Netscape Navigator and Microsoft's Internet Explorer. Management may set up an Intranet to improve operating efficiencies and productivity and to reduce operating costs (e.g., distribution expenses), time, and errors. Of course, keeping information on the Intranet current takes time and resources. Proper controls must be established to guard against unauthorized access of the company's data through the Internet. One security device is the use of firewalls (barriers) to protect the company's Intranet by unauthorized access and to prevent misuse of the Intranet by outsiders who might otherwise be able to alter accounting and financial information, steal property, obtain confidential data, or commit other inappropriate or fraudulent acts. Further, add-on security tools are available to restrict users by preventing them from performing certain acts, or from viewing certain "restricted" information.

THE INTRANET EXPLOSION

Information System (IS) and functional department managers quickly saw the power of this new communications medium as a resource to be leveraged on the corporate network. Forrester Research did a study finding that two thirds of large companies already had or are contemplating some use of Intranet business applications. Surveyed companies identified the Intranet as a powerful tool to make information more readily available within and outside the company.

With businesses under significant pressure to empower employees and to better leverage internal information resources, Intranets furnish an effective communications platform, one that is both timely and extensive. A basic Intranet can be set up in days and can eventually act as an "information hub" for the whole company, its remote offices, partners, suppliers, customers, investors, creditors, consultants, regulatory agencies, and other interested parties.

Intranets provide the following features:

- Easy navigation (internal home page provides links to information)
- Can integrate distributed computing strategy (localized web servers residing near the content author)
- Rapid prototyping (can be measured in days or even hours in some cases)
- Accessible via most computing platforms
- Scaleable (start small, build as requirements dictate)
- Extensible to many media types (video, audio, interactive applications)
- Can be tied into "legacy" information sources (databases, existing word-processing documents, groupware databases)

The benefits to these features are many, including

- An Intranet is inexpensive to start, requires minimal investment in dollars or infrastructure.
- Open-platform architecture means large (and increasing) numbers of add-on applications.

- A distributed computing strategy uses computing resources more effectively.

- An Intranet is much more timely and less expensive than traditional information (paper) delivery.

CALENDAR-DRIVEN VERSUS EVENT-DRIVEN STRATEGY

One of the key drivers in the Intranet adoption curve is that they allow businesses to evolve from a "calendar"——or "schedule"—based publishing strategy, to one of an "event-driven" or "needs-based" publishing strategy. In the past, businesses published an employee handbook once a year, whether or not policies changed to coincide with that publication date. Traditionally, even though these handbooks may have been outdated as soon as they arrived on the users' desks (and were promptly misplaced), they would not be updated until next year.

With an Intranet publishing strategy, information can be updated instantly. If the company adds a new mutual fund to the 401(k) program, content on the benefits page can be immediately updated to incorporate that change, and the company internal home page can have a brief announcement about the change. Then when employees refer to the 401(k) program, they have the new information at their fingertips. Content can be changed or updated to reflect new rules at any time.

ADVANTAGES OF INTRANET SYSTEMS

Intranets dramatically reduce the costs (and time) of content development, duplication, distribution, and usage. The traditional publication model includes a multistep process including creation of content, migration of content to desktop-publishing environment, production of draft, revision, final-draft production, duplication, and distribution.

The Intranet publishing model includes a much shorter process, skipping many of the steps involved in the 1S6 traditional publication model. In the Intranet model, revision becomes part of the updating process while the original content is available to end users, thus dramatically reducing the time it takes for the information to become available to the user. As the information is centrally stored and always presumed to be current, the company will not have to retrieve "old" information from employees, thus saving updating expenses.

This new publishing model significantly reduces both costs and the time frame. Assuming that the corporate Local Area Network (LAN) environment can support Intranet activities (and most can), the Information Technology (IT) infrastructure is already in place. Further, most popular Intranet web servers can run on platforms widely found in most companies (Intel 80486 or Pentium-class computers, Apple Macintosh, Novell NetWare, etc.), so that little if any additional infrastructure is required.

Organizations estimate that the traditional model may entail physical duplication and distribution costs as high as $15 per employee, costs separate from the content development or testing phases. An organization with 10,000 employees may find potential cost savings of moving to an Intranet policy for a single application alone—the employee policies and benefits manual—of $150,000. This cost savings does not even consider the additional value in an Intranet solution that makes information more easily available to staff, thus improving their productivity and morale.

PRACTICAL APPLICATIONS OF INTRANETS

The uses of Intranets (internal webs) by companies are unlimited, including

- Furnishing outside CPAs with accounting, audit, and tax information
- Providing marketing and sales information to current and prospective customers or clients
- Providing information to salespersons in the field and managers at different branches (e.g., sales and profit reports, product tracking, transaction analysis)
- Furnishing resource needs and reports to suppliers
- Communicating corporate information to employees, such as company policies and forms, operating instructions, job descriptions, time sheets, human-resource data and documents, business plans, newsletters, marketing manuals, phone directories, schedules, and performance reports
- Assisting in employee training, development, and technical support

- Transferring information to government agencies (e.g., Department of Commerce, SEC, IRS)
- Furnishing current and prospective investors with profitability, growth, and market-value statistics
- Providing lenders and creditors with useful liquidity and solvency data
- Providing project, proposal, and scheduling data to participating companies in joint ventures
- Providing press releases and product/service announcements
- Giving legal information to outside attorneys in litigation matters
- Providing trade associations with input for their surveys
- Accessing and searching databases and rearranging information
- Furnishing information to outside consultants (e.g., investment-management advisers, pension planners)
- Providing insurance companies with information to draft or modify insurance coverage
- Allowing for collaborative workgroups such as letting users access various drafts of a specific project document interactively and adding annotations and comments (for example, Ford's Intranet links design engineers in the United States, Europe, and Asia)
- Furnishing economic statistics about the company to economic advisers
- Facilitating database queries and document requests
- Providing spreadsheets, database reports, tables, checklists, and graphs to interested parties
- Displaying e-mail

Site maps (e.g., Table of Contents) should be included so users may easily navigate from each note (element) visible through frames or panels.

An Intranet requires web application development for its internal network such as appropriate web servers. For quick response time, there should be a direct connection to the server. Web browsers may be used to achieve cross-platform viewing and applications for a wide variety of desktops used within the company. The use of web technology (e.g., web servers) allows each desktop having a web browser to access corporate information over the existing network. Therefore, employees in different divisions of the company located in different geographic areas (e.g., buildings) can access and use centralized and/or scattered information (cross-section).

There are many client/server applications within and among companies such as cross-platform applications. The major element in an Intranet is the web-server software, which runs on a central computer and serves as a clearinghouse for all information. Web servers for the Intranet are available from many vendors, including

- IBM (800-426-2255): Internet Connection Server for MVS
- Microsoft (800-426-9400): Internet Information Server (comes with Microsoft's NT Server)
- Netscape (415-528-2555): Fast Track and Commerce Server for Windows NT
- Lotus (800-828-7086): InterNotes Web Publisher
- CompuServe (800-848-8199): Spry Web Server for Windows NT
- Quarterdeck (800-683-6696): Web Server and Web Star for Windows NT

The advantages of the Microsoft's Windows NT Server are higher security and easier capability to upgrade to more powerful hardware at a later date, as application needs increase.

Further, there are many Intranet tool vendors such as Illustra Information Technologies (http://www.illustra.com), telephone number (510)652-8000, and Spider Technologies (http://www.w3spider.com), telephone number (415)969-7149. For example, Frontier Technologies' Intranet Genie is an Intranet tool that includes a fairly secure web server, HTML authoring instructions and guidelines (discussed here), web browser, and e-mail functions. Regardless of the operating system (e.g., Windows, UNIX, Macintosh), many Intranet tools are available.

HYPERTEXT MARKUP LANGUAGE (HTML)

The Hypertext Markup Language (HTML) should be used in developing Intranets because it is an easier Graphical User Interface (GUI) to program than windows environments such as Motif or Microsoft Windows.

HTML is a good integrating tool for database applications and information systems. It facilitates the use of hyperlinks and search engines, enabling the easy sharing of identical information among different responsibility segments of the company. Intranet data usually go from back-end sources (e.g., mainframe host) to the web server to users (e.g., customers) in HTML format.

COMMON GATEWAY INTERFACE (CGI)

The majority of web applications run through a mechanism in the web server referred to as the common gateway interface (CGI). CGI is used to connect users to databases. Most CGI programs are written in TCL or Pert (a scripting language). Due to the fact that these languages involve printing a source code of the web server, however, there is an unsecured situation from a control-and-security standpoint. Other deficiencies are relative slowness in applications, nonexistent or inadequate debuggers, and maintenance problems. Consider other languages for the CGI such as C or C++.

The following CGI business applications are recommended:

1. In developing web applications for Intranets, code-management tools are needed to enable different participants in a corporate project or activity to communicate and work together. You must also use tools for database design, modeling, and debugging. In this connection, the following web sites, among others, provide helpful information to corporate managers:

   a. Basic HTTP
      (http://www.w3.org/hypertext/www/protocols/http/http2.html)
   b. HTML Browser List
      (http://www.w3.org/hypertext/www/clients.html)
   c. Web Server Comparison Chart
      (http://www.proper.com/www/servers-chart.html)
   d. HTML Specs from the WWW Consortium
      (http://www.w3.org/hypertext/www/markup/markup.html)
   e. Introduction to CGI
      (http://www.ncsa.uiuc.edu/docs/cgi:/overview.html)

2. Do not commit to a particular server or browser because new technological developments require flexibility. Set up your system so that it may accommodate many servers and browsers.

3. Make sure your HTML-user interface is separate from the database and application logic.

SETTING UP AN INTRANET

Intranet applications are scaleable—they can start small and grow. This feature allows many businesses to "try out" an Intranet pilot—to publish a limited amount of content on a single platform and evaluate the results. If the pilot looks promising, additional content can be migrated to the Intranet server.

Proposed Content

Companies must ascertain if data should be made available via a web server, via e-mail, or by some other means. If the data are of general import, such as company travel guidelines or mileage reimbursement, it can be posted on a web server so that when employees and travel agents, among others, require this information, they click on Travel Guidelines from the human-resources page and obtain the most current information.

Many businesses find building web interfaces to "legacy information" a key application. With tools such as Purveyor's Data Wizard, HTML Transit, and WebDBC, end users can build simple point-and-click access to this legacy information without any programming, making it available to nontechnical users through their web browser. Key database applications include customer records, product information, inventory, technical-problem tracking, call reports, and so forth. In addition, individuals can quickly set up seminar or training-registration forms for short-term usage, loading the registrants' information into an easily manipulated database.

Conversely, interoffice e-mail may be more appropriate for "interrupt-driven" time-sensitive information, especially for a focused group of recipients: "Our most important customer is coming in March 2, so please attend the briefing at 9 a.m." In this case, the web server can be used as an extended information resource: "Before the meeting, check the internal web-server link for Current Customers for updated information concerning this account."

Business Enhancements

Intranets can provide efficient access to other external information resources including group access to mailing lists, threaded discussion groups, and stock/bond quotes. In this way, the oft-accessed information can be aggregated at the firewall and efficiently dispersed within the company, thus reducing external bandwidth and connectivity requirements.

Multithreaded discussion-group software, or conferencing applications, can run on the same platform as the Intranet application, providing further chances to discuss company issues and the content that resides on the server.

Comparing Intranets to Groupware

Intranets and groupware are not mutually exclusive. Many companies find that groupware (work flow, collaborative computing, etc.) is appropriate for certain focused applications, while Intranets are suitable for migrating existing content to online delivery. Others find a powerful combination in groupware and a web server (Lotus InterNotes engine for publishing "Notes" databases on the web, for example).

Ultimately, each application strategy has its merits. Beyond this, Intranet applications and web servers make an excellent foundation for web-based groupware, allowing businesses to employ a web-centric Intranet system strategy and leverage the nearly ubiquitous web browser and the powerful navigational aids provided by HTML.

SETTING UP EXTRANETS

An *Extranet* is an extended Intranet creating virtual private networks among companies, business partners, and clients. It allows Intranets to interact. Security provides the appropriate level of access to users. The key point is that all three "nets"—Internet, Intranet, and Extranet—use the same technology. The only difference among them is who has access to what. The goal is to have access to what you need no matter where you are at any time of the day or night. No matter where you are when you log in, things should work the same way.

Intranets and Corporate Finance

The use of Intranets should be for corporate real-time decision support. The true competitiveness of a firm is determined by the ability of its management to make accurate, timely decisions that improve profitability and long-term prospects. To make these decisions, an organization must possess knowledge about various customers, products, and suppliers, the availability of assets, the status of commitments, and the profitability of activities.

While most companies have sophisticated transaction systems that collect operational data, the information that managers require for decision-making and performance-measurement purposes is not readily available. The challenge remains in how tremendous amounts of corporate financial data will be transformed into useful information. The problem is that there are too much data and not enough meaningful information. Firms need to access certain information with which to make smart decisions without the clutter of data. Why? Because developing a response to an emerging business situation means sifting through large amounts of data from business units or product lines. To enable large-scale data analysis, firms are increasingly using online analytical processing (OLAP).

The problem is not limited to tools for analyzing the data. Accuracy, timeliness, and accessibility of the data are also important. With management facing increasing pressure to make profitable decisions faster, they need to be free of the constraints of time and space to access distributed data from their office, home, or the road, at all hours of the day and night. The next generation of Intranet applications will be required to provide access to the full range of corporate data to make strategic decisions. This might involve developing software "intelligent agents" that pull together information from a variety of relational and legacy systems at regular intervals to construct an integrated view of business activities. These agents then transform the data into a consistent, easily accessible format and distribute it where needed for decision making (see Figure 13E–1).

This section looks into the role of Intranets in financial management and how it can allow companies to deal with all their financial information and what role it plays in the financial information-management process.

FIGURE 13E–1
DISTRIBUTED COMPUTING ENVIRONMENT

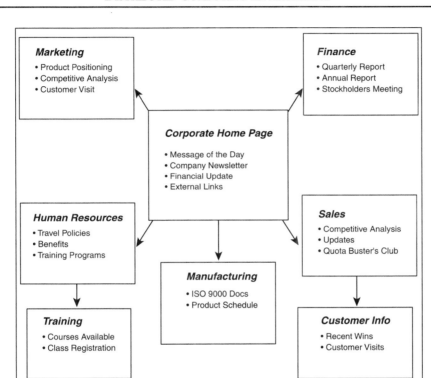

Summarized here are the business problems faced, their solution, and their benefits after the solution is applied:

Business Problems

- Nonintegrated islands of valuable information
- Nonintegrated financial and accounting applications
- Need for analysis tools and decision support for management

Solution

- Fully integrated web-based enterprise-wide financial and accounting infrastructure

Benefits

- Integrated information across business functions
- Improved data analysis and decision support
- Cost savings from increased efficiency

The competitive business environment is forcing firms to reengineer financial-management processes. General-ledger systems and spreadsheets alone prove inadequate when data are voluminous and worldwide, when corporate structures change because of mergers and acquisitions, and when timely and reliable consolidations, budgets, and forecasts are essential.

A definition of exactly what financial systems are is required to establish the setting. Financial systems encompass business processes, procedures, controls, and data dedicated to the operation and maintenance of corporate financial objectives. They incorporate reporting and analyzing financial data, simplifying the budgeting and forecasting process, enabling better planning and controlling of the financial consolidation of actual results, answering *ad hoc* requests efficiently, and improving cost control and performance measurement. Financial systems are often triggered by events facing financial consequences such as receipt of appropriations or other financial resources, acquisition of goods or services, payments or collections, recognition of guarantees, benefits to be provided, potential liabilities, or other reportable financial activities. In technical aspects, financial systems usually have the following characteristics: a common database, common data-element definitions, and standardized processing for transactions. A financial system includes multiple applications that are integrated through a common database or are interfaced to meet defined data and processing requirements.

For software developers to succeed in understanding the new business requirements that are emerging, in terms of functionality rather than technical architecture, they need to address the business issues and requirements, and not conversely. A review of what financial and accounting systems set out to do is in order. Accounting captures a firm's financial data, records and aggregates them, and statements are prepared that communicate to decision makers necessary information about business units, transactions, and events. The early accounting system processed transactions, stored historical information, and used that information to answer questions about the past, present, and future. Today's accounting systems are a collection of methods for capturing and transforming financial data. An important aspect about accounting is to report the financial position of the firm and the performance of various business units to facilitate decision making. The accounting system is usually broken up into two types: financial and management accounting. Financial accounting collects, classifies, and reports financially based transactions subject to numerous disclosure requirements. The reports are used by external sources such as shareholders, investors, creditors, financial analysts, and the IRS. Financial accounting activities in the report include collecting, processing, maintaining, transmitting, and reporting data about financial events; supporting financial planning or budgeting activities; and supporting the preparation of financial statements.

Management accounting provides a financial analysis of management decisions and activities. The reports generated by the management-accounting system are used by organizations internally. These reports prepare the report card by which operations managers are evaluated. Compared to financial accounting, management accounting is fairly new, having evolved from simple cost-accounting systems. Management-accounting activities include reporting historical transactions to internal and external parties, accumulating and reporting cost information, safeguarding the assets of a company, and providing insight with respect to the value of future transactions.

Financial Intranets

Finance and accounting software have typically been characterized as dull and not trendsetting. Accounting software, for instance, provided a way to enter transactions and manage those transactions in the form of an audit trail. The primary focus of accounting software was transaction entry and back-office management of the audit trail, critically important but not very exciting.

Today there is a lot more that business managers need from the information locked inside accounting databases. In short, the information is there but it is very difficult to obtain. Intranets can play a big role in solving this problem because they will allow the integration necessary to provide accounting information that managers need, in the specific form they need it, when they need it, and where they need it.

Well-managed companies watch their financial records carefully and set clear objectives for their managers. Providing access to important financial information securely and in an easy-to-use, online manner is a top priority. By using internal web applications, finance departments can more easily disseminate this information to key managers by securely "posting" corporate-finance information or by providing simple forms-based query capabilities. This will allow information to take the form of hundreds of specific views rather than one general view or report, such as the typical set of financial statements.

New systems technologies offer integration and make it possible for information to be put into a system once and moved to all the different places. This frees accountants from having to spend time manually moving information from one place to another because there was no other way to accomplish the task. Accountants need to recognize the inevitable changes technology is going to bring about and must look for new ways to add value to the business. This value must be in alignment with the needs of the business process.

Finally, large financial systems developed in the era of mainframes have become too costly to maintain, troublesome to document, inefficient, ineffective, or even strategically dangerous as they are difficult to change as business conditions evolve. Deloitte and Touche conducted a study of senior-level financial and accounting executives at 200 corporations. The report reveals that 68% of the respondents stated they plan to implement a new system within the next two years. From this group, 80% intend to purchase packaged solutions and 64% prefer client/server hardware platforms. These statistics reveal that systems based in new technology are well positioned to benefit from a major surge in demand expected to occur over the next few years. The rapid growth of Intranet accounting applications has been attributed partly to a replacement-cycle phenomenon. It's estimated that the average enterprise general ledger in a Fortune 100 company is believed to be about fifteen to seventeen years old. Virtually all of these are running on mainly IBM mainframes. A significant majority are internally developed applications. Replacement of these applications is being driven by high maintenance costs and the desire to enable accounting to provide decision-support data and facilitate business-process reengineering.

The Purpose of Financial Intranets

Successful Intranet implementations should help tackle four problems that existing systems are not equipped to handle: production control, the effect on short-term and long-term strategy from daily operations, cost control, and the lack of control over report-generating.

With the increasing amount of global sourcing, financial flows related to production are becoming more complicated. Currently, managers rely on a patchwork of systems to support financial-management activities, such as accounts payable, accounts receivable, fixed-asset management, purchasing, and general ledger. These systems worked well when their primary responsibility was to collect and present historical information. Not surprisingly, most of these systems are equipped to handle only routine transactions, and little consideration is given to their connection to other business activities. For example, if the general ledger and the procurement systems were linked through an integrated information process, the financial analyst would have an accurate picture of accounts payable. By integrating financial functions into decision making, the organization can assess the financial consequences of its strategic and operational decisions on a timely and accurate basis, regardless of the type of decisions or where they are made.

While many financial systems are found to be "just adequate" for accounting purposes, they often fail to give requisite operating information to line managers or provide performance information to senior management on a timely basis. To be useful, strategic information must be compiled from the overabundance of operational data being stored; overnight batch reports are no longer sufficient. Managers need to operate with a bigger role in modeling the whole business operation. The ability to construct queries on the fly and to quickly ask follow-up questions that drill deeper into the data with each successive query is necessary to allow managers to better understand the business environment before making critical decisions. Changing market conditions and specific business situations, such as inventory levels and detailed analysis of customers' behavior, can point analysts down potentially profitable paths that they could not have anticipated. For it to succeed in doing so, the systems should be developed to help managers make better strategic decisions.

New technology must be used to achieve better cost control. As businesses in the 2000s focus on downsizing and cost control as a means to survive, there is a growing need for faster, more accurate, and more useful information that allows companies to perform better financial management. In more cases than not, this is easier said than done. Many companies, especially those that are large or highly decentralized, are finding it difficult to get at the information they need to effectively manage their business. These companies are often restrained by their inflexible legacy systems and an environment surrounded by nonstandardization, creating difficulties in simple reorganization, much less in using their financial information for better management in a rapidly changing world.

In regard to the lack of control in report generating, managers are faced with problems associated with bottlenecking. The report-generating process often has difficulty integrating all the data required to make a comprehensive and informative assessment for managers to work with, often with high price tags to suit. As companies become more widespread and powerful, the balance of data-processing power has shifted away from central-information systems staffs to individuals in functional departments. By tying together desktop computers, inexpensive Intranets enable businesses to integrate their information systems to a greater extent than was previously possible.

Clearly, the need for integration is a key driver of the financial Intranet marketplace. Many organizations are planning to integrate their accounting systems into their networks over the next several years. Financial executives desire the ease of use and timeliness that this will afford. Information-systems managers, faced with scarce resources, believe this will smooth out system development and management processes, saving time and money.

Financial Analysis and Management Accounting

While managing the transaction aspects of financial flows is important, there exists another facet, namely using financial information for control purposes. The area of financial management that is essential to support the operations and strategy of the company is called management accounting. Management accounting typically includes business planning, decision making, budgeting, and controlling, including overhead-cost management, activity-based costing, product-cost controlling, and sales-and-profit analysis.

Gathering data for management accounting is quite challenging, as few companies maintain a single, integrated set of records for all their divisions and the departments within them. In practice, to consolidate their data, companies tie together data from many sources, including databases and spreadsheets. Bringing data together for periodic accounting, reporting, and budgeting has been difficult. The process adds to the time and cost required to perform consolidations at the end of a period, as well as to create and track budgets and forecasts. At the functional level, consolidation can provide the finance organization independence from the central IS organizations with a set of applications that are powerful but easy to use. This includes support for management accounting and cost accounting.

Once the data are gathered, financial-analysis tools enable people with authorized access in the organization to find the data they need, drill down as necessary, and see the results in seconds, without waiting for MIS or even corporate accounting's involvement. This information is meant not only for executives, but also for a broader set of people who want to make better decisions on a daily basis.

Online Analytical Processing (OLAP)

Analytical tools, called OLAP, transform the corporate-data warehouse information into strategic information. For instance, users of financial-data warehousing applications want better access and analysis of the data contained in the database archives. OLAP tools range from basic navigation and browsing to a multifaceted analysis of corporate data.

OLAP applications offer the advantage of spanning to a variety of organizational functions. Finance departments use OLAP for applications such as budgeting, activity-based costing, financial-performance analysis, and financial modeling. Managers use these tools to perform *ad hoc* analysis of data in multiple dimensions, thereby giving them the insight and understanding they need for better decision making. OLAP lets managers probe and access corporate data in bits and pieces, rather than by traditional means of query. This method gives the manager consistently fast access to a wide variety of views of data organized by criteria that match the real dimensions of the modern enterprise.

OLAP uses a multidimensional view of aggregate data to provide quick access to strategic information for further analysis. The key feature is the ability to transform data into so-called multidimensional form. These views are inherently representative of an actual business model. Managers typically look at financial data by scenario, organization, product-line items, and time; and at sales data by product, geography, channel, and time. Database design should not prejudice which operations can be performed on a dimension or how rapidly those operations are performed. Managers must be able to analyze data across any dimension, at any level of aggregation, with equal functionality and ease. OLAP software should support these views of data in a natural and responsive fashion, insulating users of the information from complex query syntax. After all, managers shouldn't have to understand complex computer languages to use OLAP.

CONCLUSION

The role of Intranets in supporting management is to meet their needs in acquiring comprehensive and timely business information. A company's accumulated data constitute a valuable resource, and in most organizations, those in charge are very aware of this fact, yet it is equally clear that the approach of simply collecting data has serious shortcomings. It neither succeeds in presenting data to corporate decision makers in a form they can understand and use, nor permits easy access to information.

Incompatible accounting and information systems are causing management tremendous problems. In the past companies have attempted to support financial-information systems by using mainframes that have been rigid in structure, expensive to maintain, and difficult to update when business requirements change. At the other end of the spectrum, firms generate business reports by assembling them manually by using spreadsheets and data from general ledgers and other operating systems. This approach would be incapable of handling large volumes of data primarily because it would require extensive data rekeying and manual consolidation. In addition, spreadsheets have limited capabilities for information sharing and lack the necessary control to ensure corporate consistency.

As business requirements have changed, there has been an increasing push toward the ability to analyze amounts of data in real-time. This enables management to look at different scenarios and make decisions in hours rather than in weeks. Inevitably, broad access to data and to the analytic tools that ease the analysis of the data will change the face of decision making. The speed and ease with which analysis can be completed and the inclusion of up-to-the-minute and on-the-fly accurate data are powerful competitive weapons.

Intranet technology can aid in the collection, aggregation, and consolidation of business information from fragmented computer systems and transactional databases in a number of ways, and in many cases Intranet developments will replace existing systems with more efficient alternatives.

Intranet applications can start as small "pilots" and scale upward over time, gradually providing or facilitating access to an increasing breadth of information, thus improving both employee productivity and satisfaction and eventually bolstering the company's competitive position.

13F

THE WEB AND DATABASE MANAGEMENT SYSTEMS*

This chapter covers the technologies that are required to integrate the database application with the web platform. However, before going to those parts, we present the brief fundamental concepts of the Internet, the client/server architecture, and the web architecture. Furthermore, the advantages and disadvantages of the web as a database platform, compared to the client/server platform are also presented. By presenting so, you will understand the reason why the web as a database platform is the remarkable topic for most developers and users nowadays.

THE WEB

The Internet is "a world-wide collection of interconnected computer networks providing many kinds of services such as electronic mail, remote access, World Wide Web (Web), etc." The web is "a hypermedia-based system that provides a simple point and click means of browsing information on the Internet using hyperlink."

Because the web provides a simple point and click, it is easy to use, making the web overwhelmingly successful nowadays. It consists of a network of computers that perform two roles. The first is a server-role, which provide information, and the other is a client-role, which acts as browsers to request information.

---

*This chapter was coauthored by Suttapon Kantanantha, a Long Beach, CA-based computer consultant.

247

Information on the web is stored in the HTML document format: the systematic format for marking up and publishing a document on the web. The document and locations within the document are identified by the address called Uniform Resource Locators (URL): a string of characters that represents the location or address of a resource on the Internet and how that resource should be accessed.

In other words, URL uniquely specifies where a document is located. At the client side, the browsers must understand and interpret HTML to display the document. To control the exchange of information between the web server and the browser, a protocol is needed. The protocol for the web is the Hypertext Transfer Protocol (HTTP): a generic object-oriented, stateless protocol to transmit information between server and client. HTTP is based on request and response processes consisting of these stages:

Connection: The client establishes a connection with the web server.

Request: The client sends a request message to the web server.

Response: The web server sends a response (HTML document) to the client.

Close: The connection is closed by the web server.

THE WEB AS A DATABASE APPLICATION PLATFORM

The prior section described the fundamental concept of the Internet and the web. In this section, we shall explain the concept of the database and its system architectures. Also, we shall explain the concept of integrating the web platform and the database application to be the web as a database application platform.

Database applications usually consist of four components: the database, the transaction logic, the application logic, and the user interface. In the past when most organizations used the mainframe platform, called centralized business environment, all of those components were in one mainframe computer. However, the business environment has changed. It needed the decentralized business environment that makes the system flexible to develop, operate and less expensive than that of the mainframe system. Therefore, the client/server platform was developed and now is the most popular platform most organizations deploy.

THE CLIENT/SERVER PLATFORM

The client/server system first had a two-tier architecture (see Figure 13F-1) that consisted of a client-tier and a server-tier performing different functions. The client-tier performs both user interface and business and data-processing logic functions. The server-tier or a database server performs data service functions, which are a server-side validation and a database access, to serve the client-tier requests. However, the need for enterprise scalability has changed the two-tier architecture model. During the middle 1990s many application developers realized that the applications became more complex and the client-tier incurred two main problems. The first problem was a "fat client" requiring considerable resources on the client-tier to run perfectly. The other problem was a considerable client-tier administration overhead.

To solve those problems, the three-tier client/server architecture (see Figure 13F-1) has been developed by adding one middle tier, the application server-tier. With the new architecture, the client-tier performs only the user interface functions and lets the application-tier perform business logic and data processing logic functions. Still, the database server tier performs the same function as it does in the two-tier architecture (Figure 13F-1). In

FIGURE 13F-1
THE 2-TIER ARCHITECTURE

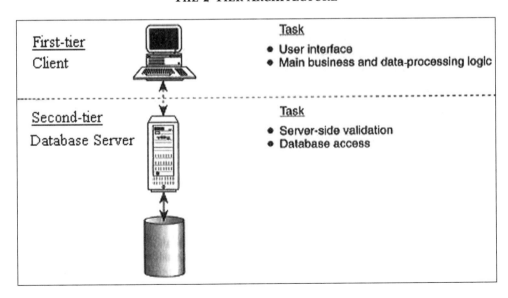

this architecture, the client-tier would not be a fat client any more, since it has moved all required resources to the application server. When developers need to upgrade the application, they can deploy the software only at the application server, thus dramatically reducing the administration overhead.

THE WEB PLATFORM

The three-tier client/server architecture (Figure 13F-2) is quite similar to the web environment. The web browser is in the client-tier and is acting as a thin client. A web server is performing the function as an application server. In addition, the three-tier can be extended to n-tiers to provide more flexibility and scalability. For instance, the second tier can be split into two: one is a web server function and the other is an application server.

FIGURE 13F-2
THE 3-TIRE ARCHITECTURE

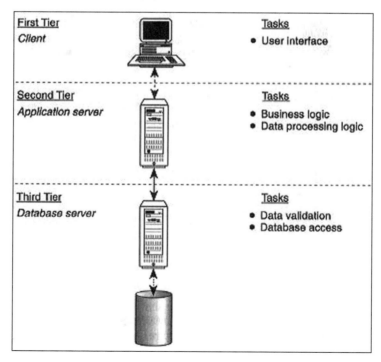

Advantages and Disadvantages of the Web as a Database Platform

Although the web as a database platform nowadays is suitable for the current inter- and intra-business environment, there are some advantages and disadvantages making developers hesitate whether to deploy the web platform.

Advantages

- **Standardization:** Since HTML is a *de facto* standard for all web browsers, it allows an HTML document on one machine to be shown on any web browser of any computer platform.

- **Platform independent:** The web-based version of a database application is highly platform independent. Web browsers use a standard HTML or Java, therefore, whichever operating system the client-tier uses, the application does not require modification to run on the different operating system. In contrast, the traditional database clients require extensive modification to port them to run on the different operating system.

- **Cross-platform support:** Because web browsers are available in almost every type of computer platform, they allow users on most types of computers to access a database from anywhere in the world. As a result, information can be disseminated with minimum of time and effort, without having to resolve the incompatibility problems of different hardware, operating systems, and software.

- **Transparent network access:** The web has the outstanding benefit of virtually transparent network access from users, except the specification of a URL. This benefit simplifies the database access. It eliminates the need for expensive networking software and the complexity of accessing data on the different platform.

- **Scalable deployment:** By storing the application on a separate server instead of clients, the web eliminates the overheads associated with application deployments. It simplifies the processes of upgrading and the administration of managing multiple platforms in an organization.

- **Innovation:** The web enables a new business service. Businesses can provide a new kind of service and reach new customers through applications that can be accessed globally.

Disadvantages

- **Immaturity of development tools:** Nowadays this issue is one of the major disadvantages that make developers hesitate to go to the web database platform. Tools that are available in the market now are not mature. There are many competing technologies and it is not clear about which technology should be the industry standard. In addition, there are no real guidelines about which technology will be better for one application than another.

- **Security:** This issue is the major concern for organizations, because it allows their database to be accessible on the web. Any potential anonymous users can access the databases, user authentication, secure data transmission, and any other security system thatare critical.

- **Performance:** Because the web browser is the interpreted language, it works slower than a traditional database client that uses a compiled language. A complied language is compiled once when developed and is not compiled anymore. For a time-critical application, the overhead of interpreted languages may be a great concern.

EXTENDING THE WEB SERVER BY WEB PROGRAMMING

As can be seen from the previous section, the web as a database platform seems to attract many application developers because of scalable deployment and platform independence. This greatly benefits system developers and the organization in the long run. Also, the disadvantages of the web will be overcome as technologies are improved.

However, a web-base application requires web programming to enhance its ability to handle the complexity of an application program. Generally, web technologies such as HTML are used to improve the structure and presentation of web pages. However, these technologies provide only a static web page: The content of the document does not change if the HTML file itself does not change. In reality, we need the dynamic web page: The content of a dynamic web page is generated each time it is accessed. It

Figure 13F-2
The Web Programming Technologies: Client-Side and Server Side

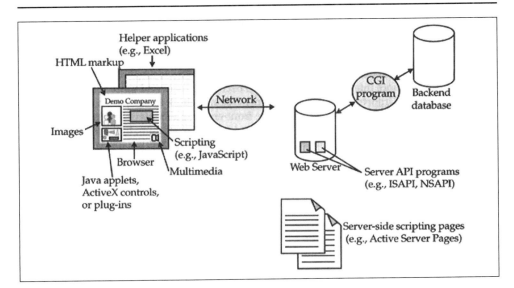

is because of that the dynamic web page performs a task similar to application software such as responding to user requests and being able to customize pages for particular users.

Nowadays, web sites are becoming more and more software-like as web programming technologies have been developed. web programming can be grouped into two basic groups: the client-side and the server-side (see Figure 13F-3). The client-side technologies are programs running on the web browser of client computers. The server-side technologies are programs running on the server called "server-side programming." Both server-side and client-side technologies are complementary. For example, to create a form on a web site to collect and store data in a database, it makes sense to verify data on the client-side to make sure that the user inputs the correct information. This reduces the network round-trip to the server just to check the input data. On the other hand, to put the data in the database, it would be best handled by server-side technologies.

Furthermore, to link a web server with a database server, the web-base system needs intermediate system software to link the web server and the database server. The intermediate system software that has a high potential to be the industry standard are JDBC from Sun Microsystems, ADO from Microsoft, and NCA from Oracle.

SERVER-SIDE PROGRAMMING

Server-side programming is the program running on a server. Examples of server-side programming technologies are CGI Scripts, Server API Program, server-side script such as Active Server Page (ASP), and ColdFusion. Each technology has its own advantages and disadvantages. However, all forms of the server-side technology share one common characteristic—control. The server is really the only part of a web platform that the developer has real control over. Server-side programs do not depend on any client-side variations. Therefore, theoretically, a site using interactivity running on the web server can deliver pages to any type of web browser.

One important thing about server-side programming is that most of the high-traffic sites rely mainly on server-side technology to develop interactive elements. This is why the major disadvantage of server-side programming is speed. Since all the interactivity takes place on the server, the users may incur delays because of a poor server response time or a network round-trip time.

As a result, a server-side program must be well designed to improve response time and to ensure that it can handle the volume of access well. We can calculate a capacity plan. For example, if you know that your web page takes 3 seconds to build and is 50K in size, you can calculate the number of simultaneous users that can be handled with 1Mbps of bandwidth.

The following are the details of server-side programming technologies.

Common Gateway Interface (CGI)

CGI, the oldest version of server-side programming, is a standard, portable, and modular method for supporting application-specific functions. Its definition is a standard way of passing data into an external program through the use of HTTP methods, which is the "Get" and "Post" method, environment variable, and passing any results back to the appropriate headers in a format that the browser can understand. A CGI program is executed in real-time so that it can create a dynamic information web page. Also, the CGI program can be written in any language that can be used on the server executing program such as C/C++, Fortran, PERL, TCL, any Unix shell, Visual Basic, and AppleScript.

To choose the CGI programming language, we should choose the language that is fast, portable, and appropriate for the web server running the program. Furthermore, the developers can write and maintain the program well.

Since a CGI program is executable by any user in the Internet, there is concern when using the CGI Program—the security. The CGI programs must be placed in a specific directory, "/cgi-bin," since the directory is usually under control of the webmaster who prohibits other users to create or modify any CGI program in the server. Also, the web server can locate and execute the CGI programs in that directory.

However, a CGI program has long been regarded as a slow execution program, since the CGI program is written in a relatively slow interpreted language such as PERL. Therefore, a serious web server needs a better server-side programming language.

Server Application Programming Languages (Server APIs)

Server APIs are developed to eliminate the problem of CGI programs. But, server APIs are bound to the particular web server software. For example, Netscape offers the API, called NSAPI, Microsoft offers the API, called ISAPI, and Apache Servers offers Apache modules. These API programming solutions provide better performance than that of a CGI and offer tight integration with the particular web server software.

In reality, server-side API programs are too complex and expensive for many development projects. However, API-oriented solutions are faster and more robust than those of a CGI program. In addition, developing software for a particular server API will lock the application into that server platform. When the developers are changing the server platform, all codes must be rewritten in the new API program. The developers must trade-off the pros and cons between the CGI- and the server API-oriented solution. The most common idea is that the developers usually use the API program for the site-critical high-performance tasks.

Server-side Scripting (or Server-parsed HTML)

Server-side Script is a special HTML file or template that contains a mixture of script and HTML that is read by the server when requested. Then the server parses the page and outputs the resulting HTML file (Figure 13F-4). This server-side technology more closely associates programming with Web pages. They are simpler than server APIs and run faster than a CGI program. There are many server-side scripting available and the three most popular ones are ColdFusion, PHP, and Active Server Page (ASP).

FIGURE 13F-4
SERVER-PARSED HTML

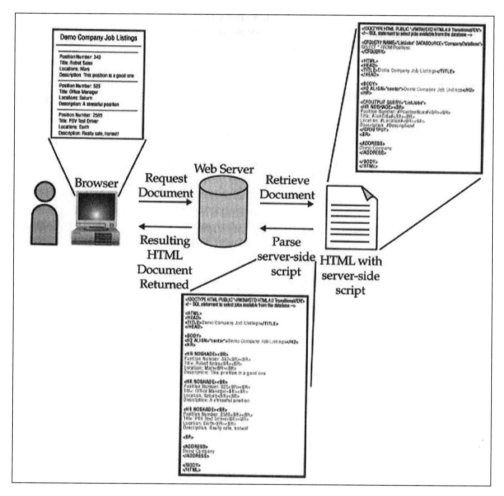

HTTP Cookies

www.cookiecentral.com defines the term of cookie as "a small piece of information sent by a web server to store on a web browser so it can later be read back from that browser." This is useful for having the browser remember some specific information. Cookies are used for storing user IDs and passwords, online ordering systems, site personalization, web-site tracking, targeted marketing, etc.

For example, when we browse through an "online shopping mall" and add items to our "shopping cart" as we browse, a list of the items we have picked up are stored by our browser. Then we can pay for all of the items at once when we are finished shopping. It's much more efficient for each browser to keep track of information like this than to expect the web server to have to remember who bought what, especially if there are thousands of people using the web server at a time.

Cookies are based on a two-stage process. First, the cookie is stored in the user's computer without the user's consent or knowledge. A command line in the HTML of a document tells the browser to set a cookie of a certain name or value. This is an example of some script used to set a cookie.

"Set-Cookie: NAME=VALUE; expires=DATE; path=PATH; domain= DOMAIN_NAME; secure"

Second, the cookie is clandestinely and automatically transferred from the user's machine to a web server. Whenever a user directs his or her web browser to display a certain web page from the server, the browser will transmit the cookie containing personal information to the Web server.

CLIENT-SIDE PROGRAMMING

Unlike server-side programs, a client-side program is usually executed quite fast to a user. It makes sense to reduce the network round-trip. However, the client-side program has the serious disadvantage of a lack of control. Because the client-side program relies on a browser, it is not covered on all different browsers. For example, when we design a web site, it is difficult to specify what kind of users will visit the web site, what browser is being used, what feature is turned on, and what kind of processors the user has. Because of this, client-side programming does not always work. The best approach is to assume that it will work. However, there should be a fallback state if it does not work.

Examples of client-side technologies are ActiveX, Java, JavaScript, and VB Script. The paragraphs below explain some interesting client-side technologies.

Plug-Ins

Since the earliest version of a web browser had limited functionality and support media beyond HTML, Netscape introduced Plug-Ins in Netscape Navigator 2 to cope with the problems. Plug-Ins are the components running within the context of the browser itself. Therefore, they are easily integrated into the design of a web page and communicated with a browser.

However, Plug-Ins have some disadvantages that users must find, download, and install. Also, the Plug-Ins are not available on every computer platform; they need to be developed for each particular operating system.

ActiveX

ActiveX is the Microsoft technology for creating small components, or controls, within the web page. It performs the same functions as the Plug-Ins from Netscape, but is different in that it supports Internet Explorer. Microsoft intends to distribute the ActiveX control through the Internet to enhance new features to Internet Explorer through automatic download and installation.

Java

The drawback of component technologies, Netscape Plug-Ins and Microsoft ActiveX, is being platform specific. Therefore, Sun Microsystems has developed Java technology. It is cross-platform development language that allows programs to *be written once and deployed to any machine, browser, or operating system* that supports the Java virtual machine (JVM). A web page uses a small Java program called "applets," that is downloaded and run directly within a browser to provide a new functionality. Now, Java is rapidly becoming the *de facto* standard programming language for web programming.

Scripting Language

Since HTML has a limitation on the functioning application code on browsers, scripting language has been created to solve this problem. The script language is embedded in the HTML and is downloaded every time the web page is accessed allowing various processes to be automated and objects to be accessed and manipulated. The scripting languages that are widely used nowadays are JavaScript and VBScript.

JavaScript

JavaScript is a scripting language originally developed by Netscape and supported by Microsoft browsers in the form of JScript, a clone language used in Internet Explorer. JavaScript is a non-compiled language, easy to use, and useful in small jobs such as checking form data; adding small bits of HTML code to a page on a fly; creating a small and performing browser, time- and user-specific computation. Furthermore, JavaScript is powerful for controlling events in browsers and accessing the HTML element themselves for manipulation.

VBScript

VBScript is a Microsoft proprietary interpreted scripting language virtually performing the same functions as those of JavaScript. It has the syntax similar to Visual Basic syntax. It is interpreted directly from source code and permits scripting within an HTML document.

QUERYING THE WEB

To access the relational database, a web server needs to access through intermediate system software. This software for a traditional client/server database system is called **O**pen **D**ata**B**ase **C**onnectivity (ODBC). It provides a common interface for accessing heterogeneous relational database systems as the standard for accessing data. For the web-based database application platform, the intermediate system software is **J**ava **D**ata**B**ase **C**onnectivity (JDBC) that is modeled after the ODBC specification for Java language. Also, there are intermediate system software from other software vendors such as Active Data Object (ADO) from Microsoft, and Network Computing Architecture (NCA) from Oracle.

JDBC

JDBC is the most outstanding and mature approach for accessing a relational database. It is a database access Application Program Interface (API) that supports basic Structure Query Language (SQL) function. It is used to manipulate and access data in a relational database. Also, JDBC enables web server access to a wide variety of relational database products.

The JDBC API consists of two main interfaces: API for application writer and a lower-level driver API for the driver writer. Application and applets can access databases using the JDBC with pure Java JDBC drivers, or using ODBC drivers and an existing database client library.

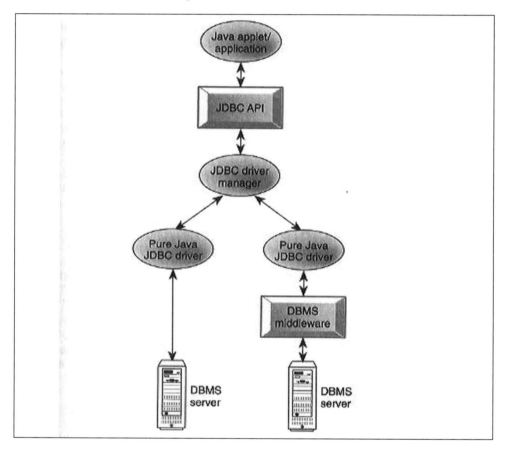

Using the pure Java JDBC driver as shown in Figure 13F-5, there are two options: the pure Java JDBC driver with a direct database connection, or the DBMS intermediate software translate. The first method will convert the JDBC calls into the network protocol used directly by the DBMS, enabling the direct calls from the client machine to the DBMS server. This approach is practical for Intranet access. For the second method, it translates JDBC calls into the intermediate software vendor's protocol, then the intermediate software server translates calls to a DBMS protocol. Generally, this is the most flexible JDBC alternative because it allows additional requirements such as accessing through firewalls.

Figure 13F-6
JDBC Using ODBC Driver

Accessing a database using ODBC drivers and an existing database client library, as shown in Figure 13F-6, has two methods: the partial JDBC driver and the JDBC-ODBC bridge. The first method converts JDBC calls on the client API for the DBMS, but requires that some database client software be loaded in each client machine. The other one provides JDBC access using the ODBC driver. ODBC binary code must be loaded on each client that uses this driver.

FIGURE 13F-7
THE ACTIVE SERVER PAGES (ASP) ARCHITECTURE

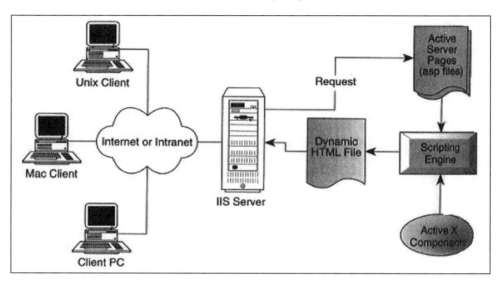

The advantage of using ODBC drivers is that they are a *de facto* standard for PC database access and are rapidly available for many popular DBMS at a very low price. Still, JDBC using the ODBC driver has some drawbacks.

First, a JDBC driver, which is not a pure Java implementation, will not necessarily work with a web browser. Next, there is a security problem when an applet has been downloaded from the Internet. Therefore, the applet should connect only to the database located on the host machine from which the applet originated. Finally, overhead costs increase because all clients need to both be installed and maintain a set of drivers.

Active Data Object (ADO)

ADO is a programming extension of Active Server Pages (ASP), introduced by Microsoft, and is developed to support the Microsoft Internet Server (IIS) for database connectivity. ADO was designed with the following features:

- Independently-created objects.
- Support for stored procedures, with input and output parameters and return parameters.

- Different cursor types, including the potential for the support of different back-end-specific cursors.

- Batch updating.

- Support for limits on the numbers of returned rows and other query goals.

- Support for multiple recordsets returned from stored procedures or batch statement.

Network Computing Architecture (NCA)

Developed by Oracle Systems, NCA is focused at providing extensibility for distributed environments. It is a three-tier architecture based on an industry standard. Also, Oracle claims that the architecture is applicable to both thin and fat clients.

As shown in Figure 13F-8, the NCA consists of:

- A plug-in "cartridge" capability that allows users to add individual pieces of functionality to their application.

FIGURE 13F-8
ORACLE'S NETWORK COMPUTING ARCHITECTURE

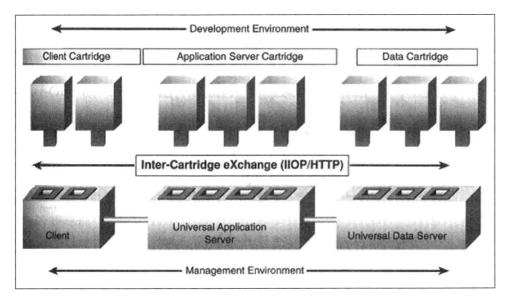

- Open protocol and standardized interfaces that allow communications among cartridge via a software bus called Inter-Cartridge eXchange (ICX).

- Extensible clients, application servers, and database servers.

- Integrated development and management cartridges.

Clients

NCA supports a wide variety of clients such as personal computers, network computers, and a mobile device. Also, cartridges can be developed in many languages such as Java, JavaScript, C/C++, Visual Basic, and SQL-based.

Universal Application Server

The Universal Application Server performs the role of the middle-tier. It was designed to allow high throughput and to provide transaction support across multiple HTTP requests. It has the Web Request Broker (WRB) architecture that allow different web servers to communicate transparently with the various application cartridges. Figure 13F-9 shows the function of the Web Request Broker that interfaces to multiple web servers and multiple Oracle-supplied cartridges, including Java, Server-side Include, X/Open Transaction API, PER, and PL/SQL cartridges.

FIGURE 13F-9
THE UNIVERSAL APPLICATION SERVER

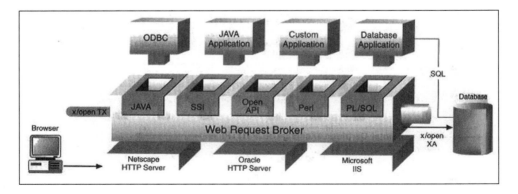

Universal Data Server

The Universal Data Server performs the role of the third-tier, the database server. Not only does it provide database management tasks as a traditional database server, but it also supports new types of data such as video, audio, and spatial. Furthermore, the NCA architecture allows clients to access the Universal Data Server in many ways such as from a fat client (traditional client) and a thin client.

Cartridges

Cartridges are component software that can be plugged into any of the three tiers to add more functionality. They can be developed to a specification by any independent software vendor (ISV) and will be operated in the NCA environment as distributed components. The benefit of the ISVs is that they can be written in virtually any language and their components will run on any operating system.

Inter-Cartridge eXchange (ICX)

ICX supports the framework for a cross application operation by acting as an object bus that enables cartridges distributed across a network to communicate with each other. ICX also allows different cartridges, which are written in different languages, to participate in the same application environment. One cartridge can call to another cartridge for further processing.

SUMMARY

In conclusion, the traditional database platform has incurred drawbacks from the fat client requirement and the high overhead of administration. Therefore, software and hardware vendors tried to solve the problem by developing the three-tier client/server platform. Since then the drawbacks of the traditional problem has been eliminated.

However, the requirements of developers and users have grown, because the business environment changes rapidly. Users require applications that are easy to upgrade or provide new kinds of services to the public. In addition, developers need the platform that is easy to upgrade, independent from any vendors, respond to the users' requirements, and provide an alternative technology in the future. The web platform is the answer for those requirements.

The web platform is desired by most developers and organizations because it has standardization, is platform-independent, and has cross-platform support. Therefore, developers do not have to be tightened with particular vendors anymore. Also, they can change the platform virtually without modification. Coupled with the new kind of service that the web-database platform can provide, the web platform enables businesses to provide services for customers around the world. Therefore, many organizations are interested in deploying web-base applications.

Still, the web as a database platform still has some drawbacks, such as the immaturity technologies and the security concern, making many developers hesitate to deploy the web platform. Integrating the web technologies with a database application is in the developing stage. To make the web server perform tasks like any application software, it needs web programming, which is separated into two sides: server-side, such as CGI, Server APIs and Server-side Scripting, and client-side, such as Plug-Ins, ActiveX, Java, VBScript and JavaScript.

Furthermore, to enable a web server communicable with a database server, the intermediate system software such as JDBC, ADO, and NCA is needed. JDBC from Java seems to be the most popular approach for linking a web server and a database server.

However, all of the client-side, server-side, and intermediate system software is in the developing stage. There is not yet a standard or matured technology for the web as a database platform. Nonetheless, from the history of the computer industry, the technologies that were an opened standard and practical to use have a highly potential to be *de facto* standards in the industry.

WEB TECHNOLOGIES

This chapter discusses a variety of web-related technologies. We start with an overview of HTML. Next, we discuss JavaScript. JavaScript may be used to create complex and dynamic web pages. We discuss how JavaScript may be used to validate forms, before form data is submitted to the web server. We discuss various Common Gateway Interface (CGI) technologies. Special attention is devoted to latest technologies using Java Servlets and Java Server Pages.

HYPERTEXT MARKUP LANGUAGE

Hypertext Markup Language (HTML) is a language used to organize and link together a variety of information, including text, graphics, audio, and video. HTML pages are the standard interface to the Internet. In this section, we will review the basic HTML "tags."

The "tags" are coded commands that tell the web browsers to appropriately format and display the information. All HTML tags begin with < and end with >. Most HTML tags have two parts: an opening tag and a closing tag. The closing tags have a / (forward slash) just after the < symbol.

The HTML tags needed to create web pages may be added using any simple text editor (capable of saving files in ASCII format), such as the Windows Notepad. The web pages should be saved using the ".htm" or ".html" extension. The web pages may be viewed using any web browser, such as Microsoft Internet Explorer or Netscape Navigator or Communicator.

267

Tags in Every HTML Page

Every HTML page must begin and end with the following tags: **<HTML>** and **</HTML>**. Putting these tags at the very beginning of a document signals that it is an HTML document.

Every HTML page has two main sections: a header section and a body section. The header section usually contains the title of the web page and other information, such as an embedded script[1]. The header section begins and ends with the following tags: **<HEAD>** and **</HEAD>**. Note that the header section is not the same as a "heading." Headings will be discussed later.

The body section is where all the content of a web page goes. The body section begins and ends with the following tags: **<BODY>** and **</BODY>**.

The title of the web page is placed in the header section. The title must be enclosed using the following tags: **<TITLE>** and **</TITLE>**. The title text appears at the very top of the window.

Figure 14A-1 puts together the tags discussed above and shows the basic skeleton of every web page. Figure 14A-2 shows a web page where the title has been set to "**A Blank HTML Page.**"

FIGURE 14A-1
SKELETON CODE REQUIRED IN EVERY WEB PAGE

```
<HTML>
<HEAD>
<TITLE>A Blank HTML Page</TITLE>
</HEAD>
<BODY>
</BODY>
</HTML>
```

---

[1]Scripts will be discussed in a later section.

FIGURE 14A-2
A BLANK WEB PAGE

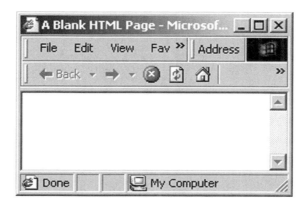

The output from the HTML code in Figure 1 is shown in Figure 14A-2. Since there is nothing in the body section, Figure 14A-2 shows a blank page.

HTML is not case sensitive. This means that the following tags are equivalent: **\<BODY>** and **\<body>**. It is up to an individual HTML author to decide whether to use uppercase or lowercase tags. In this chapter, we will be using uppercase tags.

Headings, Paragraphs, and Line Breaks

Most web pages have headings (which is not the same thing as the header section of a web page). Headings are usually larger and bolder than the rest of the text. They might be italicized or centered on the web page. Each browser has its own way of determining how a heading will appear to the user. It is possible to have multi-level headings. The second level heading will usually have a smaller font size than the main level heading. The third level heading will be even smaller.

The main level (level 1) heading begins and ends with the following tags: **\<H1>** and **\</H1>**. The second level (level 2) heading begins and ends with the following tags: **\<H2>** and **\</H2>**. The third level (level 3) heading begins and ends with the following tags: **<H3>** and **</H3>**. This may be continued for several heading levels, as illustrated in Figure 14A-3.

The HTML code for the web page in Figure 14A-3 will be formatted in Microsoft Internet Explorer as shown in Figure 14A-4.

Note that different web browsers format the same tags differently. Therefore, if you viewed the same HTML code in a different browser, the formatting might be different. The web browser will attempt to somehow differentiate between the different heading levels.

Web browsers pay no attention to line endings or the number of spaces between words in HTML pages. The words in the text are automatically separated by a single space and wrap down to the next line when the edge of a browser's window is reached. Extra spaces can be forced into the text by using "** **" (which stands for non-breaking space) for each space. Paragraphs should be enclosed using the **<P>** and **</P>** tags. To force a line

FIGURE 14A-3
HEADINGS HTML CODE

```
<HTML>

<HEAD>

   <TITLE>Heading Level</TITLE>

</HEAD>

<BODY>

<H1>First Level Heading</H1>

<H2>Second Level Heading</H2>

<H3>Third Level Heading</H3>

<H4>Fourth Level Heading</H4>

<H5>Fifth Level Heading</H5>

<H6>Sixth Level Heading</H6>

</BODY>

</HTML>
```

break, the **
** tag may be used. A horizontal rule line may be added using the **<HR>** tag.

The HTML code to generate the web page in Figure 14A-5 is shown in Figure 14A-6. The tags just discussed are shown in bold.

Ordered and Unordered Lists

Ordered lists may be created by using the **<OL>** and **</OL>** tags. Similarly, unordered lists may be generated by using the **<UL>** and **</UL>** tags. Each item in an ordered list or an unordered list should be enclosed in a list item tag: **<LI>** and **</LI>**. The HTML code in Figure 14A-7 generates the web page shown in Figure 14A-8.

FIGURE 14A-5
PARAGRAPHS, LINE BREAKS, AND NON-BREAKING SPACES WEB PAGE

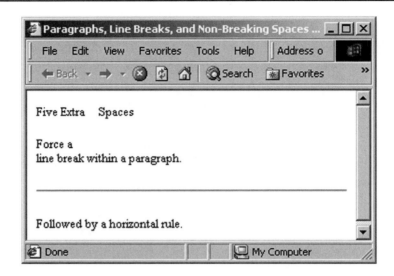

FIGURE 14A-6
PARAGRAPHS, LINE BREAKS, AND NON-BREAKING SPACES HTML CODE

```
<HTML>

<HEAD>

<TITLE>Paragraphs, Line Breaks, and Non-Breaking Spaces</TITLE>

</HEAD>

<BODY>

<P>Five Extra     Spaces</P>

<P>Force a<BR>line break within a paragraph.</P>

<HR>

<P>Followed by a horizontal rule.</P>

</BODY>

</HTML>
```

FIGURE 14A-7
ORDERED AND UNORDERED LISTS HTML CODE

```
<HTML><HEAD><TITLE>Ordered and Unordered Lists</TITLE></HEAD>

<BODY>

<H4>Ordered List</H4>

<OL>

   <LI>First Item</LI>

   <LI>Second Item</LI>

   <LI>Third Item</LI>

</OL>

<H4>Unordered List</H4>

<UL>

   <LI>First Item</LI>

   <LI>Second Item</LI>

   <LI>Third Item</LI>

</UL>

</BODY>

</HTML>
```

Links

Hypertext links take the user from one web page to another. Links may be of two types: absolute address and relative address. Absolute address links should be used to create a link to a web page external to your web site. Within your own web site, while it is possible to use absolute address links, the preferred approach is to use relative address links.

The following absolute address link will take the user to Yahoo's web site:

- <a href = "http://www.yahoo.com">Go to Yahoo!</a>

The "**a**" stands for anchor. "**href**" stands for hypertext reference. The Uniform Resource Locator (URL) is "http://www.yahoo.com." The URL is hidden from the user and does not appear on the web page. The web page only displays "Go to Yahoo!" The anchor tag is closed using **</a>**. This is an

FIGURE 14A-8
ORDERED AND UNORDERED LISTS WEB PAGE

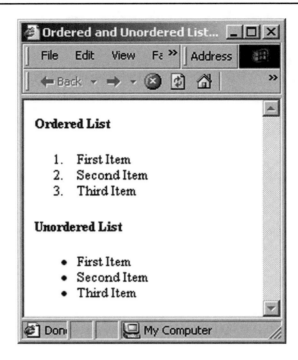

example of an absolute address link because the full web address for Yahoo was specified in the URL.

For a multi-page web site, it is generally preferable to use relative address links to connect web pages. When all the files are contained on the same machine, using relative address linking makes web management easier. First, it saves on the amount of time that is spent typing in the full web address. Second, and more importantly, it allows the web developers to move the files from one machine to another, without any modifications to the HTML code.

A relative address describes the path from one web page to another, instead of the full or absolute web address. Consider the following relative address path:

- <a href = "sales/newyork.html">New York Sales</a>

This link tells us that the file is located in the "**sales**" folder or directory. The "**sales**" folder contains a file called "**newyork.html.**" Using relative address linking, it is possible to move the entire web page structure from one computer to another without modifying the HTML code. This is especially helpful since the web pages are generally developed on one machine, such as a desktop personal computer, and then transferred to another computer, such as the web server. Figure 14A-9 shows a web page containing both an absolute address link and a relative address link.

E-mail Links

The anchor tag may also be used to add e-mail links on a web page. By clicking on the e-mail link, the default e-mail program on the user's computer opens. An e-mail link may be established as follows:

- <a href = "mailto:user@website.com">Send Email</a>

The **mailto:** command tells the browser that this is an e-mail link. The above link will send an e-mail message to user@website.com. The e-mail address will not appear on the web site. Instead, as shown in Figure 14A-10, the user will only see the words "**Send Email**."

FIGURE 14A-9
ABSOLUTE & RELATIVE ADDRESS LINKS WEB PAGE

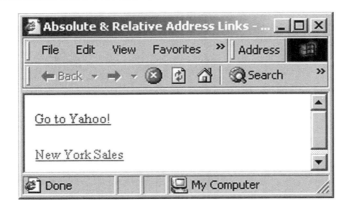

File Downloading

The anchor tag can also be used to make files available for downloading. For example, an **.exe** or a **.zip** archive file may be placed on the server so that web visitors may download the files. A zip file named **AFile.zip** may be made available for download as follows:

- <a href = "AFile.zip">Click here to download file.</a>

Figure 14A-10 shows how the above link will appear in a web page.

Tables

The ability to create tables is one of the most powerful tools in web design. Tables allow one to arrange text and graphics into multiple rows and columns. While tables may be used to organize tabular information, the real power of tables extends far beyond. Tables may be used to establish complex relationships between text and graphics. A variety of alignment options are possible. Text or graphics can be aligned as desired. Borders may be drawn around text or graphics. Complex relationships can be established by nesting tables within tables. Tables may be nested to any level desired.

Figure 14A-10
E-mail and Download Links

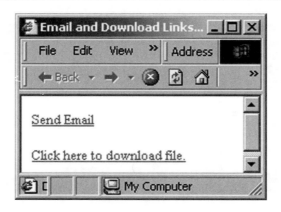

Tables are created by using the **<TABLE>** and **</TABLE>** tags. A **border** attribute may be used to specify the width of the border in pixels. A border size of zero, or leaving the **border** attribute out entirely, will make the border invisible. An invisible border is typically specified when the table is used as a page layout tool.

The table row tags, **<TR>** and **</TR>,** are used to create a table row. Each row may consist of one or more columns. The table heading tags, **<TH>** and **</TH,** are used to specify the headings of a table. Each set of table heading tags creates a single column. The table heading tags should be the first row of a table.

Each subsequent table row uses table data tags, **<TD>** and **</TD>**, rather than table heading tags, **<TH>** and **</TH>**. The table heading tags tell the browsers to highlight the heading in some way. Netscape Navigator and Microsoft Internet Explorer both display text in the table heading tags as boldface and centered. Other browsers may ignore the heading tags or format them differently. Each row should have the same number of columns as the other rows. Figure 14A-11 contains the HTML code used to generate the web page in Figure 14A-12.

Frames

Frames are a way of arranging and presenting multiple web pages at once. Frames are used to split a web page horizontally, vertically, or in both directions.

Forms

Web forms allow the web users to send data to the server. Customer feedback, web-site guest books, and online shopping carts are common examples of web forms. Every form includes a button to allow users to submit the form data. A form processing script, program, or servlet processes the user data.

A form is created using the **<FORM>** and **</FORM>** tags. Within the **<FORM>** and **</FORM>** tags, various types of input tags may be enclosed. A text input box may be used to ask the user's name as follows:

- Last Name: <INPUT TYPE= "TEXT" SIZE = "20" MAXLENGTH = "30" NAME = "lName" />

FIGURE 14A-11
TABLES HTML CODE

```
<HTML>
<HEAD>
<TITLE>Tables</TITLE>
</HEAD>
<BODY>
<TABLE BORDER="1">
  <TR>
    <TH>Column One Heading</TH>
    <TH>Column Two Heading</TH>
  </TR>
  <TR>
    <TD>Row One Column One</TD>
    <TD>Row One Column Two</TD>
  </TR>
  <TR>
    <TD>Row Two Column One</TD>
    <TD>Row Two Column Two</TD>
  </TR>
</TABLE>
</BODY>
</HTML>
```

- First Name: <INPUT TYPE= "TEXT" SIZE = "20" MAXLENGTH = "30" NAME = "fName" />

The **INPUT TYPE** is used to indicate the type of form element to display. In this case, **"TEXT"** indicates a simple one line text entry box. The

FIGURE 14A-12
TABLES WEB PAGE

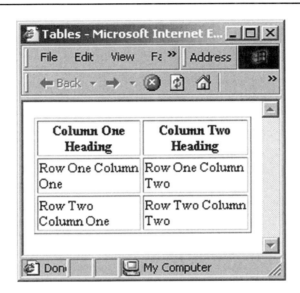

SIZE attribute indicates approximately how many characters wide the text input box ought to be. Note that this is an approximate for most proportionally spaced fonts. The **MAXLENGTH** attribute limits the maximum number of characters the user may enter into the field. This **MAXLENGTH** field may be larger than, the same size as, or smaller than the **SIZE** field.

The **NAME** attribute is used to uniquely identify each input item. If someone entered "Adam" as the first name and "Baker" as the last name, then: fName=Adam and lName=Smith.

The **INPUT TYPE** attribute may be set equal to "PASSWORD" to create a password field. A simple single line box similar to the text box is displayed. However, any information entered appears as a series of asterisks. The use of a password field is appropriate when you don't want what is typed echoed back to the user's screen. Other attributes, such as SIZE OR

NAME, are identical to a text box. The following code creates a password input box:

- Password: <INPUT TYPE="PASSWORD" SIZE="10" MAXLENGTH= "10" NAME="pass" />

A checkbox or a radio button may be created by specifying "CHECK-BOX" OR "RADIO" for the INPUT TYPE attribute. Checkboxes are used when the user is allowed to select multiple items from a list. Radio buttons are mutually exclusive. If one button is selected, the other is automatically deselected.

Both checkbox and radio have a fixed size; therefore, SIZE and MAXLENGTH attributes are not used. The following code shows an example of three checkboxes, asking the individuals which activities they enjoy:

- <INPUT TYPE="CHECKBOX" NAME="swim" />Swimming
- <INPUT TYPE="CHECKBOX" NAME="hike" />Hiking
- <INPUT TYPE="CHECKBOX" NAME="bike" />Biking

The following code shows an example of two radio buttons, asking the users to indicate their gender:

- <INPUT TYPE="RADIO" NAME="gender" VALUE= "m"/>Male
- <INPUT TYPE="RADIO" NAME="gender" VALUE= "f"/>Female

Note that the NAME attribute for both radio buttons is the same. It is used to ensure that the radio buttons are mutually exclusive; selecting one will automatically deselect the other one. The VALUE attribute is set to "m" for Male and "f" for female; this information is sent to the server to indicate which button was selected.

Each form must have a **SUBMIT** button. The SUBMIT button is used to send the data to the web server. A **RESET** button is normally included to allow the user to clear the form data and start over again. The following code shows an example of SUBMIT and RESET buttons:

- <INPUT TYPE="SUBMIT" VALUE="Send Data" />
- <INPUT TYPE="RESET" VALUE="Clear Form" />

FIGURE 14A-13
FORM DATA WEB PAGE

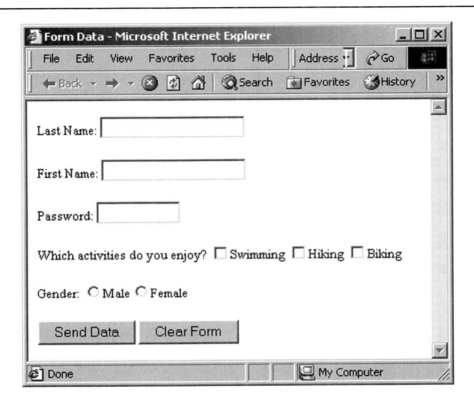

Figure 14A-13 shows an example of an input form. The code used to generate the form is given in Figure 14A-14.

The **<FORM>** tag normally has at least two attributes set. The **METHOD** attribute may be set to "**get**" or "**pos**t" and is the Hyper-Text Transfer Protocol (HTTP) method to submit the form. The **ACTION** attribute specifies the server-side form handler; it may be an HTTP URL or mailto URL.

Additional HTML Resources

The following web sites are recommended for additional information about HTML:

FIGURE 14A-14
FORM DATA HTML CODE

```
<HTML>
<HEAD><TITLE>Form Data</TITLE></HEAD>
<BODY>
<FORM METHOD = "post" ACTION = "someURL/file.cgi">
   <P>Last Name: <INPUT TYPE="TEXT" SIZE="20" MAXLENGTH="30"
NAME="Name" /></P>
   <P>First Name: <INPUT TYPE="TEXT" SIZE="20" MAXLENGTH="30"
NAME="fName" /></P>
   <P>Password: <INPUT TYPE="PASSWORD" SIZE="10" MAXLENGTH="10"
NAME="pass" /></P>
   <P>Which activities do you enjoy?
<INPUT TYPE="CHECKBOX" NAME="swim">Swimming
<INPUT TYPE="CHECKBOX" NAME="hike" />Hiking
<INPUT TYPE="CHECKBOX" NAME="bike">Biking</P>
   <P>Gender:
<INPUT TYPE="RADIO" NAME="gender" VALUE="m" />Male
<INPUT TYPE="RADIO" NAME="gender" VALUE="f" />Female</P>
   <P> <INPUT TYPE="SUBMIT" VALUE="Send Data" />
<INPUT TYPE="RESET" VALUE="Clear Form" /></P>
</FORM>
</BODY>
</HTML>
```

- http://www.pageresource.com/html/index.html
- http://www.weballey.net/index.html
- http://werbach.com/barebones/
- http://www.davesite.com/webstation/html/

JavaScript

JavaScript supports both web browser and web server scripting. JavaScript's syntax is very similar to that of Java or C/C++. JavaScript, however, is not Java; there are significant differences in the two languages.

JavaScript allows HTML to be dynamically generated. Custom event handling functions can be easily defined to handle mouse events or keyboard entries. JavaScript may also be used to control Java applets and Plug-Ins. JavaScript may be used to process form data or perform database searches.

Unlike C/C++, which is a compiled language, JavaScript is an interpreted language. The source code of JavaScript is executed directly at runtime. This offers several advantages as well as disadvantages. Interpreted languages tend to be slower than compiled languages. If performance is of prime concern, then a compiled language would be a better choice. Another disadvantage of an interpreted language is that some errors may not be caught till run-time. With a compiled language like Java, one is able to catch and fix errors at compile time, rather than at run-time.

Even with some disadvantages, interpreted languages offer a significant advantage; JavaScript is platform independent. This is especially important for web applications since there is no way to know the end-user's system configurations. It is also generally easier and simpler to write code in JavaScript. Furthermore, there is no need to recompile JavaScript code with each change or modification.

JavaScript is embedded into a HTML document using the <SCRIPT> and </SCRIPT> tags. JavaScript as well as CGI programs may be used to add considerable interactivity to web pages. HTML, by itself, is used to create essentially static pages. A significant advantage of client-side JavaScript over server-side CGI programs is that JavaScript executes on the web user's/client's machine. In general, this enhances the performance of the web application and does not overburden the server.

Additional JavaScript Resources

The following web sites are recommended for additional information about Java:

- http://www.javascriptmall.com/learn/contents.htm

- http://www.phrantic.com/scoop/tocjscript1.htm
- http://hotwired.lycos.com/webmonkey/programming/javascript/tutorials/jstutorial_index.html
- http://webteacher.com/javascript/index.html

Java

Java is an ideal language for client/server programming. Java programs are portable and the code is platform independent. This is achieved through a two-step process. First, Java source code is compiled into Java bytecode. The bytecode is used by the Java Virtual Machine (JVM) to run the program.

Java programs may be broadly classified into three categories: Applications, Applets, and Servlets. An application is a stand-alone program that executes using the Java Virtual Machine. An applet is a program that runs within a web browser such as Microsoft Internet Explorer or Netscape Communicator. Applets can be embedded in HTML documents. Applets were a major factor in Java's initial popularity and wide acceptance. Servlets extend the functionality of a web server. Servlets are primarily used to respond to the client by sending the appropriate HTML web page. Servlets may also be used to process data sent by an HTML form.

Object Oriented

Java is an object-oriented language. A Java program consists of one or more classes. A class is a template that specifies or defines an object. An object is made up of data and methods that operate on the data. Object oriented languages have the following characteristics:

- Encapsulation
- Polymorphism
- Inheritance
- Dynamic binding

Encapsulation refers to hiding data or methods. By defining data or methods as private, no object other than the class creating the object can access them. Polymorphism means that different objects are capable of reacting differently to the same message. Inheritance makes it possible to reuse code. New classes and behavior can be based on existing classes to obtain code reuse and code organization. Dynamic binding provides flexibility in writing a program since it is not necessary to know an object's specific type when writing the program.

Java Essentials

In this section, we discuss the basic concepts of Java. We assume that most Information Technology professionals have some background in programming, though not necessarily in Java.

Java supports three styles of comments. All text between /* and */ is ignored by the Java compiler. All text following // is ignored by the Java compiler. All text between /** and */ is ignored by the Java compiler; this type of comment is used to create automatic documentation in Java.

In Java, variables must be declared with both a *name* and a *type* before being used in a program. Local variables also must be initialized before being used. The names or identifiers in Java may be of any length. The identifies must *begin* with a letter, an underscore (_), or a dollar sign ($) and cannot begin with a number. The *remainder* of the identifier may consist of any characters other than those used as operators by Java. Java is case-sensitive; uppercase and lowercase characters are treated differently.

Java has eight basic data types, known as *primitive* data types:

- Two primitive data types are used to store *boolean* and *char* data types.
- Four primitive data types are used to store integer data: *byte, short, int,* and *long*.
- Two of the primitive data types are for floating point numbers: *float* and *double*.

In Java, a string is an object rather than a primitive data type. String arithmetic may be performed using the "+" operator to concatenate two strings.

Java provides six relational operators for comparing data values:

- > greater than
- >= greater than or equal to

- == equal to
- != not equal to
- <=less than or equal to
- < less than

A basic statement for making comparisons and decision making is the if statement. The syntax of the if statement is as follows:

- **if** (expression)

    statement;

where, if the value of the *expression* is true, the *statement* executes. Multiple statements may be executed by enclosing them in brackets. It is possible to nest the **if** statements to any number of levels desired. The **switch/case** statements can be used to do the work of multiple **if** statements as illustrated below:

- switch(var)

    {

       case 'A':

          // Do Something if char var is A

          break;

       case 'B':

          // Do Something if char var is B

          break;

    }

Loops allow a statement to be executed repeatedly. The **for** loop statement consists of the following format:

- for (initialization; condition; increment)

    {

    // one or more statement;

    }

The **while** loop is similar to the **for** loop. The **while** loop statement consists of the following format:

- while (condition)
  {
  // one or more statement;
  }

Java offers two ways to terminate or skip a loop. The **break** statement may be used to terminate a loop immediately or the **continue** statement may be used to skip a loop iteration.

Exceptions arise when something serious goes wrong in a program. Java requires that certain methods that might cause an exception be invoked in a try/catch/finally block or declare that the method might throw an exception.

Java Class Library

The Java Development Kit (JDK) contains a large number of standard classes grouped into packages (or directories). Additional classes are commercially available and may be imported.

Java Editions

Sun Microsystems has split its original Java 2 software development platform into three editions. Each edition is aimed at a different category of hardware deployment. The traditional Java Runtime Environment, along with its core classes, is now referred to as the Java 2 Standard Edition (J2SE). The J2SE is primarily targeted towards traditional desktop computing platforms, such as Microsoft Windows.

The Java 2 Micro Edition (J2ME) is a subset of the J2SE. It is targeted towards handheld devices, embedded processors, and information appliances. The basic aim of J2ME is to provide a Java environment of "Write Once, Run Anywhere" while requiring a minimal footprint.

The Java 2 Enterprise Edition (J2EE) adds extension classes to Java's core classes. The extension classes are targeted towards enterprise application development.

Java 2 Enterprise Edition Platform

A multi-tiered distributed application model is used by the J2EE platform. The application logic is divided into components according to functions. A J2EE component has the following characteristics:

- The functional software is self-contained.
- It is assembled into a J2EE application with its related classes and files.
- It can communicate with other components.

The J2EE has three components: client components, web components, and business components.

Client components consist of client applications and applets. A J2EE client component may be web-based or non-web-based (traditional desktop). For a non-web-based J2EE application, the application simply executes on the client's machine. In a web-based J2EE application, the application (web pages and applets) executes within the web browser. Applets are small Java client applications that execute in the web browser's Java Virtual Machine. Web pages may be created using HTML, Wireless Markup Language (WML), or Extensible Markup Language (XML).

Web Components include Java Servlets and JavaServer Pages (JSP), which may be used to create dynamic web pages. These web pages in HTML, WML, or XML are generated by servlets using JSP technology. JSP allows for a modular application design. With JSP, it is possible to separate applications programming from web page design. The main advantage of this approach is that personnel involved in web page design do not need to understand Java programming, and Java programmers do not need to have creative and artistic web design skills. Each is able to work independently and still join forces when needed.

Business component consists of code which incorporates business logic. It meets the specialized needs of particular industries such as banking or finance.

JavaBeans component architecture is used to manage the data flow between an application client or applet and components running on the J2EE server. JavaBeans components in the J2EE platform have instance variables and *get* and *set* methods for accessing the data in the instance variables.

J2EE components are created and compiled using the standard Java programming language. However, when using the J2EE platform, the components are assembled into a J2EE application, which determines compliance with the J2EE specification. They may then be deployed to production, where they are managed by the J2EE server.

A J2EE application may be *n*-tiered, where *n* represents the numbers of tiers. Most J2EE applications are three-tiered because they are distributed over three locations:

- the client machines,
- the J2EE server machine, and
- the back-end which consists of database or legacy machines.

The three-tiered model is different from the standard two-tiered client/server model. Three-tiered applications extend the two-tiered client and server model by placing a multithreaded application server between the client application and back-end storage.

Additional Java Resources

The following web sites are recommended for additional information about Java:

- http://java.sun.com/

The starting point for anyone interested in Java.

- http://java.sun.com/docs/books/tutorial/?frontpage-spotlight

This site contains several tutorials on Java topics. An excellent source for advanced topics.

- http://chortle.ccsu.ctstateu.edu/cs151/cs151java.html

This site contains an excellent Java tutorial by a professor at Central Connecticut State University. Starts with the very basics and progresses to advanced topics in about seventy chapters.

- http://home.att.net/~baldwin.dg/JavaLinks/jaxatop.htm
  Comprehensive source of Java links on a variety of topics.

DATA VALIDATION

JavaScript is often used for client-side data validation. The basic approach is to use an onSubmit handler to check each form field for constraints. The user is prohibited from submitting form data without satisfying the constraints.

The code in Figure 14A-15 shows how the data in the form shown in Figure 14A-13 may be validated. Some of the HTML code from Figure 14A-14 has been repeated here for the sake of completeness. The new code is in **bold**.

The FORM tag uses the method POST. It also uses the ONSUBMIT event handler to ensure that only valid data is sent to the server. The name of the form is "activitiesForm." The value for ACTION was left blank. The value for ACTION should contain the URL of the CGI program or the servlet to process the data.

The function *validateForm()* is called by the ONSUBMIT event handler. The *if* decision-making syntax of JavaScript is identical to that of Java, as previously discussed. The first *if* statement tests to determine if the value for Last Name (**activitiesForm.lName**) is equal to an empty string ("").

Note that the equality operator in Java and JavaScript consists of two equal signs (==), rather than a single equal sign (=). A single equal sign is used for assignment purposes only.

If the string is empty, and a value for last name has not been entered, an alert box (dialog window) pops up as shown in Figure 14A-16.

After the dialog box is dismissed, the input box for last name will have the focus to allow the user to go there directly to fix the problem.

A similar test is performed for first name and if that box is left blank, another alert/dialog box will pop up. The password field checks to see if the length of the password is at least six characters. A dialog box warns the user if the password length is less than six characters.

Finally, the function checks to determine whether the Gender field has been selected. At start-up, neither item is selected. The user is not allowed to submit the form without selecting the Gender field.

After all the data has been validated, the function returns true. If any of the items are invalid, the function returns false. The function must return true to allow the form data to be submitted to the server.

It is essential to understand that client-side validation, such as using JavaScript, is never sufficient by itself. Server-side validation is always necessary. There is no way to enforce the rules when using client-side validation. In fact, it is very easy for users to circumvent JavaScript programming by

```
<HTML>
<HEAD>
<TITLE>Data Validation</TITLE>
</HEAD>

<BODY>

<FORM METHOD="POST" ONSUBMIT="return validateForm()" ACTION NAME="activitiesForm">
<P>Last Name: <INPUT TYPE="TEXT" SIZE="20" MAXLENGTH="30" NAME="lName" /></P>
<P>First Name: <INPUT TYPE="TEXT" SIZE="20" MAXLENGTH="30" NAME="fName" /></P>
<P>Password: <INPUT TYPE="PASSWORD" SIZE="10" MAXLENGTH="10" NAME="pass" /></P>
<P>
Which activities do you enjoy?
  <INPUT TYPE="CHECKBOX" NAME="swim" VALUE="ON">Swimming
  <INPUT TYPE="CHECKBOX" NAME="hike" / VALUE="ON">Hiking
<INPUT TYPE="CHECKBOX" NAME="bike" VALUE="ON">Biking
</P>
<P>
Gender:
  <INPUT TYPE="RADIO" NAME="gender" VALUE="m" />Male
  <INPUT TYPE="RADIO" NAME="gender" VALUE="f" />Female
</P>
<P>
  <INPUT TYPE="SUBMIT" VALUE="Send Data" />
  <INPUT TYPE="RESET" VALUE="Clear Form" />
</P>
</FORM>


<SCRIPT LANGUAGE=JavaScript>
<!—
function validateForm()
  {
  // Last name has been entered
      if (activitiesForm.lName.value=="")
          {
          alert ("Please enter your Last Name");
```

```
            activitiesForm.lName.focus();
            activitiesForm.lName.select();
            return false;
            }
// First name has been entered
        if (activitiesForm.fName.value=="")
            {
            alert ("Please enter your First Name");
            activitiesForm.fName.focus();
            activitiesForm.fName.select();
            return false;
            }
// The password consists of at least 6 characters
tmpString = activitiesForm.pass.value;
passwordLength = tmpString.length
        if (passwordLength < 6)
            {
            alert ("The password must consist of at least 6 characters");
            activitiesForm.pass.focus();
            activitiesForm.pass.select();
            return false;
            }
// Either the Male or Female button has been selected
if (!(activitiesForm.gender[0].checked I activitiesForm.gender[1].checked))
            {
            alert ("Gender selection is invalid!");
            return false;
            }
// Return true if everything has been validated
return true;
            }

—>
</SCRIPT>
</BODY>
</HTML>
```

FIGURE 14A-16
ALERT BOX

creating their own form and submitting the data to the server without any validation. If the GET method is being used, the user can simply modify the URL that is submitted to the CGI program or servlet.

For any critical application, it is unwise to rely upon client-side validation. Server-side validation is under the complete control of the web developer. Accordingly, at least a check should be performed there.

Even though server-side validation is necessary, it is still often advantageous to perform client-side validation using JavaScript. One significant advantage of client-side validation is speed. The user can be given immediate feedback without having to submit the information to the server. Server-side validation can often take longer. Client-side validation, followed by server-side validation, is often the best strategy. One benefits from the quick response of client-side validation, yet still ensure that the data are valid.

ADDITIONAL RESOURCES

The following web site is recommended for additional information about web programming:

- http://www.programmingtutorials.com/main.asp

This site contains links to over 150 tutorials on many programming languages including HTML, JavaScript, and Java.

14B

SERVLETS AND JAVASERVER PAGES

SERVLETS

Java servlets have become immensely popular in recent years. An analogy may be drawn between applets and servlets. Servlets do on the server side what applets do on the client side. Servlets perform the same duties as Common Gateway Interface (CGI) programs written in PERL or C, but offer tremendous advantages.

Servlets are portable. Servlets are written in Java and therefore comply with the philosophy of "write once, run everywhere." Servlets are usable across a variety of operating systems and server implementations.

The full power of Java's Application Programming Interface (API) is available to servlets. The API is a language and message format used by an application program to communicate with the operating system. Java's API includes support for networking, multithreading, database connectivity, internationalization, remote method invocation (RMI), object serialization, data compression, security, and many other areas. A servlet author can take advantage of the Java API and select from numerous classes available from third-party Java classes and JavaBeans components.

With RMI and object serialization, Java-based applets and servlets may be used for client/server communication. Contrast this with using Common Gateway Interface (CGI) to develop a custom protocol to handle communications, which is considerably more complicated.

Servlet code is object oriented, modular, and simple. The servlet API's classes and methods handle most of the necessary tasks of servlet development. Standard classes handle cookie management and session tracking.

Servlets are highly efficient. Once loaded, a servlet remains in the server memory as a single object instance. A lightweight method invocation is used to handle the servlet. Multiple concurrent requests are handled by separate threads of the same object instance. This means that servlets are highly scaleable and efficient. There is no need for a new process to spawn or an interpreter to invoke, as would be necessary when using CGI.

Servlets are faster than CGI because unlike CGI, they are able to hold on to external resources, such as a database connection. It is possible to hold on to external resources since servlets stay in the server's memory as a single object instance.

Servlets are tightly coupled with the web server. This allows servlets to do things that CGI programs cannot. For instance, a servlet can use the server to perform a variety of tasks such as translating file paths, checking authorization, performing logging, and accessing the server's user database.

Servlets protect the server through the use of the Java security manager. The security manager ensures that poorly written or malicious servlets do not harm the server file system.

Servlets inherit strong type checking from Java. Unlike CGI programs that use string data type for most values, including numeric items, servlets use native data types. For example, a numeric value in a servlet is represented as an integer and not a string.

Servlets take advantage of Java's automatic garbage collection and memory management. Programmers do not have to deal with pointers or memory leak problems.

Errors can be handled in an elegant fashion using servlets. Servlets can take advantage of Java extensive exception-handling capabilities. By appropriately handling errors, server crashes can be prevented.

SERVLET DEVELOPMENT KIT

The *javax.servlet* package and the *javax.servlet.http* package contain the classes and interfaces necessary to define servlets. The Java Development Kit and the Servlet packages are available without charge from Sun Microsystems (http://java.sun.com/products).

To test servlets, one must have a web server with servlets support. Tomcat is a free, open-source implementation of Java Servlet and JavaServer Pages technologies. It was developed under the Jakarta project at the Apache Software Foundation. Tomcat is also available for commercial use in both binary and source versions. The Sun website provides complete instructions for downloading and installing the necessary software.

Another option is to download *VisualAge for Java* from IBM. The entry edition of the software is available without charge at the following web site:

- http://www7.software.ibm.com/vad.nsf/Data/Document4293

The remainder of our discussion will be based on software available from Sun Microsystems, as explained above. After the Tomcat software has been properly installed and configured, you may test it by pointing the web browser to:

- http://localhost:8080/

If everything is functioning as it should, the web browser's screen should look similar to Figure 14B-1.

SERVLET API

All servlets must implement the servlet interface. The methods of the servlet are automatically invoked by the server on which the servlet is installed. The servlet interface defines five methods:

- void init (ServletConfig config)
- ServletConfig getServletConfig()
- void service (ServletRequest req, ServletResponse res)
- String getServletInfo()
- void destroy()

The servlet packages define two abstract classes that implement the servlet interface: the GenericServlet class and the HttpServlet class. Both classes provide default implementations of all the methods enumerated above.

FIGURE 14B-1

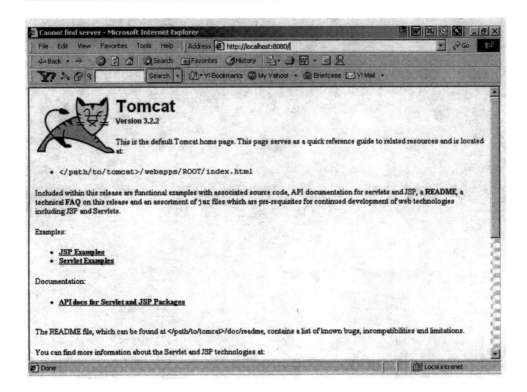

A protocol-independent servlet should extend GenericServlet. A Hyper-Text Transfer Protocol (HTTP) servlet should extend the HttpServlet class. Note that HttpServlet is a subclass of GenericServlet with HTTP functionality.

Most servlets extend the HttpServlet and override methods to provide appropriate behavior. The most important method is the *service* method. The *service* method receives both a *ServletRequest* and a *ServletResponse* object. The HttpServlet class overrides the original *service* method to distinguish between the two most common types of requests received from a web browser: *GET* and *POST*. An HTTP servlet generally does not override the *service* method; instead it overrides the *doGet()* and *doPost()* methods. An HTTP servlet extending HttpServlet class should not override the *service* method since that method handles the setup and dispatching to other methods.

GET AND POST

The GET method is designed to get information, such as a document or the results of a database query. The POST method is designed to post information, such as store new data in a database. While the GET method was designed to read information, it can include, as part of its request, some information that better describes what information to retrieve. For instance, the GET method may send an individual's social security number as part of its request to get information about the individual.

In other words, while the primary purpose of the GET method was to retrieve information, it is also possible to use the GET method to send information to the server. The information is sent by appending the information to the URL. This means that one can bookmark the URL generated by the GET request. It is also possible for one to e-mail the URL to another individual. The GET method, however, should not be used to send large amounts of information. In fact, some servers, especially the older ones, limit the length of URL and query strings.

The POST method is used to send virtually unlimited information to the server over socket connections as part of the HTTP request body. Unlike the GET method, the POST method does not affect the URL. Therefore, POST requests cannot be bookmarked or e-mailed. Since the POST method does not affect the URL, only the POST method should be used to send sensitive information to the server. For instance, it would be unwise to use the GET method to send credit card numbers since the credit card number would become part of the URL. Similarly, the GET method should not be used to place an order or modify a database since one may accidentally place an order or modify a database by simply clicking on the URL.

OTHER HTTP METHODS

Besides GET and POST, there are several other infrequently used HTTP methods. The HEAD method is used when the client only wants to see the headers of the response. This is frequently used to determine the modification time or document's size.

The OPTIONS method may be used to determine the options supported or resources available on a server. The TRACE method is used as a debugging tool. This method returns the exact content of the request to the client.

The PUT method is used to place documents on the server. The DELETE method is used to remove documents from the server. These two methods are not widely supported by most servers.

FIGURE 14B-2
A SIMPLE SERVLET

```
import javax.servlet.*;

import javax.servlet.http.*;

import java.io.*;


public class SimpleServlet extends HttpServlet {

    public void doGet(HttpServletRequest req, HttpServletResponse

res) throws ServletException,

                                    IOException {

        res.setContentType("text/html");

        PrintWriter out = res.getWriter();

        out.println ("<HTML>");

        out.println ("<HEAD><TITLE>Simple Servlet</TITLE><HEAD>");

        out.println ("<BODY>");

        out.println ("<H1>A Very Simple Servlet</H1>");

        out.println ("</BODY></HTML>");

    }

}
```

GENERATING AN HTML PAGE

The simplest type of an HTTP servlet simply generates a HTML page. Such servlets can do everything that a traditional CGI program could do plus more. Figure 14B-2 shows the Java source code for a basic servlet. This servlet just displays "A Simple Servlet" as a heading on the browser's screen. This servlet should be compiled just like any Java code using *javac*. To execute the servlet, the web browser should point to:

- http://localhost:8080/servlet/SimpleServlet

For the servlet to execute properly, it is necessary to ensure that the class path variables are set correctly. It is also necessary to append */servlet/* to the URL before the servlet's class name.

The servlet imports classes from two packages: *javax.servlet* and *javax.servlet.http*. The servlet also imports classes from the *java.io* package. The servlet SimpleServlet is a subclass of HttpServlet. The SimpleServlet servlet overrides the *doGet()* method. It receives both a HttpServletRequest object and a HttpServletResponse object. This servlet just ignores the HttpServletRequest object; in most servlets one would not do this. The HttpServletResponse object is used to send information of type "Text/HTML" back to the client browser. The servlet generates the HTML code shown in Figure 3. The servlet below may easily be modified to generate a more complex HTML page.

The HTML code in Figure 14B-3 generates the web page shown in Figure 14B-4.

FIGURE 14B-3
SERVLET-GENERATED HTML CODE

```
<HTML>
<HEAD><TITLE>Simple Servlet</TITLE><HEAD>
<BODY>
<H1>A Very Simple Servlet</H1>
</BODY></HTML>
```

```
<HTML>
<HEAD><TITLE>Phone Number</TITLE></HEAD>
<BODY>
<FORM METHOD="GET"
ACTION="http://localhost:8080/servlet/PhoneServlet">
<P>
   Phone Number: <INPUT TYPE="text" NAME="phone" SIZE="12">
   <INPUT TYPE="radio" VALUE="home" NAME="location">Home
   <INPUT TYPE="radio" NAME="location" VALUE="work">Work
</P>
<P>
   Select State <SELECT SIZE="1" NAME="state">
     <OPTION VALUE="NY">New York</OPTION>
     <OPTION VALUE="NJ">New Jersey</OPTION>
   </SELECT>
</P>
<P>
   <INPUT TYPE="submit" VALUE="Submit" NAME="submit">
   <INPUT TYPE="reset" VALUE="Reset" NAME="reset">
</P>
</FORM>
</BODY>
</HTML>
```

PROCESSING FORM DATA

Java servlets are often used to perform the work of traditional CGI programs written in PERL or C. A common use of these programs is to handle data submitted by a form using the GET or POST method. Consider the HTML code for a simple form in Figure 14B-5.

The <FORM> tag in Figure 14B-5 shows that it uses the GET method. The ACTION is set equal to the URL of the servlet:

- http://localhost:8080/servlet/PhoneServlet

On clicking the SUBMIT button, the form data will be sent to the URL set in ACTION using the GET method. The HTML in Figure 14B-5 results in the output shown in Figure 14B-6.

The data submitted using the form in Figure 14B-6 may be processed using the servlet code in Figure 14B-7. The HttpServletRequest object's ***req.getParameter("phone")*** method is used to find out the phone number. Similarly, the ***req.getParameter()*** method is used to retrieve the location and state.

Figure 14B-8 shows the output from processing the form data using the servlet. The URL of the web page in Figure 14B-8 is as follows:

- http://localhost:8080/servlet/PhoneServlet?phone=123-555-1234&location=work&state=NJ&submit=Submit

FIGURE 14B-6
PHONE NUMBER FORM

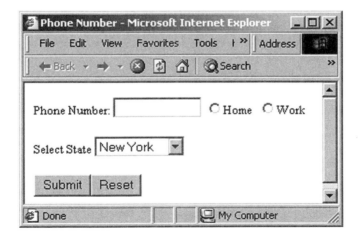

FIGURE 14B-7
PHONESERVLET TO PROCESS FORM DATA

```java
import javax.servlet.*;
import javax.servlet.http.*;
import java.io.*;

public class PhoneServlet extends HttpServlet {
public void doGet (HttpServletRequest req, HttpServletResponse res)
        throws ServletException, IOException {
    String phone = req.getParameter("phone");
    String location = req.getParameter("location");
    String state = req.getParameter("state");
    res.setContentType("text/html");
    PrintWriter out = res.getWriter();
    out.println ("<HTML>");
    out.println ("<HEAD><TITLE>Phone Servlet
Response</TITLE><HEAD>");
    out.println ("<BODY>");
    out.println ("<H1>The telephone number is:" + phone + "</H1>");
    out.println ("<H1>This is your" + location + " telephone number.</H1>");
    out.println ("<H1>You selected" + state + " state.</H1>");
    out.println ("</BODY></HTML>");
  }
}
```

FIGURE 14B-8
PHONE SERVLET WEB PAGE

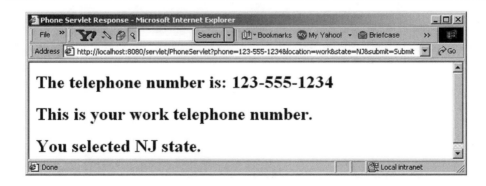

Appended to the URL is the information that was submitted by the HTML form. The URL and the data are separated by a "?" and the various parameter values are separated by the "&" sign.

SERVLET INSTANCE PERSISTENCE

Traditional CGI programs exist as separate programs, external from the HTTP server. This means that a new process is spawned by the server for each request. While this allows the server to handle multiple requests simultaneously, this creation process tends to be resource intensive in most operating systems. Memory as well as other system resources must be allocated. Program code and data must also be loaded. Most CGI programs execute quickly since they are designed to respond to a single request. After the program has executed, additional operating system resources are needed to destroy the process.

In short, considerable system resources are devoted to simply creating and destroying the process in order to execute a simple program. Java servlets, in contrast, handle multiple requests by using threads, rather than creating a new process. Threads require considerably less overhead to create and destroy than full-fledged processes. Threads are, therefore, more efficient than processes. They are sometimes referred to as lightweight processes.

The code in Figure 14B-9 illustrates how servlets have instance persistence and are not destroyed after each request.

The output generated by the servlet in Figure 14B-9 is shown in Figure 14B-10 and Figure 14B-11. The variable *count* is incremented with each request. If the servlet had been destroyed after the first request, the *count* variable would not have incremented. The same servlet instance was used to process both requests.

Hitting the browser's REFRESH button will update the browser window as shown in Figure 14B-11.

It is important to note that the code shown in Figure 14B-9 is not thread safe. If multiple threads are executing, there may be an interaction between threads that might corrupt the *count* data. For instance, it is possible that two or more threads increment the *count* variable before any thread gets a chance to output the *count* value. This may have an undesired effect of incrementing the *count* variable by two, three, or more. This code may be made thread safe through various means, such as by using the synchronized keyword to limit access to certain parts of the code to a single thread at a time.

FIGURE 14B-9
INSTANCE PERSISTENCE OF A SERVLET

```
import javax.servlet.*;

import javax.servlet.http.*;

import java.io.*;

public class CounterServlet extends HttpServlet {

    int count =0;

    public void doGet(HttpServletRequest req, HttpServletResponse res)

            throws ServletException, IOException {

    res.setContentType("text/html");

    PrintWriter out = res.getWriter();

    count++;

    out.println ("<HTML>");

    out.println ("<HEAD><TITLE>Counter Servlet</TITLE><HEAD>");

    out.println ("<BODY>");

    out.println ("<H1>This servlet has been accessed" + count + " times.</H1>");

    out.println ("</BODY></HTML>");

    }

}
```

SINGLE THREAD MODEL INTERFACE

It is possible for a pool of servlet instances to be created instead of a multi-threaded single servlet instance. This may be done by implementing the *javax.servlet.SingleThreadModel* interface. Any servlet implementing this

FIGURE 14B-10
SERVLET-ACCESSED WEB PAGE

FIGURE 14B-11
SERVLET-ACCESSED WEB PAGE

interface is considered thread-safe. Its instance variables do not have to be synchronized because multiple threads are not allowed to concurrently execute the service method of the servlet.

Note that such an approach would be useless for the CounterServlet example discussed in Figure 14B-7. If a new servlet instance is created for each request, it would not be possible to increment the count instance variable with a new request.

BACKGROUND PROCESSING

Since multi-threaded servlets can persist between accesses, they can also execute between accesses. A servlet may continue executing even after a response has been sent. This allows a long-running task to be executed on a servlet. The incremental results from this task may be made available to multiple clients, as necessary.

SERVLET INIT AND DESTROY METHODS

A servlet's init() and destroy() methods are automatically called by the server. The init() method is used to initialize the servlet. The destroy() method is called when the servlet is about to be unloaded.

The init() method is called when the server starts, or when the servlet is first requested, or when the server administrator requests it. The init() method is guaranteed to be called before the servlet handles its first request.

The destroy() method should be used to free resources that are not automatically destroyed by the garbage collector. The destroy() method is also used to write out its unsaved cached information or information that will be required by the init() method when the servlet is reloaded.

SESSION MANAGEMENT

The HTTP protocol is stateless. There is no way for the server to recognize that a sequence of requests are from the same client. There are several techniques available to overcome this shortcoming. Traditionally, CGI programs have used techniques such as hidden form fields, URL rewriting, and cookies. While these techniques may be used by Java servlets, session tracking can be easily managed using Java servlet's Session Tracking API.

A *javax.servlet.http.HttpSession* object is associated with each user. The servlet can use that object to save or retrieve information about a user. The *getSession()* method is used to retrieve the current session object, or to create it if it does not exist. The method takes a boolean argument; if the argument is set to true, then a new session is created if there isn't an existing valid session. To add data to the *HttpSession* object, use the *putValue()* method. Data may be retrieved using the *getValue()* method.

Once created, a session may be invalidated automatically after a fixed period of time. A session may also be manually invalidated. Any information saved in the user's session object is lost when the session is invalidated. The information may be saved if needed in an external file or a cookie.

Like conventional CGI programs, Java servlets support the use of cookies to store information on the client's computer. Cookies are small files sent by the servlet as part of a response to the client. The cookies are stored and retrieved using the header portion of an HTTP interaction.

It is possible to set the maximum age of a cookie. Cookies are automatically deleted when they expire. Most browsers limit the number of cookies. Generally, a web site may set a maximum of 20 cookies. The total number of cookies per user is generally limited to 300. Cookie size is often limited to 4096 bytes each. There are several ways to overcome the 20-cookie limit. One way is to combine several fields into one long string.

JAVASERVER PAGES

JavaServer Pages (JSP) are an integral part of developing web-based Java applications. JSP make it possible to separate content presentation from the programming logic implementation. This separation greatly facilitates web development by allowing web designers to work independently of web programmers, yet allowing the work of the team to be integrated using a well-defined interface.

JSP are somewhat similar to Microsoft's Active Server Pages (ASP). Both allow web developers to use a scripting language to access the server and its extensions. While ASP are efficient at generating dynamic web content, ASP are essentially limited to Microsoft platforms. Moreover, a minor scripting mistake can crash or hang the server.

JSP offer all of the advantages of developing Java using a script-like environment. JSP are dynamically assembled into servlets, just like other Java classes.

JSP tend to be more efficient than other scripting languages due to Java's use of threads to handle requests. Java's error handling can help prevent server hangs and crashes.

JSP functionality is implemented using the servlet technology. When the web server receives a request for a JSP, it forwards the request to a servlet or JSP container. The servlet then compiles the JSP file into a servlet.

To compile the page, several steps are involved:

- The JSP compiler parses through the page content to identify JSP tags.
- The tag content is converted to Java code. This is used to generate the dynamic content.
- Static HTML content is converted to Java strings.
- The newly generated source code is used to create a servlet. Its service methods are written to produce the content requested by the JSP.

Figure 14B-12 contains the code for a simple JSP. A JSP generally consists of HTML code mixed with Java code. The file name of a JSP must end with ".jsp" extension. The code should be placed in the appropriate subdirectory of the server. For the previously discussed Tomcat server, the JSP should be placed in the ***webapps/ROOT*** directory. By placing it in this directory and giving it the ".jsp" extension, the server automatically knows it is a JSP which must first be compiled into a servlet.

FIGURE 14B-12
A SIMPLE JSP PAGE

FIGURE 14B-12
A SIMPLE JSP PAGE

```
<HTML>
<HEAD>
<TITLE>A JSP Page</TITLE>
</HEAD>
<BODY>
<H1>A JSP Page</H1>
</BODY>
</HTML>
```

JSP supports two basic styles of delimiting its scripting elements from the HTML content. The first style is similar to ASP and uses <% and %>. The second style to create JSP is XML compliant.

Java is case-sensitive. Therefore, the name of the file should be entered in the exact case desired. We named our file "JSPintro.jsp."

The web page output from the above code is shown in Figure 14B-13. Since Java, unlike HTML, is case-sensitive, it is essential to type the web address correctly as follows:

- http://localhost:8080/JSPintro.jsp

FIGURE 14B-13
JAVASERVER PAGE GENERATED USING ONLY HTML CODE

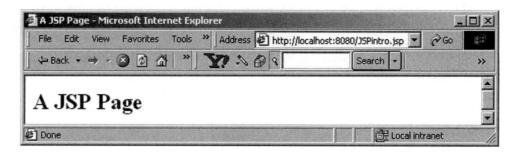

Notice that code in Figure 14B-12 consists entirely of HTML. While unnecessary to create a JSP for this code, it is completely legal. A JSP may consist of nothing more than HTML code.

As the previous example illustrated, it is possible for a JSP to consist entirely of HTML. However, this would be pointless. The strength of JSP is the ability to add dynamic content. A slightly more complex JSP with dynamic content is presented in Figure 14B-14.

The dynamic content in the code in is written in Java. To separate it from HTML, the Java code appears in **bold**. The Java code appears inside **<%** and **%>**. The string variable **phone** is assigned the value from **request.getParameter("tel")**. The value for "tel" may be specified as part of the URL and will be retrieved by the servlet using the GET method. The value in string **phone** is outputted using the **=phone** expression.

The following URL will load the default version of file "JSPphone.jsp" in the web browser (see Figure 14B-15):

- http://localhost:8080/JSPphone.jsp

FIGURE 14B-14
PHONE JSP

```
<HTML>
<HEAD>
<TITLE>JSP Phone</TITLE>
</HEAD>
<BODY>

<% String phone = request.getParameter("tel");
if (phone==null) phone = "No Phone Number Entered!"; %>
<H1>The Telephone Number is: <%=phone %>! </H1>

</BODY>
</HTML>
```

FIGURE 14B-15
DEFAULT PHONE JSP

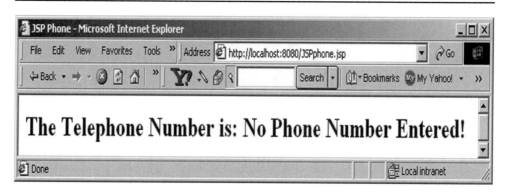

The following URL contains the **tel** parameter. The dynamically generated version of file "JSPphone.jsp" will be displayed in the web browser as shown in Figure 14B-16:

- http://localhost:8080/JSPphone.jsp?tel=222-555-1234

FIGURE 14B-16
DYNAMICALLY GENERATED JSP

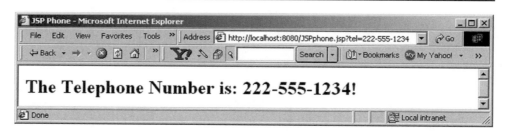

17

CONTINGENCY PLANNING

Sixty percent of businesses are unable to continue following a major disruption. Lack of contingency planning can cause businesses to lose a majority of their customers. An organization is most likely to recover if it has a contingency plan and has trained its staff to respond appropriately following a disruption.

It is difficult to estimate the probability of the occurrence of a disruption. A contingency plan provides a level of assurance. It tells the organization what needs to be done before, during, and after the disruption to minimize loss. Contingency planning

- Enhances the safety and welfare of personnel
- Ensures backup and recovery of critical data
- Helps determine the probability of occurrence of various types of disruptions
- Identifies potential loss exposures
- Minimizes the effect of disruptions on daily operations
- Minimizes reliance on key personnel
- Protects the assets of an organization
- Reduces insurance premiums
- Reduces legal liability and exposure to lawsuits

Disruptions may affect an organization at any time. Contingency planning helps minimize the effects of disruptions. A disruption is defined as any event that can adversely affect

- Health, safety, or welfare of personnel or general public
- Business operations
- Physical facilities or environment

Disruptions may be classified as malfunctions, disasters, or catastrophes. Examples of various types of disruptions include

- Acts of terrorism or sabotage
- Breakdown of communication systems
- Earthquakes
- Electrical problems
- Fires
- Flooding
- Hazardous-materials emergency
- Hurricanes
- Riots
- Snowstorms
- Tornadoes

Minor disruptions are referred to as malfunctions. Malfunctions may involve problems with hardware, software, or data files. Malfunctions typically have a narrower scope, and most organizations are able to recover from them relatively quickly. On-site backup of software and data files is typically sufficient to recover from a malfunction or minor disruption. Hardware backup may be accomplished by having either redundant facilities or using alternate on-site processing facilities.

A disruption affecting the entire facility is referred to as a disaster. A disaster may require the use of off-site facilities to recover operations. A disaster may disrupt facilities for an extended period of time.

Catastrophes are the most devastating types of disruptions. The entire facility may be destroyed in a catastrophe. In the short run, an organization needs to use alternate facilities for processing data. In the long run, it is frequently necessary to rebuild or establish new facilities.

Contingency planning allows an organization to resume its activities in a timely and efficient manner. Loss of human life, data, and capital can be prevented with proper preparedness. Contingency planning should focus on the continuity of the business. Many organizations limit contingency planning to primarily recovering their computer technology. Undue emphasis on recovery of computer technology is a mistake. An organization's focus should be on recovering its business operations quickly. Sometimes, manual procedures might be best for quick recovery. Committing too many resources to providing redundant computer-processing facilities may not satisfy the cost-benefit criterion.

Contingency planning should reduce the risk of financial loss and enhance an organization's ability to recover from a disruption. All facets of an organization including its staff, computer programs, data, workspace, and vital records should be considered. Insurance requirements should be evaluated to recover investment in computers and equipment. Consideration should be given to the type of losses that may be uninsurable. Succession planning and backup training should be used to recover from loss of key personnel.

It is generally preferable to take preventive action, not corrective action. Nonetheless, it is virtually impossible to anticipate each and every problem. Even if problems can be anticipated, the cost-benefit criterion may not justify taking preventive actions. Preventive measures may also prove to be ineffective because of human or other error. Productivity and efficiency may be reduced if preventive procedures are taken too far.

MANAGEMENT'S FIDUCIARY RESPONSIBILITIES

Top management might be unwilling to commit resources to develop a recovery plan. The low probability of a disaster or catastrophe, as well has the high costs of developing a contingency plan, may serve as a deterrent. Determining the scope of contingency plans is difficult, and some organizations may not be able to justify the benefits to be derived from contingency planning. Top management hesitant about committing resources for contingency planning should consider the cost of damages associated with being unprepared. Most organizations are heavily dependent upon computer technology. The damages from a disruption can be high, and even a minor business interruption may have significant financial consequences.

Management's support is essential in contingency planning. Senior management has the final responsibility for developing, testing, regulating, and monitoring contingency plans. Top management should recognize that they have a fiduciary responsibility to protect the assets of their organization. Top management and the board of directors could be held personally liable for damages that could have been prevented or minimized by adequate contingency planning.

Government regulation, such as the Foreign Corrupt Practices Act of 1977 (FCPA), requires all publicly held organizations to maintain adequate controls over their information systems. Civil and criminal penalties may be imposed on a company's management or board of directors for failure to take reasonable precautions to ensure the integrity of their records and the internal-control structure.

Management should appoint a committee to develop and test an organization's contingency plans. The contingency-planning committee should define the scope of the contingency plan. The committee should be responsible for performing risk analysis to identify the effects of major and minor disruptions. The committee should establish guidelines to help an organization recover from disruptions. The information-systems or information-technology manager should be a key member of the committee. Other members of the committee should consist of individuals from key functional areas throughout the organization. The committee should obtain input from each department and consult with specialists both within and outside the organization. Specialists and experts include

- Accounting and finance specialists
- Doctors and medical experts
- Internal auditors
- Lawyers
- Public-relations personnel and media specialists
- Sales and marketing specialists
- Security experts

The operations of accounting and finance departments are likely to suffer considerably in the event of a disruption in information technology. The planning committee should work with these departments to develop alternate processing procedures.

Doctors and medical specialists should be consulted to ensure human health and lives are not compromised. Medical specialists can recommend the type of first-aid equipment that should be available. They can also train staff to provide basic first aid. Medical specialists should be consulted about the effects of fire extinguishers, such as Halon, or carbon dioxide, and other chemicals on human health and life.

Internal auditors have two main roles in an organization. Internal auditors evaluate an organization's internal-control structure and conduct operational audits to ensure efficiency of operations. Internal auditors also frequently work with external independent auditors in audits of financial statements.

The legal consequences of various types of disruptions should be discussed with the legal department or lawyers. Special attention should be given to complying with federal, state, and local government regulations, such as the Foreign Corrupt Practices Act.

All communications with the media should go through the public-relations department. Personnel outside the public-relations department should not be granting interviews or otherwise communicating with the media.

The security department should be responsible for coordinating the recovery efforts of various departments. It should take precautions to prevent a security breach and to respond following a breach.

BUSINESS-IMPACT ANALYSIS

Business-impact analysis (BIA) is used to determine the effect of a significant disruption to an organization. BIA helps an organization

- Determine the effect of an information-technology disruption on the functional areas of an organization.
- Consider worst-case scenarios.
- Assess the costs associated with disruptions.
- Set priorities to restore critical operations.
- Identify specific recovery strategies.
- Evaluate its backup strategy, including the use of off-site facilities.

A business-impact analysis requires collecting information about all potential disruptions, the organization's planned response, and the organization's recovery capabilities. An estimate should be made about the probability of the occurrence of various types of disruptions, emergencies, and risks. The effect on the well-being of personnel should be assessed. The assessment should include the effect of serious injury or death. Potential property loss or damage should be assessed.

The effect on continuity of business operation should be determined. A determination should be made about the effect of the disaster on data-processing and business operations. How long will the service be interrupted and at what level would the company be able to operate?

The total effect of a disruption can be understood only by involving the various information-systems users. Users should be interviewed to obtain an understanding about the effects of the failure on

- Service levels
- Cash flow and other financial resources
- Information resources

Emergency-planning agencies of the federal, state, and local governments should be consulted when performing a business-impact analysis and in developing contingency plans. It is essential to ensure that your organization is not violating any of the federal, state, or local regulations. Other entities, such as utility companies, will also provide important information that should be incorporated into an organization's contingency planning. Volunteer groups that may help out in an emergency should be identified and consulted.

The business-impact analysis will help identify shortfalls in the organization's ability to deal with disruptions. To achieve this purpose, data collected from interviews should be categorized, classified, and summarized. The summarized report should include a detailed risk analysis and recommendations for mitigating losses in the event of a disruption. The report should specifically address actions that should be taken by the company's management.

Appendix K contains a BIA worksheet.

DEVELOPING THE CONTINGENCY PLAN

Senior management should play an integral part in developing the plan. The contingency plan should contain guidelines to be followed before, during, and after an emergency. Senior management should appoint the planning committee responsible for developing contingency guidelines. The planning committee should consist of individual teams from various functional areas. Each team should be assigned specific responsibilities. Each team should have a manager; an alternate should also be designated. Senior management should review and approve the contingency plan.

Personnel Safety

The health and safety of personnel should be the primary concern in contingency planning. The contingency plan should have procedures in place for

- An emergency evacuation
- Alerting the fire department and other emergency response authorities
- Health and safety concerns unique to the business (such as hazardous materials in a manufacturing plant)

Preparing an Outline

Before writing the actual contingency plan, an outline should be prepared to guide the plan's development. The outline should be modified as necessary during the plan's development. Appendix I contains a comprehensive contingency-planning checklist.

The plan should be clear and succinct. It should not be too narrow in scope. It should consider not only computer processing, but also other functions and operations. It should comprehensively address a variety of emergency scenarios and disruptions.

The writing of the plan is greatly facilitated if a standard format is used. A standard format is especially helpful if several individuals are working on different sections of the plan. The use of a standard format enhances its development and ensures consistency. Consistency makes it easier to maintain the plan on an ongoing basis. Key management officials should be assigned the responsibility for keeping the plan up-to-date.

Making Assumptions

Certain assumptions are necessary when developing the plan. For example, the plan should consider "worst-case" scenarios. The worst-case scenario assumes that the disruption has destroyed primary processing and operations facilities. If the plan is able to effectively deal with worst-case scenarios, then it is considerably easier to deal with lesser disruptions. Other assumptions or considerations include

- What files or records have been destroyed by the disruption? What data or materials are available to reconstruct files and records? Have off-site backup records been affected?

- Which facilities have been affected? Is the hardware functioning? Have the off-site facilities and equipment been affected?

- What voice and data communication facilities will be available?

- What personnel are likely to be available to assist in recovery efforts? Will personnel need to relocate to alternate off-site facilities?

- Following a disruption, what level of support may be expected from suppliers to meet the needs of your customers?

- Are adequate inventory and supplies stored off-site, or will they be available at short notice from vendors?

- Is the contingency plan flexible enough to cover a wide variety of disasters and catastrophes?

- What will be the effects of a single disruption, such as a fire, on your facilities versus the effects of a community-wide disaster, such as an earthquake or flood?

- Will the resources needed to help your organization in a community-wide disaster be severely limited?

Access to Facilities

What will be the effect of delayed access to facilities after a disaster or catastrophe? After a fire, for example, no one may be allowed inside the building until an assessment of the structural damage has been made. A criminal investigation, such as arson or murder investigation, may have to be conducted, and the building may be a crime scene. In a manufacturing plant, there may be the danger of toxic or noxious chemical contamination. Access into the geographical area in which your facilities are located may be restricted following community-wide disasters, such as those caused by earthquakes, floods, or tornadoes. Your organization must be prepared for delayed access to your primary facilities. Depending upon the severity and type of disruption, the delay may be anywhere from a couple of hours to several weeks or more.

It is essential to determine in advance if urgent access to certain areas of the facilities will be required. This will expedite the process of making damage assessment. If priority access is required, appropriate authorities should be contacted in advance of the disruption to ascertain the proper procedure. Under special circumstances, access may be granted to qualified individuals.

Backup Policy

The short-term as well as the long-term backup needs of the organization should be specified in the contingency plan. Contingency planning should consider organizational needs beyond simply keeping a backup of records for short-term recovery. Contingency planning should focus on the long-term needs of the entire organization, not simply on the data centers.

This is especially important because of the changes in technology. The traditional focus of backup policy in contingency planning is to aid in the recovery of records from centralized data centers. The use of decentralized information systems mandates that the focus of contingency planning extend to the entire organization and not simply to information-processing centers or data centers.

The plan should clarify backup procedures to prevent operational errors. The plan should specify the backup schedule for each type of data file. It should specify how long each generation of data files must be kept.

Vital Records

Vital records must be recovered quickly from the off-site backup location. The contingency plan should specify which documents and records are likely to be needed first. It should specify the location where the vital records will be stored. Consider whether any special equipment or other resources will be needed to restore or recover the vital records. Once vital records have been recovered, where will these records be stored and how will they be protected?

Emergency Organizational Structure

The contingency plan should define the organizational structure in an emergency. The organizational structure may not necessarily be the same in an emergency as it is during normal times. Major functional areas such as computer processing, data backup, and data restoration should be considered.

Procedure

The contingency plan should describe the procedures to be followed. It should indicate which procedures take precedence over others. It should indicate which procedures are to be performed sequentially or simultaneously. A flowchart or diagram can greatly simplify the recovery process.

There should be standardizations and uniformity in the procedures described. Preprinted "fill-in" forms should be used whenever possible. Procedures that require approval or authorization should cite the title or position of the individual responsible for granting approvals. Names of specific individuals should not be used; using an individual's title or position makes it easier to maintain and update the plan when employees leave, retire, transfer out, or get promoted. A list of sources for additional information or reference material should be included.

Testing

The contingency plan should be tested on a regular periodic basis. Testing will help identify problem areas that should be fixed. Testing also provides a way to train employees for an emergency. The guidelines for testing the contingency plan should be defined within the plan. The testing of the plan should be documented.

Emergency Funding

The contingency plan should contain the procedure for funding acquisitions during and immediately after a disruption. Consider taking the following actions:

- A list of emergency supplies should be preauthorized.
- Individuals responsible for emergency acquisitions should be specified.
- The dollar limit for such individuals should be determined, and procedures should be in place to authorize expenditure in excess of preauthorized limits.

LEGAL CONSIDERATIONS

Contingency planning is necessary not only to recover from a disruption, but also because it may be legally required. Contingency planning may be required under common law, statutory law, and contract law.

The common law is comprised of legal rules that have resulted from court decisions. Most of the law concerning negligence and fiduciary responsibilities of management and directors resulted from the common law. Senior management and directors of organizations are required to be prudent and exercise reasonable business judgment. This means that if an organization lacks a contingency plan, or its contingency plan is not prudently designed, there may be financial repercussions. Shareholders, creditors, and third parties such as customers may sue for damages.

It is relatively easy for an organization to design and develop contingency plans to combat a disruption. The technology for redundant processing and backup storage is relatively inexpensive, and computer equipment is typically reliable. The failure of an organization to obtain such technology would therefore be considered negligent. The courts typically balance the cost of taking precautions, which is relatively small, against the harm that would result from not taking appropriate precautions, which can be significant.

There are innumerable federal, state, and local laws. Many laws, directly or indirectly, require organizations to develop, maintain, and test contingency plans to recover from disruptions. For example, the Securities and Exchange Commission requires publicly held companies to maintain adequate accounting records. The Foreign Corrupt Practices Act requires businesses to maintain adequate internal controls. The Internal Revenue Service requires taxpayers to maintain adequate records for at least three years for audit purposes. If the IRS believes that fraud has been committed, the IRS audit may go back for more than three years, since there is no statute of limitations for tax fraud.

Business contracts may require performance, regardless of a disruption. Customers, for example, may demand that your organization honor its commitment to supply their needs. Your organization may be sued for breach of contract if it is unable to meet customers' demands. Larger businesses typically require their suppliers to have appropriate business-resumption capabilities. Similarly, organizations are frequently required to have appropriate contingency plans for disruptions if they wish to do business with government agencies.

Business contracts often contain clauses disclaiming liability for a variety of events. A clause disclaiming liability as a result of a computer disruption is not likely to be supported by the courts. Such clauses allow one to disclaim liability for events beyond an entity's reasonable control. Damages caused by computer disruptions are frequently controllable, and hence, an organization may not be able to successfully disclaim liability. The law does not allow one to limit liability for willful misconduct or gross negligence.

Attorneys should be involved in every phase of contingency planning. The effect of federal, state, and local laws on contingency planning should be discussed with legal counsel. Attorneys should review corporate documents, such as the corporation's Articles of Incorporation and by-laws. Violation of laws may prevent recovery of damages from insurance policies. The attorneys should help the contingency planners steer clear of potential liability. They should assist the contingency planners by researching legal requirements, which may affect the contingency plan.

For example, the Worker Adjustment and Retraining Notification Act limits the right of an employer to lay off personnel or close a plant. At least sixty days' notice must be provided to the state and local officials as well as the employee. Natural disasters, such as earthquakes and floods, are excluded from the notification requirement. However, other types of disruptions, such as a fire, are not excluded from the notice requirement. Hence, an organization may be unable to lay off personnel. It has to continue paying salaries and benefits. Without adequate insurance coverage, your organization may be unable to meet its legal obligation.

Sometimes, following a disaster, it is necessary to move computer facilities to another state or locality. The new locality, city, or state may have its own legal requirements that should be considered at the contingency-planning stage. It may be necessary for an organization to file papers or obtain permission before doing business at the new location. The tax consequence of moving should be considered. There may be different withholding requirements and other taxes at the new location.

OBTAINING ADEQUATE INSURANCE COVERAGE

Insurance coverage should be obtained to protect against disruptions in business. It is essential to obtain coverage with the right endorsements. The purpose of insurance is to indemnify an organization for loss resulting from disruptions. Insurance needs, both before and after the disruption, should be considered. Insurance coverage should be obtained for damages if it is not possible to access the facilities for a considerable period of time after a disaster.

Most insurance policies treat computer equipment like industrial equipment. Insurance coverage is provided for the same threats faced by the facilities where the equipment is located. Threats specific to computer equipment, such as power outages or electrostatic discharges that may delete or destroy electronically stored information, are not covered by standard insurance policies.

An Electronic Data Processing (EDP)-specific policy generally provides coverage for risks involving computers. Such a policy will provide coverage for replacing or repairing computer equipment. It is essential to obtain a "replacement-cost" endorsement for computer equipment and other high-technology assets. Computer equipment, unlike industrial machinery and other assets with a long useful life and low depreciation rate, tends to depreciate rapidly and lose its value. An organization might be unable to replace its computer equipment if the replacement-cost endorsement is lacking.

EDP policies generally do not cover damages due to the inaccessibility or loss of computer equipment. Business-interruption and out-of-pocket-expenses insurance should be purchased to cover such damages. Business-interruption insurance covers both current losses and future business losses if operations are unable to resume speedily. Many insurance companies require their customers to have a business-recovery plan in order to obtain business-interruption insurance. Some insurance companies give discounts to customers with recovery plans. Out-of-pocket-expenses coverage should be obtained to provide for the use of alternate computer facilities. Insurance coverage should extend to data-processing operations at the facilities of the outsourcing vendor.

Valuable-papers and records coverage would include the cost of recreating documents, such as reentering data and restoring damaged items. Software products are often excluded from insurance policies unless there is a specific endorsement. Coverage should be obtained if there is a breakdown in equipment, such as a system crash.

Many organizations keep on renewing their insurance policies and do not bother reviewing them to ensure that the policies are up-to-date. The rapidly changing business environment dictates that policies be reviewed periodically. A comprehensive list of organizational assets should be kept. The list should be updated as assets are added or retired. The list should contain the appraised values of the assets. Is the list complete and asset values accurate? A copy of the list should be stored off-site. The off-site copy should be updated at the same time as the primary copy.

Your organization may be penalized if it fails to maintain the proper level of insurance. Many insurance policies require policyholders to insure their property to 80, 90, or 100 percent of its value. Assets should be periodically appraised and insured to the value required by the policy to reduce your organization's chances of being penalized by the insurance company.

FIRE-CONTINGENCY PLAN

Fire is one of the most common disruptions to business operations. The contingency plan should consider local fire codes and regulations. The organizational facilities should be inspected for potential fire hazards.

Insurance policies should be reviewed to ensure adequate coverage. The insurance carrier should be asked to recommend actions that may be taken to reduce the likelihood of fire. Implementing these measures will frequently help reduce your insurance premiums.

Your organization's representatives should meet with fire-department officials to discuss the fire department's capabilities and your organization's fire-hazard plan. Any special substances or materials on your organization's premises that could cause or accelerate a fire should be discussed. Any substance that could pollute or contaminate the environment should also be discussed.

FireTracer and WinTracer

FireTracer and WinTracer products (http://www.emss.net) may be used to identify the exact location of a developing fire. They can be installed in computer cabinets or rooms. Using air-sampling techniques, they can also be used in air-handling units, return air grills, ducts, and other large, open areas.

FireTracer uses a pump to draw air into a series of micro-bore tubes. The micro-bore tubes may be located in a computer cabinet, room, or compartment being protected. The sample of air is then analyzed for the presence of either smoke particles or gas. If the smoke level reaches a preset trace level, FireTracer switches from an air-sampling mode to a search mode. It uses the search mode to identify the exact location of the source of the smoke. The system triggers alarms at three separate stages. Each of the three alarms may be connected to a fire panel for control purposes.

- The first alarm level is triggered when the trace cycle is initiated.
- A prealarm is triggered to warn that a potential fire exists in the identified area.
- The final alarm indicates that a full incipient fire condition is present.

The FireTracer products can be monitored and controlled using the WinTracer control software. WinTracer provides

- Action sequences and hazard indications
- Bar graphs that display the current levels of smoke or gas
- Color-coding that indicates when current levels exceed the alert/alarm levels
- Data logging and recording of significant events
- Display of site status (tracers that are on-/off-line, etc.)

- Historical trends
- Location of the alarm
- Remote control (reset, off-/on-line and changing functions, such as alarm levels, etc.)
- Warning when smoke levels exceed preset limits

In the event of an alarm, there is a text description of the alarm source. A site map shows the location of the alarm. Actions to be taken for different alarm types and locations (e.g., notes to tell operator to phone fire station, clear room, etc.) are provided. A list of hazards near the alarm location is also given.

WinTracer's advanced features allow the administrator to customize WinTracer and analyze data. The administrator has remote programming access to control functions. Alarms may be acknowledged or canceled. Trend graph may be plotted for compliance-monitoring purposes. Text descriptions, action sequences, and hazard lists may be programmed.

Training Personnel

Employees should be trained to respond in a fire emergency. Employees should know how to

- Prevent fires.
- Keep fires from spreading.
- Evacuate the facilities in the event of an emergency.
- Trigger fire alarms.

Fire drills should be conducted on a periodic basis. Employees should know the best way to evacuate the facilities. Elevators should never be used in a fire. Doors should be kept closed in a fire to retard the spread of fire. In a smoke-filled room, it is best to stay near the floors and crawl out. Floor plans highlighting the evacuation route should be posted at all exits and other prominent locations. Unless employees have been specifically trained, they should be instructed not to fight a major fire. All employees, however, should know the basics of using a fire extinguisher.

An alarm system should be installed in the facilities for warning personnel in an emergency. The warning system should consider the needs of persons with disabilities. For example, a flashing light may be used in addition to an audible alarm. The alarm system should have a backup power supply. The system should be tested on a periodic basis.

EARTHQUAKE CONTINGENCY PLAN

Earthquakes can seriously disrupt business operations. Earthquakes generally strike without any advance warning. Certain geographical regions are more vulnerable to earthquakes. Aftershocks can frequently occur for days and weeks following an earthquake.

Special precautions should be taken if your facilities are located in an earthquake-prone region. Governmental agencies can provide seismic information about the region in which your facilities are located. Adequate insurance coverage should be obtained to recover from damage caused by an earthquake. Insurance carriers can frequently provide safety information; implementing safety measures recommended by your insurance company may help reduce premiums.

The safety code should be adhered to strictly. Organizational facilities should be inspected and evaluated by structural engineers. The structure of the facilities should be reinforced, if necessary. Common techniques to strengthen the structure include

- Installing steel braces to the frame
- Reinforcing building foundation
- Securing pipes
- Installing braces to support suspended ceilings
- Using safety glass

Nonstructural items should be inspected to identify anything that might fall, break, or cause damage in an earthquake. Major considerations are

- Large and heavy objects should not be hung, but rather should be kept on the floor.
- If it is essential to hang large or heavy objects, they should be kept as far away as possible from areas where humans may be present.

- Shelves, cabinets, and heavy equipment should be secured or anchored.

- Hazardous chemicals and materials should be given special attention. Chemicals that may react with each other to produce a dangerous mix should be stored in separate locations.

Earthquake-emergency drills should be conducted on a periodic basis. Staff should be provided with basic safety instructions:

- If personnel are indoors during an earthquake, they should remain indoors and cover should be taken. It is essential to try to protect one's head and neck.

- If personnel are outdoors during an earthquake, they should move to an open area. They should stay away from buildings, trees, street lights, and electric-power wires.

- After an earthquake, personnel should be instructed to stay away from windows, chandeliers, and other items that may become loose and fall.

- Only stairways should be used to evacuate the buildings. Elevators should not be used.

- Special areas should be designated in which personnel should gather after an earthquake.

- Procedures should be established to determine whether evacuation is necessary following an earthquake.

WINTER-STORM CONTINGENCY PLAN

Snow, ice, and strong winds can shut down roads and facilities. It can cause physical damage, and electrical power is frequently affected. Monitoring weather forecasts will give you advance warning of winter storms. If a severe winter storm is expected, the facilities should be shut down and personnel should be allowed to go home early.

The facilities should be equipped with a backup power source, such as a generator, to avoid interrupting essential functions. Emergency supplies such as canned food, water, candles, flashlights, radios, batteries, blankets, first-aid supplies, and so forth, should be available in case personnel get stranded at your facilities.

HURRICANE CONTINGENCY PLAN

The hurricane season begins around June and ends around November. Hurricanes are severe tropical storms. They cause torrential rains and powerful ocean waves, which can damage coastal areas. Hurricanes may produce tornadoes. The National Weather Service monitors hurricanes and issues the following advisories:

> A *hurricane watch* means that a hurricane is possible in the next twenty-four to thirty-six hours.

> A *hurricane warning* means that a hurricane will hit in the next twenty-four hours.

A hurricane watch requires you to follow the weather to learn if a hurricane warning will be issued. If a hurricane warning is issued, immediate action is generally required.

The local emergency office may require that residents and businesses evacuate the community. Procedures should be established for closing the facility and evacuating as necessary.

- Personnel stranded at your facilities may need to be transported to a shelter.
- The external structure of the facilities should be protected.
- Any outside equipment should be protected or moved inside, if possible.
- Anything that may fly off and cause damage should be moved inside if possible, or secured to the ground.
- Windows are most vulnerable to damage. They should be protected using plywood. If your facilities are located in an area prone to hurricanes, a better solution is to install permanent storm shutters.
- Automatic water-activated pumps should be installed to remove flood water. Hurricanes frequently damage power lines, and electricity may not be available to power the pumps. Backup power source, such as a generator, is essential. Alternately, consider installing a gasoline-powered pump. When buying a gasoline-powered pump, check the fuel capacity and determine how long it will power the pump before requir-

ing refueling; it may not be possible for someone to refuel the pump during a hurricane.

TORNADO CONTINGENCY PLAN

Tornadoes are violent whirling windstorms with speeds reaching hundreds of miles per hour. The path of the tornado may be a mile wide and several miles long. While tornadoes frequently occur in the southern and the midwestern states, tornadoes can hit in any state. Tornadoes have the power to uproot trees and destroy buildings. Anything in the path of a tornado can instantly turn into a deadly missile.

Procedures should be established to deal with a tornado emergency. Personnel should be told to immediately take shelter if a tornado warning is issued. The best shelter from a tornado is some type of underground area. If it is not possible to take shelter in an underground area, interior rooms on the lowest floors should be considered. Ideally, the interior rooms should not have any windows. The room should be constructed of concrete, brick, or block.

It is preferable to be in a small room rather than in a large room. In fact, large rooms such as auditoriums and cafeterias with a level, widely spread roof are not considered safe and should not be used. Interior hallways on the lowest floors are a relatively safe place; personnel should, however, stay away from doors and windows. Personnel should be instructed to evacuate lightweight modular-office buildings immediately.

A structural engineer should be asked to evaluate and designate areas in your facility where shelter may be taken in the event of a tornado. If your facilities are located in an area frequently subjected to tornadoes, it is essential to conduct tornado drills.

FLOOD CONTINGENCY PLAN

Most areas in the United States experience some flooding. Certain areas are, however, more prone to significant flooding; greater precautions against flooding should be taken if your facilities are located in an area with a history of flooding.

Flooding may occur due to heavy rainfall or thawing of snow. While most floods develop slowly, flash floods can occur suddenly. Flash floods are typically caused by a dam failure. In certain regions with proximity to rivers or streams, flash floods may result from intense rain.

Personnel should be aware of your organization's evacuation plan in case of a flood emergency. Transportation arrangements may need to be made for the personnel.

Flood insurance should be purchased if your facilities are located in an area that is susceptible to flooding. Typical property and casualty insurance contracts specifically exclude flooding.

If your facilities are located in a flood zone, consider

- Relocating out of the flood zone
- Flood-proofing your facilities

If it is not possible or feasible to relocate, certain actions may be taken to flood-proof your facilities. The structure may be modified to resist flood-water pressure and seepage. Doors, windows, and other openings can be made of water-resistant materials such as bricks or concrete.

Sometimes it is not feasible to waterproof the entire facility. Building waterproof walls around the work areas or equipment can help protect essential equipment or work areas. Levees may be constructed to channel away floodwater. Water pumps should be installed to remove floodwater. If new facilities are being constructed in a flood zone, consider elevating the structure. During a flood emergency, building a wall of sandbags or other material can help minimize water damage.

HAZARDOUS-MATERIALS CONTINGENCY PLAN

Hazardous materials can threaten health and life and damage the environment and property. Hazardous materials may be toxic or noxious. They may pose a fire or explosion hazard. They may also be radioactive.

The accidental release of hazardous materials may require the evacuation of an entire community. The legal consequences of accidental release of hazardous materials are likely to be significant. A number of federal, state, and local laws regulate the use of hazardous materials. Some of the major laws include

- Clean Air Act
- Hazardous Materials Transportation Act
- Occupational Safety and Health Act
- Resource Conservation and Recovery Act of 1976
- Superfund Amendments and Reauthorization Act of 1986
- Toxic Substances Control Act

To minimize danger from accidental discharge of hazardous material, it is essential to label all hazardous materials. Employees should be trained in the proper handling of material. Safety guidelines for each specific material should be followed strictly. Procedures should be established to report and respond to an accidental discharge of hazardous material.

DEVELOPING A BACKUP STRATEGY

It is critical to have a backup strategy for functions that are essential for the survival of the organization. All vital records, including records on non-electronic media, should be backed up to recover from a disruption. Data files should be backed up on a periodic basis. The backup strategy should consider recovery not only of data files, but also of hardware, software, and documentation. Without a backup strategy, it would be time consuming and expensive to reconstruct lost information.

On-site and Off-site Backup Facilities

Both on-site and off-site backup must be planned for hardware, software, data, and documentation. The advantages of on-site backup include convenience and immediate access. Generally, a fire-resistant safe on the premises will suffice for on-site backup. It should be used to store the most current copy of the backup files. On-site backup is useful when there is a need to recover from a minor disruption, such as the malfunction of hardware equipment or the corruption of a data file.

For more significant disruptions, such as a disaster or catastrophe, however, on-site backup protection may be inadequate. In a disaster, such as a fire, an earthquake, or a tornado, there is a significant probability that whatever will affect the primary hardware, software, or data files will also affect the backup hardware, software, or data files. Off-site backup facilities are essential in recovering from a significant disruption.

Off-site facilities may be located nearby for convenience or far away for greater protection. A disruption, such as a fire, may not affect your nearby backup facility. However, a widespread disaster such as a hurricane, a flood, or an earthquake may damage your nearby off-site backup facilities, as well.

A balance must be struck between convenience and protection. One compromise is to have both a local off-site facility and a remote off-site facility. Consider the following:

- A fire-resistant safe in a building within a few miles of your primary facilities can serve as a local off-site facility. This will provide reasonable protection against disasters such as a fire. A local off-site facility offers the convenience of accessing data files on a daily basis. Files may be kept in this location for a few days.

- A remote off-site facility provides the greatest protection. The greater the distance, the greater the protection. The remote off-site facility should be at least several miles from the primary facility. Ideally, it should be at least a hundred miles from the primary facilities. The remote off-site facility should have a fire-resistant storage area. It may be used to house data files for several weeks or longer.

Several generations of backup files should be kept. An organization should have procedures in place to move data files between different backup facilities. The logistics of moving files to different facilities can become complex very quickly. It is essential to ensure that data files are correctly backed up and transported.

The organization should make an attempt to utilize standard technology. Recovery in a disaster can be expedited if the organization does not use unique hardware or software. Hardware equipment and software should be kept current to make it easier to replace equipment and software after a disruption.

Hot, Warm, and Cold Backup Sites

Hot sites are capable of becoming fully operational on a short notice, often in a matter of hours. Warm sites can be made operational in a matter of days or weeks. Cold sites typically have only a skeleton structure in place;

it may take anywhere from several days or weeks to even months to get a cold site operational.

Hot sites are suitable for critical applications. If a delay in computer processing will cause significant financial loss, an organization should consider using a hot site. Hot sites are used when even a partial degradation in processing is considered unacceptable.

The fast recovery time of a hot site comes at a significant price. It is essential all hardware and software at the hot site be completely compatible with the primary processing site. Whenever equipment or software is updated at the primary site, it must be updated at the hot site.

Warm sites tend to be less expensive than hot sites. The trade-off is that warm sites require more time to become fully operational. An organization may be able to use older or less expensive equipment at its warm site. More expensive equipment and software may be purchased or leased if necessary after a serious disruption. Warm sites are suitable when a partial degradation in processing output is considered acceptable.

Cold sites are suitable for longer-term computing needs. A cold site may not necessarily have any hardware equipment or software. A cold site may consist of nothing more than a basic skeleton facility. The cold site provides the infrastructure for a computer facility, such as cables for voice and data transmissions, air-conditioning/heating units, humidity controls, electrical wiring, flood- and fire-protection systems, and so forth.

The three types of backup sites do not have to be mutually exclusive. It often makes sense to utilize two or three types of sites in contingency planning. A hot site may be used for initial short-term processing until a warm site or cold site is ready to meet long-term processing needs.

Identifying the best recovery strategy is a complex issue. It requires a thorough technical analysis to identify the cost of hardware equipment and software applications. Cost-benefit analysis should be performed for each strategy option. The cost-benefit analysis should consider not only the direct cost of hardware and software, but also the indirect costs, such as wiring, air-conditioning, and fire prevention systems.

Selecting a Commercial Hot Site

Many organizations choose to subscribe to a commercial third-party hot site, rather than set up one of their own. While commercial hot sites tend to be expensive, the hot-site vendor will normally guarantee that your organization will receive properly configured hardware and software.

The cost of commercial hot sites varies considerably. Most vendors charge a monthly subscription fee, and when the hot-site facilities are actually used, an activation fee plus an hourly rate is typically charged. Some vendors have a high activation fee to discourage nonemergency use. Other vendors encourage the subscribers to make use of the hot-site facilities on a regular basis, such as for overload processing. Insurance may be purchased to cover the cost of the activation fee as well as the hourly rates.

For most organizations, use of a commercial hot site for an extended period of time is not economically feasible. Commercial third-party warm sites or cold sites offer a better alternative for a longer duration. Basic computer facilities and hardware are typically included in a warm-site subscription. A third-party cold-site subscription typically will not provide any hardware or software.

You should ask several questions before committing to a specific hot-site vendor.

- What are the activation fees?
- Does the vendor encourage or discourage the use of facilities for overload processing?
- What are the annual subscription fees?
- What is the hourly usage rate?
- What is the minimum contract period? What is the maximum contract period for locking in subscription fees?
- Is there a penalty for early termination of a contract?
- What networking capability does the vendor have?
- How is the vendor's customer service?
- Does the vendor charge for technical assistance?
- What hardware and software does the vendor provide?
- How will the vendor upgrade its hardware and software as your organization's hardware and software needs change?
- Does the vendor have the financial and technical capability to upgrade hardware and software?

- What is the vendor's expertise and experience in your specific industry?
- What security protections does the vendor offer?
- What is the vendor's experience with actual disasters and catastrophes?
- How are the references, especially from subscribers who have actually experienced a disaster?
- What other services does the vendor provide?

The following two questions are critical in selecting a hot-site vendor:

- How many subscribers does the vendor have?
- Where are its subscribers' geographical locations?

A vendor with too many hot-site subscribers may be unable to provide services when the need arises. A vendor will be unable to survive financially with too few subscribers. If there is a significant geographic concentration of subscribers, the hot-site vendor may be unable to meet the needs of all its subscribers in the event of a common natural disaster.

Some vendors can provide mobile sites for use in an emergency. Mobile sites typically consist of trailers equipped with computer hardware and software. A mobile site should be considered when it would be difficult for the personnel to move or commute to a remote backup location.

Mutual-Aid Agreements

Mutual-aid agreements are used by organizations to meet emergency needs. Two or more companies agree to help each other in the event of an emergency. Mutual-aid agreements offer a low-cost alternative to commercial hot sites. Mutual-aid agreements may not necessarily be legally enforceable; they should not be relied upon exclusively.

Mutual-aid agreements are appropriate for organizations with unique equipment/application requirements. Mutual-aid agreements, however, are not limited to computer processing only. They may also be appropriate for:

- Responding to a fire or hazardous-material incident
- Providing emergency equipment, shelter, storage, supplies, staff

- Assisting in an evacuation, such as by transporting personnel

Before entering into a mutual-aid agreement, consider the following:

- How will the agreement be activated?
- What constitutes an emergency?
- What costs will be incurred?
- How will the costs be accounted for?
- Which party will bear which costs?
- What is expected of each party during an emergency?
- Is the hardware and software between the two parties compatible?
- How will compatibility be maintained if one party decides to upgrade its hardware or software?
- How will compatibility be tested?
- How often will compatibility tests be conducted?
- How will processing time be shared at the host partners' facilities?
- Is your organization allowed processing time only if there is excess capacity available?
- Will the host partner be willing to delay its own processing to meet the needs of your organization?
- If there are multiple mutual-aid partners, how will the processing time be allocated among partners?
- Which partners will be used, and in what order?
- What is the level of technical assistance that the host partner's staff will provide?
- What hardware equipment and software may the parties use in an emergency?
- Will the mutual-aid parties be using each other's staff?
- How long may the host partner's facilities be utilized?

Relocating Facilities

An organization may need to relocate either temporarily or permanently after a disaster or a catastrophe. It may take the organization a significant amount of time to recover from a disruption if relocation needs are not specifically addressed in the contingency plan. Factors to consider in relocating include

- How many square feet will be needed?
- Will the new facility have adequate voice- and data-communication capabilities?
- How will the various departments be assigned space?
- Will there be adequate security at the new facility?
- Will there be sufficient storage area at the new facility?
- Is there access to public transportation for personnel and customers?
- Is there sufficient parking for personnel and customers?
- Will the new site meet staff needs, such as
  - Housing
  - Schools
  - Day care
  - Shopping

Consideration should be given to interim measures if only a portion of the facilities is affected by the disruption. The contingency plan should identify departments and functions that must be restored first. The plan should identify the type of support that each department will need. The possibility of splitting up large departments should be considered so they may be able to operate out of two or more locations. Departments that must be located at the same facility should be considered.

Hardware Selection

Backup of hardware equipment is one of the most important elements of contingency planning. Backup hardware is needed for both on-site and off-site facilities. A minor malfunction of the hardware that delays or disrupts a critical processing could cause significant financial loss. Some element of redundancy should be built into hardware-equipment planning. The use of older or slower equipment for backup purposes is often acceptable, especially if there are budgetary constraints. Partial processing capability may be enough to survive until hardware equipment can be fixed or replaced.

When replacement equipment or a component is needed, the best source is generally hardware vendors. However, the vendor may not always be able to supply the equipment quickly, especially if the equipment is in demand and inventories are low. The used-hardware market should be considered in such a situation; used-hardware dealers may be able to supply the critical components on short notice.

Software Selection

The backup strategy should include keeping copies of all software, including operating-system, utilities, and application programs. It is not necessary to keep backup copies of older-generation software. It is critical to keep backup copies of any upgrades or patches to fix bugs. Backup should be made of software configuration files or other special settings. Backup copies of system manuals and program documentation (online or hard copy) should be kept.

Backup copies of software, upgrades, patches, configuration files, and user manuals should be kept at both the organization's primary computer facilities and at off-site facilities. Backup copies should be kept in a fire-resistant safe.

When upgrading software at the primary facilities, backup copies of the software at the off-site facilities should also be upgraded. Procedures should be established to ensure that copies of maintenance patches to the software are kept at the off-site location. The licensing requirements for making backup copies should be considered.

Data Recovery

Rapid recovery of data is a critical part of contingency planning. Data include

- Source documents

- Data files and databases
- Output documents

Data records are stored on all types of media, including electronic media and hard copies. Backing up data poses a unique challenge for organizations. Unlike software or hardware, data are continually evolving. In an online, real-time system, each transaction modifies some element of the data. The backup strategy must consider the inherent nature of data. Procedures must be in place to ensure that the most recent data records are backed up.

Caution must be exercised when recovering data from backup files. It is advisable to always duplicate the original backup files before attempting recovery to minimize the likelihood of accidentally damaging the backup files. Controls should be used to ensure the integrity of the data in the recovery process.

Several techniques may be used to back up data. Smaller files, which are not continuously updated, may be duplicated in their entirety on backup magnetic or optical media. Larger files, especially those that are frequently updated, require alternate backup strategies; typically, it is not practical or cost effective to back up the entire file.

Updating the original master file with transactional changes, in a batch-processing system, creates a new master file. By keeping copies of the original master files and the transaction files for two or three generations, a new master file can be recreated if necessary.

Different backup procedures must be used in real-time, online processing systems. The continuously changing nature of data files necessitates the use of techniques such as the duplicate logging of transactions or keeping before-and-after images of master records. Copies of individual records may have to be kept before updating. Database-management systems typically contain specialized backup procedures for recovery of data in online, real-time systems.

Backup copies of vital records should be stored at an off-site location. Vital records include

- Corporate records
- Customer and supplier information
- Engineering plans

- Financial records

- Formulas and trade secrets

- Insurance information

- Inventory lists and specifications

- Patent designs

- Personnel files

In every organization, there are likely to be numerous documents that have not been backed up. For example, recently received source documents, such as invoices or purchase orders that originate outside the organization may contain critical information that cannot be easily reconstructed in the event of the document's destruction.

Remote backup using the Internet is available from several companies. Data files are automatically backed up on a daily basis. Data are stored in an encrypted format. Remote backup using the Internet is inexpensive. It is especially useful for small businesses that may not be keeping backup copies of their data on a regular basis at an off-site location. Appendix L contains a sample listing of companies offering remote backup using the Internet.

Another more expensive option is to transmit a copy of each transaction to a remotely located computer facility. Mirror processing not only transmits the data, but also updates a backup duplicate database, always keeping the backup current.

EMERGENCY COMMUNICATIONS AND NOTIFICATIONS

A failure in communications can significantly disrupt an organization's operations. Emergency-notification procedures should be established as part of every contingency plan. Communications must be operational to

- Warn personnel.

- Report emergencies.

- Coordinate emergency response with officials.

- Keep management, personnel, customers, and suppliers up-to-date.

Some of the issues to consider in planning emergency communications and notifications include

- What effect would there be on business operations if communications systems failed?

- Have procedures been established for personnel to report an emergency?

- Who must be notified (emergency response teams, key management officials, key personnel, families of personnel trapped in a disaster, key customers, key suppliers, media)?

- What are the legal requirements for notification of an emergency? Which governmental agencies must be notified?

- What are the potential health and safety effects of an emergency on the general public?

- Where is the primary notification list kept? Where is the backup list kept?

- How frequently is the notification list updated?

- Who is responsible for the notification process?

- How is communication expected to take place? (What if phone lines and other communication channels are not working?)

- How will functions requiring voice and data communications be supported?

- What communications equipment will be needed to provide notification?

- How are the communications facilities prioritized? Which communications facilities should be restored first?

- How will the restoration take place? What emergency support will be available from vendors of communication equipment?

Appendix M contains a list of federal and state emergency-management offices. Appendix N lists vendors for contingency-planning/disaster-recovery software.

Appendix A

GENERAL-SECURITY-ISSUES WORKSHEET

(A *NO* response indicates a potential vulnerability)	Yes	No	Don't Know or Not Applicable
1. Is there a written policy on security management?	❏	❏	❏
2. Is responsibility for computer security assigned to a specific individual or a department?	❏	❏	❏
3. Is each software purchased by the company reviewed for security requirements?	❏	❏	❏
4. Are there written procedures to protect a company's copyrights, patents, and trade secrets?	❏	❏	❏
5. Are contracts with governmental entities reviewed for special security and confidentiality requirements?	❏	❏	❏
6. Are management controls being followed?	❏	❏	❏
7. Is management concerned about anti-social behavior?	❏	❏	❏
8. Does management seem to have ethics?	❏	❏	❏

Appendix B

ACCESS-SECURITY
WORKSHEET

(A *NO* response indicates a potential vulnerability)	Yes	No	*Don't Know or Not Applicable*
1. Is access restricted to sensitive data files?	❏	❏	❏
2. Is access to program documentation and source code restricted?	❏	❏	❏
3. Are the password procedures adequate?	❏	❏	❏
4. Are guards used to monitor access to sensitive areas?	❏	❏	❏
5. Are dogs used to restrict access to sensitive areas?	❏	❏	❏
6. Are all employees required to carry an ID card?	❏	❏	❏
7. Is there a security officer?	❏	❏	❏
8. Is there a written security policy?	❏	❏	❏
9. Are password files encrypted?	❏	❏	❏
10. Are controls in place to prevent and detect security violations?	❏	❏	❏
11. Are users given the minimum access to perform their duties?	❏	❏	❏

(A *NO* response indicates a potential vulnerability)	Yes	No	*Don't Know or Not Applicable*
12. Is user access restricted to specific files, applications, or servers?	❏	❏	❏
13. Is modem access secure? Are techniques such as callback used?	❏	❏	❏
14. Is access to live files restricted to programmers?	❏	❏	❏
15. Is file maintenance restricted to specific individuals?	❏	❏	❏
16. Is there a process in place to grant access?	❏	❏	❏
17. Are access levels reviewed by internal auditors on a periodic basis?	❏	❏	❏

SECURITY-CONTROLS
WORKSHEET

(A *NO* response indicates a potential vulnerability)	*Yes*	*No*	*Don't Know or Not Applicable*
1. Are audit trails maintained throughout the application systems?	❏	❏	❏
2. Is there an independent review and testing of application controls?	❏	❏	❏
3. Is authorization required for changes to computer programs?	❏	❏	❏
4. Is there segregation of activities between programming and computer operations?	❏	❏	❏
5. Is there segregation of activities between clerical controls and computer operations?	❏	❏	❏
6. Is program development separate from program testing?	❏	❏	❏
7. Are personnel assignments rotated?	❏	❏	❏
8. Are dual controls used so that it is not possible to commit fraud in the absence of collusion?	❏	❏	❏
9. Are personnel bonded?	❏	❏	❏

349

(A *NO* response indicates a potential vulnerability)

	Yes	No	Don't Know or Not Applicable
10. Is there separation of duties?	❏	❏	❏
11. Is there rotation of duties?	❏	❏	❏
12. Are surprise inspections made?	❏	❏	❏
13. Are there periodic internal audits?	❏	❏	❏
14. Does the company have a written policy that prohibits full-time personnel from obtaining outside employment or moonlighting?	❏	❏	❏
15. Does the company have a written policy prohibiting the acceptance of gifts or entertainment from suppliers, vendors, contractors?	❏	❏	❏
16. Does the company have a written policy prohibiting the bribing of customers?	❏	❏	❏
17. Does the company have a written policy prohibiting the fixing of prices with competitors?	❏	❏	❏
18. Does the company have a written policy prohibiting gambling on the job?	❏	❏	❏
19. Does the company have a written policy prohibiting drug and alcohol abuse?	❏	❏	❏
20. Does the company have a written policy prohibiting the playing of computer games or surfing the net?	❏	❏	❏
21. Does the company have a written policy prohibiting the lending of keys, ID cards, badges, etc., to unauthorized individuals?	❏	❏	❏

(A *NO* response indicates a potential vulnerability)	Yes	No	*Don't Know or Not Applicable*
22. Does the company have a written policy prohibiting the disclosure of computer passwords to unauthorized individuals?	❏	❏	❏
23. Are there controls for smoke and fire detection?	❏	❏	❏
24. Are there controls for water detection?	❏	❏	❏
25. Are there redundant components in the computer system?	❏	❏	❏
26. Are management controls properly designed?	❏	❏	❏
27. Are there audit controls?	❏	❏	❏

Appendix D

FIREWALL-PERSONNEL-SECURITY WORKSHEET

(A *NO* response indicates a potential vulnerability)	Yes	No	*Don't Know or Not Applicable*
1. Are employees required to sign a confidentiality agreement?	❏	❏	❏
2. Are an applicant's references and background fully checked before employment?	❏	❏	❏
3. Are new personnel trained on company security practices?	❏	❏	❏
4. Are all materials, including ID cards, keys, and passes returned by employees upon termination?	❏	❏	❏
5. Are educational achievements of applicants verified?	❏	❏	❏
6. Are references of applicants checked?	❏	❏	❏
7. Are previous employers of applicants contacted?	❏	❏	❏
8. Are applicants checked for criminal convictions?	❏	❏	❏
9. Are applicants in sensitive positions required to undergo a polygraph test or voice-stress analysis?	❏	❏	❏

(A *NO* response indicates a potential vulnerability)	Yes	No	Don't Know or Not Applicable
10. Are psychological diagnostic tests used?	❑	❑	❑
11. Are new employees required to undergo mandatory security-orientation training?	❑	❑	❑
12. Are there written rules of ethical employee behavior?	❑	❑	❑
13. Are there job enrichment programs?	❑	❑	❑
14. Is there tuition reimbursement for employees?	❑	❑	❑
15. Are there written job descriptions?	❑	❑	❑
16. Are there standards for performance?	❑	❑	❑
17. Are performance appraisals conducted on a regular periodic basis?	❑	❑	❑
18. Are personnel penalized for violating the company's security policies?	❑	❑	❑
19. Is there a background security check performed for temporary, part-time, or contract employees?	❑	❑	❑
20. Is a log kept for personnel working after normal business hours?	❑	❑	❑
21. Are personnel guided when performance is below acceptable levels?	❑	❑	❑
22. Are rewards such as pay, benefits, job security, promotion opportunities, etc., perceived to be inadequate?	❑	❑	❑
23. Are job responsibilities clearly defined?	❑	❑	❑
24. Is there accountability in job assignments?	❑	❑	❑
25. Is there recognition for good performance?	❑	❑	❑

(A *NO* response indicates a potential vulnerability)	Yes	No	Don't Know or Not Applicable
26. Is feedback on job performance adequate?	❏	❏	❏
27. Is mediocre performance considered unacceptable?	❏	❏	❏
28. Are resources needed to meet requirements provided?	❏	❏	❏
29. Do personnel have enough time to complete assignments?	❏	❏	❏
30. Is management fair and impartial in recruiting, compensating, and evaluating employees?	❏	❏	❏

Appendix E

COMPUTER-FACILITIES-PROTECTION WORKSHEET

(A *YES* response indicates a potential vulnerability)	Yes	No	*Don't Know or Not Applicable*
1. Are computer facilities located in the basement or lower floors of a building?	❏	❏	❏
2. Are computer facilities located on the top floor? (Top floors should be avoided due to the possibility of a roof leak.)	❏	❏	❏
3. Is there a danger of flooding due to poor drainage?	❏	❏	❏
4. Are there exterior windows in the computer room?	❏	❏	❏
5. Are computer facilities located near water mains?	❏	❏	❏
6. Are computer facilities located near boilers, gas tanks, compressors, or other explosive or flammable materials?	❏	❏	❏
7. Is the computer area carpeted? (Carpets should be used only if they are fireproof and nonstatic.)	❏	❏	❏
8. Are water-protection measures, such as a pumping system, lacking?	❏	❏	❏

Appendix F

COMMON SERVICES, FEATURES, AND DEFINITIONS RELATED TO THE INTERNET SERVICE-PROVIDER MARKET

Dial-up service—Dial-up service gives up to 56Kbps telephone-modem access, which must be dialed into and connected each time it is used.

Leased Line—A leased line is a telephone line that has been leased for private use. In some contexts, it's called a dedicated line. A leased line is usually contrasted with a switched line or dial-up line.

Typically, large companies rent leased lines from the telephone message carriers (such as AT&T) to interconnect different geographic locations in their company. The alternative is to buy and maintain their own private lines or, increasingly perhaps, to use the public switched lines with secure message protocols. (This is called *tunneling*.)*

Virtual Private Network—A virtual private network (VPN) is a private *data network* that makes use of the public telecommunication infrastructure, maintaining privacy through the use of a *tunneling protocol* and security procedures. A virtual private network can be contrasted with a system of owned or leased lines that can be used by only one company. The idea of the VPN is to give the company the same capabilities at much lower cost by sharing the public infrastructure. Phone companies have provided secure shared resources for voice messages. A virtual private network makes it possible to have the same secure sharing of public resources for data. Companies today are looking at using a private virtual network for both *Extranets* and wide-area *Intranets*.

---

*Available at <http://www.whatis.com/>

Using a virtual private network involves encrypting data before sending them through the public network and decrypting them at the receiving end. An additional level of security involves encrypting not only the data but also the originating and receiving network addresses. Although as yet there is no standard protocol, Microsoft, 3Com, and several other companies have proposed a standard protocol, the Point-to-Point Tunneling Protocol (*PPTP*), and Microsoft has built the protocol into its Windows NT server. VPN software such as Microsoft's PPTP support as well as security software would usually be installed on a company's *firewall* server.*

Tunneling—Relative to the Internet, tunneling is using the Internet as part of a private secure network. The "tunnel" is the particular path that a given company message or file might travel through the Internet.

A protocol or set of communication rules called Point-to-Point Tunneling Protocol (PPTP) has been proposed that would make it possible to create a *virtual private network* through tunnels over the Internet. This would mean that companies would no longer need their own leased lines for wide-area communication but could securely use the public networks.

PPTP, sponsored by Microsoft and other companies, and Layer 2 Forwarding, proposed by Cisco Systems, are among the main proposals for a new Internet Engineering Task Force (IETF) standard. With PPTP, which is an extension of the Internet's Point-to-Point Protocol (PPP), any user of a PC with PPP client support will be able to use an independent service provider (ISP) to connect securely to a server elsewhere in the user's company.**

Secure Communications—Secure communications password protection and data encryption measures used to keep private communications private over the public Internet.

Internet Protocol—The Internet Protocol (IP) handles the address part of each data packet that is transmitted from one computer to another on the Internet. (A protocol is the set of rules computers use to talk to each other.) Each computer (or host) on the Internet has a unique address containing four numbers separated by periods (for example, 199.0.0.2). Each file you request (for example, someone's web home page) is identified in part by a domain name that maps to the Internet address of its computer. The file you request is in turn sent to you at your associated Internet address by the IPs at either end of the exchange.†

---

*Available at <http://www.whatis.com/index.htm>

**Available at <http://www.whatis.com/tunnelin.htm>

†Available at <http://www.jyu.fi/~eerwall/ip.htm>

The Internet Protocol, together with the Transmission Control Protocol (TCP), which manages the assembly and reassembly of data into the information packets sent over the Internet, form a program, TCP/IP, that each computer on the Internet uses to communicate with any other computer.

Intranet—An Intranet is a *network* of networks that is contained within an *enterprise.* It may consist of many interlinked *local area networks* and also use *leased lines* in the *wide-area network.* Typically, an Intranet includes connections through one or more *gateway* computers to the outside Internet. The main purpose of an Intranet is to share company information and computing resources among employees. An Intranet can also be used to facilitate working in groups and for teleconferences.

An Intranet uses *TCP/IP, HTTP,* and other Internet protocols and in general looks like a private version of the Internet. With *tunneling,* companies can send private messages through the public network, using the public network with special encryption/decryption and other security safeguards to connect one part of their Intranet to another.

Typically, larger enterprises allow users within their Intranet to access the public Internet through *firewall* servers that have the ability to screen messages in both directions so that company security is maintained. When part of an Intranet is made accessible to customers, partners, suppliers, or others outside the company, that part is called an *Extranet.** It has been described as a "state of mind" in which the Internet is *Extranet.*

Extranet—An Extranet is a private network that uses the Internet *protocols* and the public telecommunication system to securely share part of a business's information or operations with suppliers, vendors, partners, customers, or other businesses. An Extranet can be viewed as part of a company's Intranet that is extended to users outside the company, perceived as a way to do business with other companies as well as to sell products to customers. The same benefits that *HTML, HTTP, SMTP,* and other Internet technologies have brought to the Internet and to corporate Intranets now seem designed to accelerate business between companies.

An Extranet requires security and privacy. These require *firewall* server management, the issuance and use of *digital certificates* or similar means of user authentication, *encryption* of messages, and the use of virtual private networks (*VPNs*) that tunnel through the public network.**

---

*Available at <http://www.whatis.com/>
**Ibid.

Point-of-Presence—A point-of-presence (POP) is the location of an access point to the Internet. A POP necessarily has a unique Internet (*IP*) address. Your independent service provider (*ISP*) or online service provider (*OSP*) has a point-of-presence on the Internet. POPs are sometimes used as one measure of the size and growth of an ISP or OSP.

A POP may actually reside in rented space owned by a telecommunications carrier such as *Sprint.* A POP usually includes *routers,* digital/analog call *aggregators, servers,* and frequently *frame relay* or *ATM* switches.*

Remote Access—Remote access is the ability to get access to a computer or a network from a remote distance. In corporations, people at branch offices, telecommuters, and people who are traveling may need access to the corporation's network.**

Virtual Hosting—On the Internet, virtual hosting is the provision of a web *server* and other services so that a company or individual doesn't have to purchase and maintain its own web server *host* with a line to the Internet. A virtual hosting provider is sometimes called a web or Internet "space provider." Some companies providing this service simply call it "hosting." Typically, virtual hosting provides a customer who wants a web site with domain-name registration assistance, multiple domain names that map to the registered domain name, an allocation of file storage and directory setup for the web-site files (*HTML* and graphic-image files), e-mail addresses, and, optionally, web-site creation services. The virtual hosting user (the web-site owner) needs only to have a File Transfer Protocol (*FTP*) program for exchanging files with the virtual host.†

E-commerce—E-commerce (electronic commerce or EC) is the buying and selling of goods and services on the Internet, especially the World Wide Web. In practice, this term and a new term, *e-business,* are often used interchangeably. For online retail selling, the term *e-tailing* is sometimes used.

E-commerce can be divided into:

- E-tailing or "virtual storefronts" on web sites with online catalogs, sometimes gathered into a "virtual mall"
- The gathering and use of demographic data through web contacts

---

*Available at <http://www.whatis.com/pointofp.htm>
**Available at <http://www.whatis.com/>
†Available at <http://www.whatis.com/index.htm>

- Electronic Data Interchange (*EDI*), the business-to-business exchange of data

- *E-mail* and *fax* and their use as media for reaching prospects and established customers (for example, with newsletters)

- Business-to-business buying and selling

- The security of business transactions*

Encryption/decryption—Encryption is the conversion of data into a form, called a cipher, that cannot be easily intercepted by unauthorized people. Decryption is the process of converting encrypted data back into its original form, so it can be understood.

The use of encryption/decryption is as old as the art of communication. In wartime, a cipher, often incorrectly called a "code," can be employed to keep the enemy from obtaining the contents of transmissions. (Technically, a code is a means of representing a signal without the intent of keeping it secret; examples are Morse code and *ASCII*.) Simple ciphers include the substitution of letters for numbers, the rotation of letters in the alphabet, and the "scrambling" of voice signals by inverting the sideband frequencies. More complex ciphers work according to sophisticated computer *algorithms* that rearrange the data bits in digital signals.

In order to easily recover the contents of an encrypted signal, the correct decryption key is required. The key is an algorithm that "undoes" the work of the encryption algorithm. Alternatively, a computer can be used in an attempt to "break" the cipher. The more complex the encryption algorithm, the more difficult it becomes to eavesdrop on the communications without access to the key.

Encryption/decryption is especially important in *wireless* communications. This is because wireless circuits are easier to "tap" than their hardwired counterparts. Nevertheless, encryption/decryption is a good idea when carrying out any kind of sensitive transaction, such as a credit-card purchase online, or the discussion of a company secret among different departments in the organization. The stronger the cipher—that is, the harder it is for unauthorized people to break it—the better, in general. However, as the strength of encryption/decryption increases, so does the cost.

---

*Available at <http://www.whatis.com/>

Firewall—A firewall is a set of related programs, located at a network *gateway server,* that protects the resources of a private network from users from other networks. (The term also implies the security policy that is used with the programs.) An enterprise with an *Intranet* that allows its workers access to the wider Internet installs a firewall to prevent outsiders from accessing its own private data resources and for controlling what outside resources its own users have access to.

Basically, a firewall, working closely with a *router* program, *filters* all network *packets* to determine whether to forward them toward their destination. A firewall also includes or works with a *proxy server* that makes network requests on behalf of workstation users. A firewall is often installed in a specially designated computer separate from the rest of the network so that no incoming request can get directly at private network resources.

There are a number of firewall-screening methods. A simple one is to screen requests to make sure they come from acceptable (previously identified) *domain names* and *IP* addresses. For mobile users, firewalls allow remote access to the private network by the use of secure logon procedures and authentication certificates. A number of companies make firewall products. Features include logging and reporting, automatic alarms at given thresholds of attack, and a graphical user interface for controlling the firewall.*

ATM Technology—ATM combines the reliability of circuit switching with the efficiency of packet switching, giving you the best way to deliver all types of diverse traffic: data, image, voice, and video. Through simplified packet-switching techniques, ATM segments packets into 53-byte cells containing a 48-byte information field and a 5-byte header. The header identifies cells belonging to the same virtual channel and is used in appropriate routing. ATM speeds the cells of data over the public network, makes quick connections, and accurately reassembles the transmission at its destination.

ATM is an attractive Internet access option because it provides cost-effective access for companies requiring higher speeds than DS1 leased lines (1.544 Mbps), but not needing the full speed of DS3 leased lines (45 Mbps). Unlike DS3 lines, ATM has no distance-based pricing component.**

---

*Available at <http://www.whatis.com/firewall.htm>
**Available at <http://public.pacbell.net/business.html>

Appendix G

Selecting a
Value-Added Network
(VAN)

- What are the basic fees? What are the startup costs? What are the ongoing costs?
- What are the additional costs besides basic fees?
- Are there discounts for volume?
- What kind of billing data are provided?
- What communication speeds and protocols are supported?
- What security features are offered?
- What type of compliance testing is performed to ensure data integrity?
- What data backup and recovery services are offered?
- What types of transmission status reports are provided? What other types of reports are provided?
- What types of transaction-filtering services are offered to receive only desired solicitations?
- Is the VAN certified by Department of Defense for trading with the U.S. government?
- Does the VAN provide consulting services?
- Does the VAN provide training services?
- Does the VAN limit the number or type of transactions?
- How reliable is the service?

- When is customer support available? Is support provided twenty-four hours a day? What are the support hours?
- Does the VAN offer profiling of business transactions?
- What translation software is used by the VAN? Are customers provided with a choice?
- What is the frequency with which transaction data are forwarded by the VAN?
- How long is transaction data kept for retrieval?
- Will I need to join multiple VANs to reach all trading partners?
- Who is liable for lost transmission data?
- What references are there of entities similar to yours and what has been their experience?
- What additional special services does the VAN offer?

Appendix H

CONTINGENCY-PLANNING WORKSHEET

(A *NO* response indicates a potential vulnerability)	Yes	No	*Don't Know or Not Applicable*
1. Has the responsibility for creating and maintaining contingency plans been established?	❏	❏	❏
2. Is there a long-term contingency plan?	❏	❏	❏
3. Is there a short-term contingency plan?	❏	❏	❏
4. Are there "Hot-sites," "Warm-sites," or "Cold-sites" contingency facilities?	❏	❏	❏
5. Has a cost-benefit analysis been conducted to determine insurance needs?	❏	❏	❏
6. Is an uninterruptible power supply (UPS) used?	❏	❏	❏
7. Is a full-scale standby power facility available for long-term power outages?	❏	❏	❏
8. Are data files backed up periodically?	❏	❏	❏
9. Are backup copies of data files stored in a secure remote site?	❏	❏	❏

(A *NO* response indicates a potential vulnerability)	Yes	No	*Don't Know or Not Applicable*
10. Are vital records and documentation stored in a secure remote site?	❏	❏	❏
11. Are there redundant pathways in transmission lines?	❏	❏	❏
12. Are there backup dial lines?	❏	❏	❏
13. Have natural disasters, such as earthquakes, floods, and tornadoes, been considered in contingency planning?	❏	❏	❏
14. Has consideration been given to vital-records management, including backup of data files and software?	❏	❏	❏
15. Has consideration been given to intentional and accidental threats such as strikes, sabotage, disgruntled employees, terrorism, and human errors or omissions?	❏	❏	❏
16. Are preventive actions taken to reduce threats and vulnerabilities?	❏	❏	❏
17. Is there a written plan for taking action during an emergency?	❏	❏	❏
18. Have insurance-company requirements to maintain coverage been met?	❏	❏	❏
19. Is management aware of its responsibilities under the Foreign Corrupt Practices Act (FCPA)?	❏	❏	❏
20. Is management aware of its responsibilities for retaining records for tax and regulatory purposes?	❏	❏	❏
21. Have software-related failures and malfunctions been considered?	❏	❏	❏

(A *NO* response indicates a potential vulnerability)	Yes	No	*Don't Know or Not Applicable*
22. Has the contingency plan been adequately tested?	❏	❏	❏
23. Has recovery time been determined?	❏	❏	❏
24. Is the contingency plan updated at periodic intervals as necessary?	❏	❏	❏
25. Are personnel aware of their responsibilities under the contingency plan?	❏	❏	❏
26. Are personnel trained on the contingency plan, including when subsequent changes are made?	❏	❏	❏
27. Is there equipment insurance coverage when it is in a remote site (such as at a client's office) or in transit?	❏	❏	❏
28. Is there business-interruption and extra-expense insurance coverage?	❏	❏	❏
29. Is there insurance coverage for professional liability?	❏	❏	❏
30. When leasing equipment, has the liability for each party been determined?	❏	❏	❏
31. Are insurance needs reviewed on a periodic basis to prevent under or over insurance?	❏	❏	❏
32. Is there crime insurance?	❏	❏	❏
33. Is there errors-and-omissions insurance?	❏	❏	❏
34. Is there insurance for electrical disturbance?	❏	❏	❏
35. Are there emergency measures in place for recovery after disaster?	❏	❏	❏

Appendix I

CONTINGENCY-PLANNING CHECKLIST*

GENERAL OVERVIEW

1. If a major disaster to your data center occurred today, could your organization survive?
2. Have you recently completed an Impact/Risk Analysis?
3. Do you know the total dollar amount of your exposure?
4. Have you prioritized all of your programs?
5. Have you listed the maximum downtime for all of your systems?
6. Have you listed the objectives of a disaster plan and the assumptions it includes?
7. Do you have a disaster plan, and is it current?
8. Does the plan include backup facilities?
   - Hot backup site?
   - Cold site?
   - Reciprocal agreement?
9. Does the backup facility inform you when there is a change in hardware or software?
10. Have you determined the cost of a disaster plan, including

---

*This appendix is taken from *Disaster Recovery Journal*'s sample contingency plan (<http://www.drj.com/articles/drpall.html>).

371

- Initial cost?
- Development cost?
- Maintenance cost?

11. Has the plan been approved by top management?

12. Do you have a Disaster Planning Coordinator?

13. Is someone assigned to update the plan?

14. Does the plan use a team approach?

15. Do you have people assigned to lead each team?

16. Is the same person assigned to lead more than one team?

17. Are names and phone numbers updated regularly?

18. Has the plan been reviewed by the Internal Audit, Security, and Insurance Departments?

19. Does the plan provide for recovery from a major disaster, and can it be adjusted for a less severe occurrence?

20. Has the plan been tested using only material stored off-site?

21. Is the plan tested at least every six months?

22. Has the plan been updated as a result of the testing?

23. Have you ever initiated a surprise test?

24. Does the plan provide instructions for
    - Emergency procedures?
    - Organizational structure following a disaster?
    - Off-site storage for all recovery material?

25. Does the off-site storage have twenty-four-hour access, physical security, vaulting, fire protection, courier service, round-trip travel time of less than one hour, and access only by authorized persons?

26. Are the tapes secured in a separately controlled room within the secured area?

27. Is all system documentation, except program listings, kept in fireproof storage when not in use?

28. Are there written instructions that define the responsibilities that personal computer (PC) users have for backing up and protecting their files?

29. Have these instructions been given to all PC users?

30. Have all data-center personnel been advised about the confidentiality of all information they work with?

DATA CENTER FACILITY

1. Are there signs outside identifying the data center?

2. Is the building protected by security guards, fences, alarm systems, and/or closed-circuit monitoring?

3. Is wiring for all security and alarm systems passed through conduit?

4. Do guards make scheduled rounds of the building?

5. If no guards are used, are the people responsible for security trained by security professionals?

6. Has someone been assigned the responsibility for security of the data center, company, or building?

7. Are security personnel or computer-room personnel on-site at all times?

8. Is there card access to the facility and various areas in the facility?

9. Are identification badges worn by all employees?

10. Are visitors required to sign in and sign out?

11. Is there security at the receiving area?

12. Is there an Office/Building Emergency Booklet published that includes

    - Medical emergencies?
    - Fire-emergency procedures?
    - Evacuation procedures?
    - Bomb threats?
    - Security violations?
    - Electrical failures?

13. Has someone been assigned to provide information, instruction, and supervision for the list in Item 12?

14. Are evacuation-route drawings posted in all hallways?

15. Have all occupants been instructed and trained in emergency procedures?

16. Are fire drills conducted on a regular basis under the supervision of your local fire marshal?

17. Is there a written termination procedure that includes a checklist of items to be returned to the company, such as keys, ID badges, card access, etc.?

18. Are all employees required to take vacation time so others can perform their duties?

19. Do all areas of all buildings have a fire-alarm system?

20. Has the fire-detection and extinguishing equipment been tested and/or inspected in the past six months?

21. Does the insurance company or fire department make annual fire inspections?

22. Is the storage area for forms and supplies protected with sprinklers?

23. Are smoke detectors located in the storage area?

DATA ENTRY

1. Are there alternatives for entering input normally keyed online?

2. Have you made provisions to have keying done on the outside in emergencies?

3. Is a copy of the keying instructions stored off-site?

4. Is a software package used for keying, and is it available to outside services?

5. Have arrangements been made to have your affiliates or divisions key your input?

6. Are all manual procedures performed by data entry documented and a copy stored off-site?

7. Are source documents batched and controlled by another department?

8. Are source documents stamped with date, time, and operator after keying?

9. Are source documents maintained in their original batches for a short time so they can be rekeyed if necessary?

10. Are source documents returned to the data-control department after keying?

11. Can the data-entry department be reestablished in another location in a reasonably short time, if necessary?

DATA CONTROL

1. Is access to the data-control department restricted?

2. Are all source documents and computer reports routed through this department for control and balancing?

3. If communication fails for transmitted reports, has an alternate method for sending reports to users been established?

4. Is this department responsible for the control of check forms?

5. Is there a written procedure for issuing a supply of blank checks outside the computer room?

6. Are checks signed by a different person from the person balancing and distributing them?

7. Can the check signer be replaced overnight?

8. Is there any special office equipment critical to the operation of the data center?

9. Are backup signature facsimiles secured off-site?

10. Is there a formal custom-form system that identifies all forms, their reorder point, their supplier, and an alternate supplier?

11. Is a small supply of all critical custom forms maintained on-site?

12. Is a copy of all form specifications and a copy of the final proof maintained off-site?

13. Is a fact sheet maintained on all suppliers of office equipment and forms?

14. Has an alternate point-to-point pickup and delivery been planned for if the primary method is not operational?

15. Is there an output distribution report form for every printed report—defining number of copies, method of shipping, recipient name, and recipient phone number?

COMPUTER ROOM

1. Is access to the computer room restricted?
2. Are only the computer operators allowed to operate the computer?
3. Is the room protected from halon, carbon dioxide, or sprinklers?
4. Are smoke detectors located
   - In the ceiling?
   - Under the raised floor?
   - In the air-conditioning ducts?
5. Will the smoke detectors operate even if there is a power outage?
6. Are fire extinguishers located at all exit doors?
7. Are water detectors located under the floor?
8. Are waterproof covers stored in the computer room for emergencies?
9. Is an uninterrupted-power-supply system installed for short power outages?
10. Is a generator available for extended power outages?
11. Is there emergency lighting in the computer room?
12. Is there an emergency power-off switch located at the exits?
13. Is there more than one cooling system that will support the computer hardware should one system fail?
14. Will an alarm sound if the air-conditioning system is turned off?
15. Is the temperature and humidity monitored?
16. Will some type of visible or audible alarm sound if the limits are exceeded?
17. Are fire doors installed at all entrances to the computer room?
18. Are check forms stored in a secured room?

19. Are there written instructions for powering up and powering down the system?

20. Are there written instructions for actions to take in an emergency?

21. Is there a copy of the Management Information System Contingency Plan in the computer room?

22. Is a procedure library used that contains all the job control necessary to execute job streams?

23. Is there a formal scheduling system, either computerized or manual?

24. Is someone assigned to review the schedule and enter all control-record information?

25. Is the entering of control records and similar job-control functions eliminated from operator intervention?

26. Are tape mounts controlled by a tape-librarian system?

27. Does a supervisor review reasons why an operator overrides the tape-librarian system?

28. Does operations management review the console log and error listing to ensure that identifiable errors are corrected and recurring errors are prevented?

29. Are there written restart procedures for all production systems?

30. Do the restart procedures indicate that other systems may have to be reprocessed even though they are completed successfully?

31. Do all high-priority systems have detail recovery procedures documented?

32. Are all problems in the computer room documented?

33. Are metered hours correlated to lapsed time, if practical?

34. Is there a formal problem-management system, where computer-room problems are reviewed by members from operations and programming and remedies assigned?

35. Is all down time reviewed by operations management?

36. Is all production-job control reviewed by the operations department after testing is completed and before programs are turned over for production?

37. Are there run manuals for all production applications?

38. Do the operators have easy access to the run manuals?

39. Are duplicate copies of the run manuals stored off-site?

40. Is all special processing for quarterly or annual runs properly documented?

41. Are batch jobs scheduled for each shift?

42. Is there a computerized job-accounting system?

43. Is the job-accounting report reviewed to determine any unusual run patterns?

44. Are all new systems reviewed for proper file rotation to off-site storage?

45. Is there a list of all computer hardware including serial numbers, communication equipment and lines, power requirements, cooling requirements, floor-space requirements, and acceptable substitute equipment for all the above; and is a copy of this list stored off-site?

46. Is there a cable-layout diagram and plug connector description for the current equipment, and is a copy stored off-site?

47. Is a vendor-information sheet maintained for all vendors supplying computer equipment and supplies?

48. Have you asked a used hardware vendor for a list of available equipment in preparation for an emergency?

49. Are the following backed up daily and rotated off-site?
    - Procedure library?
    - Tape library?
    - Job schedule?

50. Is there a formal procedure for obsoleting a program?

51. Are the microfiche procedures documented and a copy stored off-site?

52. Are there any water pipes near or above the computer room?

53. Is there a threat of water leakage from nearby areas: kitchen, rest rooms, janitor closet, drinking fountain?

TAPE LIBRARY

1. Is the tape library protected by sprinklers?

2. Are smoke detectors located in the tape library?

3. Does the entrance to the tape library have a fire door?

4. Does the tape library have emergency lights?

5. Is access to the tape library restricted by card access or other security?

6. Is a fire extinguisher mounted outside the door to the tape library?

7. Has the tape library become a storage area for items other than tapes?

8. Does the off-site storage for tapes have security, fire protection, twenty-four-hour access, bonded pickup and delivery?

SYSTEMS AND PROGRAMMING

1. Is all application software backed up and stored off-site?

2. Do all changes to programs need authorization?

3. Are there audit trails that identify any program that has been copied for modification or any new program in development?

4. Is all application software responsible for distributing funds, such as payroll and accounts payable, password protected?

5. Do the systems have adequate controls, such as batch totals, hash totals, run totals, and dollar amounts?

6. Are checks outside the normal range flagged on an audit-trail report?

7. Does an accounts-payable audit-trail report list the payee for all checks?

8. Do all financial applications have complete audit-trail reports?

9. Is all of the on-site system documentation stored in fireproof cabinets?

10. Are users asked to assist in the preparation of test data?

11. Is there a formal methodology for design and programming?

12. Is the design phase completed before the programming phase begins?

13. Are there written design standards and programming standards?

14. Are permanent files categorized as critical, important, useful, and non-essential?

15. Do the standards require the backing up of all critical files?

16. Are the three most current generations of all important and critical files maintained (current, father, grandfather)?

17. Do the standards require all programs to include proper controls and totals for complete auditing and for the detection and correction of errors?

18. Are test data with predetermined results saved and used for heavily maintained systems such as payroll?

19. Are program changes always made to the source code?

20. Is the source code maintained on a library that is backed up and rotated off-site?

21. Are the program link-edit reports reviewed for errors and filed with the source code listing?

22. Are programs always tested even when they have minor modifications?

23. Does management randomly review program changes and test results?

24. Do user departments sign off on program modifications and review test results?

25. Is there a formal procedure for making a program in development a production program?

26. Are operation run manuals required as part of the program turnover to operations?

27. Are all modifications to purchased software fully documented and coded in a way that will not disturb the pure supplied code?

28. Is a list available of all systems with the person responsible noted?

29. Is there a list that identifies all programs in a system?

30. Does each system have a backup person?

31. Is documentation kept current?

32. Is documentation maintained on the computer, backed up, and rotated off-site?

33. Is there a listing of all technical manuals so they can be replaced if necessary?

34. Does your company policy state the file retention period for asset information, stockholder information, tax records, employee information, and other vital records?

35. Are record layouts maintained for the retention period along with the file media?

36. Has the source information been identified that created the retained data?

TECHNICAL SUPPORT

1. Is the operating system backed up and rotated off-site?

2. Is a list maintained of all operating-system software?

3. Are the people in the department cross-trained so that everyone has backup?

4. Are all responsibilities, duties, and procedures documented and a copy stored off-site?

5. Is a vendor-information sheet maintained for all vendors supplying software?

6. Have provisions been made for purchased software to execute on another system during an emergency?

7. Is a copy of the SYSGEN parameters stored off-site?

8. Is there complete documentation explaining how to bring up the operating system at the backup facility?

9. Is the utilization of all disk devices documented?

10. Has a plan been formulated on how alternate disk devices would be utilized?

11. Is there documentation explaining how to modify the job-control-language to execute at the backup facility?

DATABASE ADMINISTRATION

1. Are all databases identified?

2. Are all programs that update each database identified?

3. Is the activity that updates the database continually logged?

4. Are all programs that access each database identified?

5. Are databases backed up and rotated off-site?

6. Are audit trails available that identify databases that are filing up, and are these reports available on a daily basis?

7. Are there documented procedures on how to test the validity of each database after it is restored?

8. Is there documentation that identifies multiple databases that must be kept synchronized with one another?

INTERNAL AUDIT

1. Have you reviewed the MIS Contingency Plan?

2. Have you observed a recovery test that used only material stored off-site?

3. Do you periodically review the data-center operation and make written recommendations on improvements to procedures, security, and controls?

4. Are user departments required to balance computer output to manual-control totals for audit and security?

5. Do you save test data to process through cash disbursement systems producing predetermined results?

INSURANCE

1. Has the data-center management been informed as to the do's and don'ts concerning insurance following a disastrous event?

2. Does the insurance policy include business-interruption coverage?

3. Is another department in the organization responsible for insurance protection?

4. Do you have a copy of the insurance policy?

5. Have you reviewed the coverage in the past year?

6. Do you have an annual formal review of your insurance coverage with the insurance carrier?

7. Does the insurance coverage include data-processing hardware and software?

8. Did you perform a risk/impact analysis for the data center?

BACKUP FACILITY

1. Do you currently subscribe to a fully equipped backup facility?

2. Is the backup facility located at a distance that will ensure that an area-wide disaster will not affect the facility?

3. Is the security at the backup facility at least as good as the security at your current facility?

4. Have you ever used the backup facility as part of a mock disaster?

5. Does the backup facility have adequate hours available for testing?

RECIPROCAL AGREEMENTS

1. Do you have a formal reciprocal agreement currently in effect?

2. Does the other organization's computer have time available to share with you?

3. Does your computer have time available to share with another organization?

4. Are both computer systems compatible?

5. Do both computer systems have the capacity to process critical applications for both organizations at the same time?

6. Is the operating-system software compatible?

7. Is there sufficient tape and disk capacity and compatibility?

8. Will your communication network quickly connect with the other organization's computer?

9. Does either data center have specialized hardware such as laser printers or cartridge-tape drives?

10. Have both organizations agreed to notify the other about changes in hardware or software?

11. Will your purchased software execute at the other data center?

12. Have you tested a critical application at the other data center?

13. Is there temporary storage available at the other data center for printer forms?

14. Is there temporary storage available at the other data center for your tape library?

15. Is there temporary office space available at the other data center for operations-support personnel?

Appendix J

FIRE-PROTECTION WORKSHEET

(A *NO* response indicates a potential vulnerability)	Yes	No	Don't Know or Not Applicable
1. Are hand extinguishers for smaller fires available in convenient locations?	❏	❏	❏
2. Is fireproof metal furniture used in computer facilities?	❏	❏	❏
3. Are paper supplies and other combustible materials stored separately?	❏	❏	❏
4. Are personnel trained in fire emergency?	❏	❏	❏
5. Is smoking prohibited in the computer room?	❏	❏	❏
6. Are emergency procedures posted?	❏	❏	❏
7. Are fire drills conducted on a periodic basis?	❏	❏	❏
8. Is electrical power to computer equipment cut off automatically after extinguishing systems are activated (but in an orderly fashion to allow work in progress to be saved)?	❏	❏	❏
9. Is a grid system of detection devices used so that a single malfunction in a unit does not automatically trigger an extinguishing agent?	❏	❏	❏

(A *NO* response indicates a potential vulnerability)

	Yes	No	*Don't Know or Not Applicable*
10. Is there adequate fire-insurance coverage?	❏	❏	❏
11. Is smoke vented to prevent buildup of corrosive fumes?	❏	❏	❏
12. Are raised floors made of noncombustible material?	❏	❏	❏
13. Is acoustic material fireproof?	❏	❏	❏
14. Are water extinguishers marked, "Danger. Do not use on electrical fires."?	❏	❏	❏
15. Are automatic carbon-dioxide extinguishing systems avoided in personnel-occupied enclosed areas? (Carbon dioxide can be dangerous to personnel, and automatic extinguishers should be used only in areas that contain equipment, but not personnel.)	❏	❏	❏

Appendix K

BUSINESS-IMPACT ANALYSIS WORKSHEET*

What would be the effect of a "worst-case scenario" (any kind of disaster or calamity) if it occurred at your work facility? It is important to try and calculate the "impact value" of a crisis because that will tell you how damaging a "critical incident" will be if there is no crisis intervention.

AMOUNT OF SCRUTINY THE CRISIS MIGHT GENERATE

- What kind of news coverage might ensue?
- What kind of agencies might get involved? Occupational Safety and Health Agency? Environmental Protection Agency?
- How would stockholders and creditors react?
- What about senior management's evaluation?

On a scale of 1 to 10, how much scrutiny would your crisis incur? _____

EFFECT ON EMPLOYEE MORALE/PRODUCTIVITY

- How would the crisis affect employee productivity?
- Absenteeism?

---

*This appendix is taken from "Estimating the Impact Value of a Crisis" by Dan Paulk (available through http://www.disaster-resource.com/) and is based upon the research of Steven Fink, *Crisis Management: Planning for the Inevitable,* American Management Association. New York, 1986.

- How much time might be spent dealing with the crisis at the expense of other work/business functions?
- What about employee morale during this time? Stress? Outrage?

On a scale of 1 to 10, estimate the amount of business interference the crisis might generate. _____

COMPANY'S PUBLIC IMAGE

- How will the public view the crisis and your handling of it?
- Will the company be seen as culpable? Liable?
- What about customers' reactions?
- Community reaction?
- Employees' families' reactions?

On a scale of 1 to 10, estimate the potential damage to company image/reputation in the aftermath of the crisis. _____

DAMAGE TO THE COMPANY'S BOTTOM LINE

- Concerning "hard" dollars, what might be the cost to the company?
- How much would be covered by insurance?
- Concerning "soft" dollars, what will employee unrest, stress, absenteeism, lowered morale, and lowered productivity cost the company?
- How would it affect the company's ability to get products to market on time? Meet payroll? Pay creditors?
- What about the costs of increased workers' compensation claims?
- Unemployment insurance claims?

Combining hard and soft dollar costs together, what is your opinion (1 to 10) of the cost of the crisis? _____

LEGAL LIABILITY/VULNERABILITY

- Was this incident "foreseeable"?

- If so, did we take enough reasonable precautions to prevent such a calamity?

- Did we have any specific controls or policies in place meant to prevent such a crisis?

- Is there any "discoverable" information regarding this incident that could be interpreted in a "damning" way by outsiders?

- Would an aggressive plaintiff attorney "smell" an opportunity here?

Considering the potential degree of legal liability, what is your estimate, on a scale of 1 to 10, of legal vulnerability regarding this incident? _____

IMPACT VALUE OF THE CRISIS = Total of 5 scores, divided by 5 = _____

The effect of crisis on business functions increases as the Impact Value score increases. The score tells you how damaging a "critical incident" will be if there is no crisis intervention.

Appendix L

REMOTE-BACKUP SITES

The following is a sample listing of companies offering remote backup through the Internet.

- At Backup Inc
  http://www.atbackup.com/
- Atrieva
  http://www.atrieva.com/
- BACKUP Data Protection Agency
  http://members.aol.com/backupdpa/index.htm
- Connected Corporation
  http://www.connected.com/
- CYBeRGEM Remote Backup System
  http://www.cybrgem.com/backup/
- DataLock Remote Data Services
  http://datalock.com/
- DataSaver Online Backup Service
  http://datasaver.com/
- Filetron
  http://www.back-up.com/
- Guardian Computer Service
  http://www.guardiancomputer.com/

- NetSafe
  http://www.evault.com/
- Offsite Data Management Remote Backup Service
  http://odms.com/
- Saf-T-Net
  http://www.trgcomm.com/
- SafeGuard Interactive
  http://www.sgii.com/
- TeleBackup Systems Inc
  http://www.telebackup.com/

EMERGENCY-MANAGEMENT OFFICES

FEDERAL EMERGENCY MANAGEMENT AGENCY (FEMA) HEADQUARTERS

Federal Emergency Management Agency, 500 C Street SW, Washington, DC 20472; (202)646-2500.

FEMA Regional Offices

- Region I: Boston
  (617)223-9540

- Region II: New York
  (212)225-7209

- Region III: Philadelphia
  (215)931-5500

- Region IV: Atlanta
  (770)220-5226

- Region V: Chicago
  (312)408-5500

- Region VI: Denton, TX
  (817)898-5104

- Region VII: Kansas City, MO
  (816) 283-7061

- Region VIII: Denver
  (303) 235-1813

- Region IX: San Francisco
  (415) 923-7100

- Region X: Bothell, WA
  (206) 487-4604

State Emergency-Management Agencies

Alabama Emergency Management Agency
5898 S. County Rd.
Clanton, AL 35045
(205) 280-2200

Alaska Division of Emergency Services
New Anchorage Armory
Fort Richardson Bldg. 49000, Suite B-210
Fort Richardson, AK 99595-5750
(907) 428-7000

Arizona Division of Emergency Services
National Guard Bldg.
5636 E. McDowell Rd.
Phoenix, AZ 85008
(602) 231-6245

Arkansas Office of Emergency Services
P.O. Box 758
Conway, AR 72032
(501) 329-5601

California Office of Emergency Services
2800 Meadowview Rd.
Sacramento, CA 95823
(916) 427-4990

Colorado Office of Emergency Management
Camp George West
Golden, CO 80401
(303)273-1622

Connecticut Office of Emergency Management
360 Broad St.
Hartford, CT 06105
(203)566-3180

Delaware Division of Emergency Planning and Operations
Delaware City, DE 19706
(302)834-4531

District of Columbia Office of Emergency Preparedness
200 14th St. NW, 8th Floor
Washington, DC 20009
(202)727-3150

Florida Division of Emergency Management
2740 Crestview Dr.
Tallahassee, FL 32399
(904)488-1900

Georgia Emergency Management Agency
P.O. Box 18055
Atlanta, GA 30316-0055
(404)624-7205

Hawaii State Civil Defense
3949 Diamond Head Rd.
Honolulu, HI 96816-4495
(808)734-2161

Idaho Bureau of Disaster Services
650 W. State St.
Boise, ID 83720
(208)334-3460

Illinois Emergency Management Agency
110 E. Adams St.
Springfield, IL 62706
(217)782-2700

Indiana Emergency Management Agency
State Office Bldg., Room E-208
302 W. Washington St.
Indianapolis, IN 46204

Iowa Emergency Management Division
Hoover State Office Bldg.
Level A, Room 29
Des Moines, IA 50319
(515)281-3231

Kansas Division of Emergency Preparedness
P.O. Box C300
Topeka, KS 66601
(913)266-1400

Kentucky Disaster and Emergency Services
Boone Center, Parkside Dr.
Frankfort, KY 40601
(502)564-8682

Louisiana Office of Emergency Preparedness
Department of Public Safety
LA Military Dept.
P.O. Box 44217
Capitol Station
Baton Rouge, LA 70804
(504)342-5470

Maine Emergency Management Agency
State Office Bldg., Station 72
Augusta, ME 04333
(207)289-4080

Maryland Emergency Management and Civil Defense Agency
Two Sudbrook Ln., East
Pikesville, MD 21208
(301)486-4422

Massachusetts Emergency Management Agency
400 Worcester Rd.
Framingham, MA 01701
(508)820-2000

Michigan Emergency Management Division
Michigan State Police
300 S. Washington Sq.
Suite 300
Lansing, MI 48913
(517)334-5130

Minnesota Division of Emergency Services
Department of Public Safety
State Capitol, B-5
St. Paul, MN 55155
(612)296-2233

Mississippi Emergency Management Agency
P.O. Box 4501, Fondren Station
Jackson, MS 39296
(601)352-9100

Missouri State Emergency Management Agency
P.O. Box 116
Jefferson City, MO 65102
(314)751-9779

Montana Emergency Management Specialist
Disaster and Emergency Services
P.O. Box 4789
Helena, MT 59604-4789
(406)444-6911

Nebraska Civil Defense Agency
National Guard Center
1300 Military Road
Lincoln, NE 68508-1090
(402)473-1410

Nevada Division of Emergency Services
2525 S. Carson St.
Carson City, NV 89710
(702)887-7302

New Hampshire Governor's Office of Emergency Management
State Office Park South
107 Pleasant St.
Concord, NH 03301
(603)271-2231

New Jersey Office of Emergency Management
P.O. Box 7068
W. Trenton, NJ 08628-0068
(609)538-6050

New Mexico Emergency Planning and Coordination
Department of Public Safety
4491 Cerrillos Rd.
P.O. Box 1628
Santa Fe, NM 87504
(505)827-9222

New York State Emergency Management Office
Public Security Bldg. #22
State Campus
Albany, NY 12226-5000
(518)457-2222

North Carolina Division of Emergency Management
116 West Jones St.
Raleigh, NC 27603-1335
(919)733-3867

North Dakota Division of Emergency Management
P.O. Box 5511
Bismarck, ND 58502-5511
(701)224-2113

Ohio Emergency Management Agency
2825 W. Granville Rd.
Columbus, OH 43235-2712
(614)889-7150

Oklahoma Civil Defense
P.O. Box 53365
Oklahoma City, OK 73152
(405)521-2481

Oregon Emergency Management Division
Oregon State Executive Department
595 Cottage St., NE
Salem, OR 97310
(503)378-4124

Pennsylvania Emergency Management Agency
P.O. Box 3321
Harrisburg, PA 17105-3321
(717)783-8016

Puerto Rico State Civil Defense
Commonwealth of Puerto Rico
P.O. Box 5127
San Juan, PR 00906
(809)724-0124

Rhode Island Emergency Management Agency
State House, Room 27
Providence, RI 02903
(401)421-7333

South Carolina Emergency Management Division
1429 Senate St., Rutledge Bldg.
Columbia, SC 29201-3782
(803)734-8020

South Dakota Division of Emergency and Disaster Services
State Capitol, 500 East Capitol
Pierre, SD 57501
(605)773-3231

Tennessee Emergency Management Agency
3041 Sidco Dr.
Nashville, TN 37204-1502
(615)741-0001

Texas Division of Emergency Management
P.O. Box 4087
Austin, TX 78773-4087
(512)465-2183

Utah Division of Comprehensive Emergency Management
State Office Bldg., Room 1110
Salt Lake City, UT 84114
(801)538-3400

Vermont Emergency Management Agency
Dept. of Public Safety
Waterbury State Complex

103 S. Main St.
Waterbury, VT 05676
(802) 244-8271

Virgin Islands Office of Civil Defense and Emergency Services
131 Gallows Bay
Christiansted, VI 00820
(809) 773-2244

Virginia Department of Emergency Services
310 Turner Rd.
Richmond, VA 23225-6491
(804) 674-2497

Washington Emergency Management Division
Building 20, M/S: TA-20, Camp Murray
Tacoma, WA 98430-5122
(800) 562-6108 or (253) 512-7000

West Virginia Office of Emergency Services
State Capitol Complex
Room EB80
Charleston, WV 25305
(304) 558-5380

Wisconsin Division of Emergency Government
4802 Sheboygan Ave., Room 99A
Madison, WI 53707
(608) 266-3232

Wyoming Emergency Management Agency
P.O. Box 1709
Cheyenne, WY 82003
(307) 777-7566

Computer Software for Contingency Planning*

DATA-BACKUP SYSTEMS

Computerm Corporation
111 Wood Street
Pittsburgh, PA 15222
Tel: (412)391-7804; Fax: (412)391-9512
www.computerm.com
E-mail: moreinfo@computerm.com

Inrange Technologies Corp.
One Waterview Drive
Shelton, CT 06484
Tel: (203)925-7531; Fax: (203)924-6400
www.inrange.com
E-mail: prod.info@inrange.com

DATA-MIRRORING SYSTEMS

Comdisco, Inc.
6111 North River Road
Rosemont, IL 60018

---

*The information in this appendix is taken from Disaster Resource Guide Online (http://www.disaster-resource.com/)

Tel: (800)272-9792
www.comdisco.com

Computerm Corporation
111 Wood Street
Pittsburgh, PA 15222
Tel: (412)391-7804; Fax: (412)391-9512
www.computerm.com
E-mail: moreinfo@computerm.com

DATA-RECOVERY SERVICES/SYSTEMS

Arcus/Iron Mountain
10811 Main St.
Bellevue, WA 98004
Tel: (800)800-8110
www.dbi.com

Computer Conversions, Inc.
8910 Activity Rd., Ste. A
San Diego, CA 92126
Tel: (619)693-1697; Fax: (619)693-6003
www.computer-conversions.com

Data Rescue Services
P.O. Box 411196
San Francisco, CA 94141-1196
Tel: (888)2DATAGURU (232-8248)
Fax: (415)282-6499; Voice (415)282-6464
E-mail: help@datarsq.com

Ontrack Data International
6321 Bury Drive
Eden Prairie, MN 55346
Tel: (800)872-2599; Fax: (612)937-5750

Tradelink-DR, c/o Tradetech Americas, Inc.
1030 North Avenue
Des Plaines, IL 60016
Tel: (847)298-5070; Fax: (847)298-5066

www.tradetech-americas.com/tradelinkdr.htm
E-mail: barry@tradelinkdr.htm

ELECTRONIC VAULTING

Arcus/Iron Mountain
10811 Main St.
Bellevue, WA 98004
Tel: (800)800-8110
www.dbi.com

AT&T
900 Rts. 202/206 N., Room 3A205Q
Bedminster, NJ 07921
Tel: (908)234-8605; Fax: (908)234-5583
www.att.com

Computerm Corporation
111 Wood Street
Pittsburgh, PA 15222
Tel: (412)391-7804; Fax: (412)391-9512
www.computerm.com
E-mail: moreinfo@computerm.com

IBM Business Recovery Services
300 Long Meadow Road
Sterling Forest, NY 10979
Tel: (888)837-8277; Fax: (845)759-4562
www.brs.ibm.com

ENVIRONMENTAL MONITORING

Datasite, Inc.
1827 Parc Vue
Mt. Pleasant, SC 29464
Tel: (843)884-6077; Fax: (843)884-9863
www.datasiteinc.com

Intra Computer Inc.
Tel: (718)297-5500; Fax: (718)297-5518
www.intracomp.com

INTERNET BACKUP/RECOVERY

IBM Business Recovery Services
300 Long Meadow Road
Sterling Forest, NY 10979
Tel: (888)837-8277; Fax: (845)759-4562
www.brs.ibm.com

Intessera Technologies Group
4700 S. Syracuse Street, Suite 100
Denver, CO 80236
Tel: (303)267-6100; Fax: (303)267-6176
www.filehaven.com
E-mail: sales@intessera.com

MEDIA PROTECTION AND STORAGE

Perm-a-Store Inc.
105 S. Broadway, #640
Wichita, KS 67202-4275
Tel: (316)264-4144; Fax: (316)264-0055
www.turtlecase.com
E-mail: turtles@turtlecase.com

Schwab Corp.
Lafayette, IN 47905
Tel: (800)428-7678; Fax: (765)447-8278
www.schwabcorp.com

Univault
Universal Safe Deposit Corporation
New York, NY 10170
Tel: (212)687-9100; Fax: (212)972-7877
www.Univault.com

GENERAL CONTINGENCY PLANNING SOFTWARE

Cliffside Software, Inc.
P.O. Box 82262
Portland, OR 97282-0262
Tel: (888)252-6489; Fax: (503)232-3450
www.cliffsidesoftware.com
E-mail: info@cliffsidesoftware.com

Geosphere Emergency Response Systems Inc.
100 South Main Street, Suite 200
Doylestown, PA 18901
Tel: (215)340-2204; Fax: (215)340-2205
www.plantsafe.com
E-mail: inquire@plantsafe.com

BUSINESS IMPACT ANALYSIS

CSCI, a HARRIS Recovery Group Co.
590 Danbury Road
Ridgefield, CT 06877
Tel: (800)925-CSCI; Fax: (203)431-8165
www.csciweb.com
E-mail: info@csciweb.com

Strohl Systems
500 North Gulph Road
King of Prussia, PA 19406
Tel: (610)768-4120; Fax: (610)768-4135
http://www.strohlsystems.com

BUSINESS RECOVERY AND CONTINUITY

Binomial International
Tel: (888)BINOMIA; Fax: (613)692-2425
www.binomial.com
www.disasterrecovery.com

BUSINESS PROTECTION SYSTEMS

Business Protection
5041 LaMart Drive, Suite 130
Riverside, CA 92507
Tel: (800)594-3714; Fax: (909)341-5049
www.businessprotection.com
E-mail: INFO@businessprotection.com

Comdisco, Inc.
6111 North River Road
Rosemont, IL 60018
Tel: (800)272-9792
www.comdisco.com

CSCI, a Harris Recovery Group Co.
590 Danbury Road
Ridgefield, CT 06877
Tel: (800)925-CSCI; Fax: (203)431-8165
www.csciweb.com
E-mail: info@csciweb.com

Disaster Recovery System (DRS™)
by TAMP Computer Systems, Inc.
1732 Remson Avenue
Merrick, NY 11566
Tel: (516)623-2038; Fax: (516)223-2128
www.ccsinet.com/drs/drspres.htm

McGladrey and Pullen, LLP
445 Minnesota Street, Suite 1800
St. Paul, MN 55101-2170
Tel: (800)648-4030; Fax: (651)293-8497
www.disaster.mcgladrey.com
E-mail: disaster@rsmi.com

MLC & ASSOCIATES
Tel: (949)222-1202; Fax: (949)651-8220
www.mlc2resq.com

Strohl Systems
500 North Gulph Road

King of Prussia, PA 19406
Tel: (610)768-4120; Fax: (610)768-4135
http://www.strohlsystems.com

BACKUP AND RECOVERY SOFTWARE

21st Century Software, Inc.
940 West Valley Road, Suite 1604
Wayne, PA 19087-1823
Tel: (800)555-6845 or Tel: (610)971-9946
Fax: (610)964-9072
www.drvfi.com

ASPG, Inc.
3185 Horseshoe Drive South
Naples, FL 34104-6138
Tel: (941)649-1548
Fax: (941)649-6391
www.aspg.com

Computer Associates International
1815 S. Meyers Rd.
Oakbrook Terrace, IL 60181
Tel: (800)442-6861
www.platinum.com

Emergency/Crisis-Management Software
Essential Technologies, Inc.
1401 Rockville Pike, Suite 500
Rockville, MD 20852
Tel: (301)284-3000 or Tel: (800)999-5009
Fax: (301)284-3001
www.essentech.com

Integrated GPS Technologies
4173 Bluebonnet Drive
Stafford, TX 77477
Tel: (281)494-4771; Fax: (281)494-4747
www.gpsgis.com

Softrisk Technologies Inc.
St. Simons Island, GA
Tel: (912)634-1700; Fax: (912)638-3340
www.softrisk.com
E-mail: jfraser@softrisk.com

INDEX

409